ADDITIONAL PRAISE FOR

BRINGING ADAM HOME

"Novelist Les Standiford and former Miami Beach police detective Joe Matthews combine forces to provide the definitive account of Adam's death. . . . [A] well-written and well-told book. . . . Readers willing to confront the horrifying nature of this crime will come away . . . with a solid understanding of why it took so long to solve and where the investigation went terribly astray."
—*Washington Post*

"[A] heartbreaking story of incompetent police and determined parents. . . . Novelist and nonfiction author Les Standiford does a masterful job of re-creation, reporting and research. . . . Readers will be haunted by the maladroit investigation and the added anguish this caused the Walshes."
—*Los Angeles Times*

"Standiford and Matthews relate Matthews' quest skillfully. . . . Hoffman and some of his police colleagues are portrayed as so venal and incompetent that deep breaths might be in order among some readers who implicitly trust detectives. . . . Reading the book near bedtime could be inimical to sound sleep."
—*Dallas Morning News*

"Compelling, bittersweet. . . . The book is hardly a light, casual read, due to the subject matter and overwhelming sense of injustice that pervades the entire story. But Standiford, in his seventh nonfiction title and fifteenth book overall, more than acquits himself here. He ably fleshes out the difficult yet familiar story with style, pathos and relevant historical detail."
—*Miami Herald*

"A riveting, harrowing, tautly suspenseful book that reads like a crime novel . . . but is all the more chilling for being fact, not fiction."
—*St. Petersburg Times*

"Intertwined with this true-crime chronicle is the important story of how Adam's abduction turned his parents into powerful advocates for crime victims and how law enforcement agencies across the country changed their response to missing children cases."
—*Orlando Home & Leisure* magazine

"*Bringing Adam Home* is compelling. It is a measure both of Standiford's skill and his humanity that a reader who picks up the book will be unable to set it aside before turning the final page. Standiford skips no fact, avoids no avenue of inquiry, fears no wrong-headed and officious law enforcement officer. The Adam Walsh case was sensational if ever a case was. Yet, Standiford never stoops to sensationalism: He writes with a restraint that will leave readers—and other writers—marveling, wondering how he did it. Even a person of tender sensibilities will find this book not only palatable, but impossible to put down."
—*Daily Jeffersonian* (Ohio)

"This is the ultimate cold case—tragic, high-profile, and, finally, successfully solved. . . . [*Bringing Adam Home*] gives readers the ultimate insider's account of the grueling search for Adam's killer. . . . While many true-crime books claim to shine a light on society by examining one particular case, this account actually does. No reader can come away from this without appreciating what it takes to keep pursuing an investigation, against the obstacles of police politics and bureaucracy. Wrenching and riveting."
—*Booklist*

"Novelist and nonfiction author Standiford (*Last Train to Paradise*) charts with devastating precision the decades-long search for the killer and the evolution of Revé and John Walsh (John was executive producer and host of *America's Most Wanted*) from grieving parents into powerful advocates for missing children. . . . Standiford's account is riveting, heartbreaking, and supports John Walsh's statement: 'It's not about closure; it's about justice.'"

—*Publishers Weekly* (starred review)

"An essential read for those interested in forensic science and true crime."
—*Library Journal*

"[M]ystery writer Les Standiford, in collaboration with Detective Sgt. Joe Matthews, has written a riveting and page-turning account of this heart-wrenching story." —BookReporter.com

"This tale of the most significant missing child case since the Lindberghs'—that of TV host John Walsh's son Adam and the twenty-seven-year search for his killer—is truly terrific. A taut, compelling, and often touching book about a long march to justice."
—Scott Turow, author of *Presumed Innocent*

"I didn't live far from the mall where Adam Walsh was kidnapped. I remember that story as if it were yesterday. It terrified me as a kid. But it's the details that Les Standiford has found that terrify me as an adult. Insightful, horrifying, and just beautifully written." —Brad Meltzer, *New York Times*
bestselling author of *The Book of Fate*

"*Bringing Adam Home* is a maddening, terrifying, and ultimately triumphant book. Les Standiford explores the injustice and finally justice surrounding the murder of Adam Walsh. You will cry and rage but you will not be able to put this book down until you finish it. My God! What a book!"

—Ann Hood, author of *The Red Thread*
and *The Knitting Circle*

"Not since *In Cold Blood* has the story of a terrible crime been told with such elegance and power. At once heartbreaking and hypnotically suspenseful, *Bringing Adam Home* brings vividly to life the agony of a bungled investigation and the dogged persistence of a heroic police detective determined to solve the mystery of Adam Walsh's abduction once and for all."

—Joseph Finder, *New York Times* bestselling author of *Vanished*

"*Bringing Adam Home* is a riveting account of a child abduction and murder that goes unsolved for twenty-seven years—both an unsettling exposé of police incompetence and a portrait of an extraordinary and dedicated detective."   —Joyce Carol Oates

"*Bringing Adam Home* is a gripping and scrupulously detailed account of what it takes to bring closure to a horrific crime that should not have taken decades to solve. Joe Matthews has put aside all the politics, jealousy, and years of mistakes to prove without a doubt the identity of the killer of Adam Walsh. Should be required reading for anyone in law enforcement."

—Chief Thomas Hunker, Bal Harbour (Florida) PD

"The scene-setting, the character-sketching, and the social and historical contextualization are in full gear in this book. . . . An especially heartbreaking and cogent story."

—Madeleine Blais, author of *Uphill Walkers*
and winner of the Pulitzer Prize

BRINGING

ADAM

HOME

BRINGING

ADAM

HOME

THE ABDUCTION THAT CHANGED AMERICA

Les Standiford

with Detective Sergeant Joe Matthews

An Imprint of HarperCollinsPublishers

HarperCollins books may be purchased for educational, business, or sales promotional use. For information please write: Special Markets Department, HarperCollins Publishers, 10 East 53rd Street, New York, NY 10022.

A hardcover edition of this book was published in 2011 by Ecco, an imprint of HarperCollins Publishers.

FIRST ECCO PAPERBACK EDITION PUBLISHED 2012.

Designed by Mary Austin Speaker

Library of Congress Cataloging-in-Publication Data

Standiford, Les.
   Bringing Adam home : the abduction that changed America / Les Standiford with Detective Sergeant Joe Matthews. — First edition.
       p.   cm
     ISBN 978-0-06-198390-0
     1. Walsh, Adam. 2. Kidnapping—Florida—Case studies. 3. Murder—Investigation—Florida—Case studies. I. Matthews, Joe, detective sergeant, author. II. Title.
   HV6603.W35S73   2011
   364.15'23092—dc22

                                                                    2010043572

ISBN 978-0-06-198391-7 (pbk.)

12 13 14 15 16   OV/RRD   10 9 8 7 6 5 4 3 2 1

*This book is dedicated to the memory of
Alexander Standiford, 1991–2009;
to Mama Margaret Matthews, 1914–2008;
and, of course, to Adam Walsh, 1974–1981,
as well as all the other sons and daughters
taken long before their time.*

After the first death, there is no other.

—DYLAN THOMAS

I-10

TALLAHASSEE

JACKSONVILLE

STARKE
PENITENTIARY

FLORIDA
TURNPIKE

75

95

ORLANDO

VERO BEACH

MM 130
ADAM'S REMAINS FOUND

LAKE
OKEECHOBEE

FT. LAUDERDALE

HOLLYWOOD

MIAMI BEACH

N
W   E
S

0   50   100
MILES

CONTENTS

ACKNOWLEDGMENTS

Sincere thanks are due to Mitchell Kaplan, who saw from the beginning what this endeavor might become; to agent-without-peer Kimberly Witherspoon, who has yet to accept no for an answer; to Jeanne Wilmot, who got it right, right off; and to Dan Halpern and Bill Strachan, who brought this book lovingly into the light.

The authors would also like to offer thanks to Revé and John Walsh, not only for their assistance but for everything they have done on behalf of children and parents everywhere; to Susan Schindehette, who blazed this literary trail, for her advice and encouragement; to the gracious volunteer staff at the Hollywood (Florida) Historical Society; to indefatigable Florida International University reference librarian Adis Beesting; to indispensable adviser Robert Rotstein, Esq.; and to irreplaceable reader Rhoda Zelda Kurzweil.

Particular thanks are also due to any number of individuals within the community of law enforcement and justice, but especially to Joseph Kaplan, attorney for the Miami Beach Fraternal Order of Police, and former Broward County prosecutor Kelly Hancock.

Les adds his own special thanks to Kimberly, Jeremy, and

Hannah Standiford, who believed in and encouraged him and reminded him each day why this story simply must be told. We trust that "Z" would have been proud.

And, from Joe Matthews: How do I begin to thank my wife, Ginny, for her love, dedication, and loyalty? Her encouragement from the moment of Adam's abduction drove me not to give up. Thanks to my children—Joey, Greg, Michael, and Christina— their spouses, and all of my grandchildren for reminding me what is really important. To my brother Peter Matthews for being my big brother, and to my kid sister Mariann Kresge and her son Emir for being very special to me. To my dear friends and colleagues Tom Hunker, Pat Franklin, and Bernie Winer for their advice and support, and to my lifelong friends Tom Panza and Dick Brickman for being there for me always. To my assistant, Mary Alvarez, for having the patience of a saint, and to John and Revé Walsh for their unquestioning trust, which allowed me to give them the justice they so much deserved. And to Hollywood Chief of Police Chad Wagner and Broward County Chief Assistant State Attorney Chuck Morton for their integrity and their desire to put justice first.

BRINGING

ADAM

HOME

CHAPTER ONE

In the Beginning

HOLLYWOOD, FLORIDA—JULY 27, 1981

Shortly after lunch on what seemed an ordinary summer afternoon, a young South Florida housewife set out on a shopping trip with her six-year-old son in tow. It was the sort of outing that millions of other mothers all across the country might have taken on any given day. Her husband, a sales and marketing manager for a local hotel company, had noticed an ad in that morning's newspaper and called home to say that the brass barrel lamps they had been looking for had just gone on sale at the local Sears store. Maybe she ought to run over and take a look.

She was happy to do it—they'd been wanting the lamps, and the chance to save a few dollars seemed too good to pass up. She freshened herself up, dressed her son in shorts, a polo shirt, flip-flops, and his favorite way-big boat captain's hat, and set out for the store.

It was a Monday, typical ninety-degree weather with humidity just as high, but that was July in South Florida for you. Come January, when the rest of the country was in a deep freeze, Floridians would have payback. Besides, traffic in their suburban town of Hollywood was light that early afternoon, and it was less than a two-mile drive to the Sears Mall. As a bonus, the parking space she liked to use—near the receiving dock, on the building's north side, where the whole family could remember it—was open.

Just inside the doors, at the entrance to the toy department, her son spotted a video display with a demo of the new Asteroids game running, and he begged his mother to let him play.

She hesitated, but home furnishings was just a couple of aisles away, and besides, the world had not yet turned upside down. She pointed out to her son where she was going and told him she'd be back in a few minutes to pick him up. She gave her son a kiss, then, and hurried off to see about those lamps.

She would relive the moment a hundred—perhaps a million—times. Had she just said no to him, "Stay with me"; had she simply returned to the game display a minute sooner; had any one of a thousand things happened differently in the slightest—as it is said that the flapping of a butterfly's wings in the Amazon can form a tsunami in a distant time and place—perhaps what occurred might not have occurred at all.

But there is no changing what did happen that day. The mother found a salesperson in home furnishings easily, but there was a bit of a problem: they searched up and down the bright aisles but could find none of the barrel lamps on display. The clerk was happy to check in the back, of course—it would only take a moment. Which turned into something more.

When the clerk finally returned, her downcast expression said it all. The store had not received any of the advertised lamps, but they would be happy to call the moment they came in. The mother quickly gave her name and number and hurried back to where she'd left her son.

She could hear the clamor of spaceships and cannon fire tearing the air as she hurried down the aisle, and smiled at her son's passion for such games. But when she rounded the corner, she stopped short. The game was running, but its stations were deserted, the sounds issuing mechanically from the demo loop. She glanced about, puzzled, hoping she would see her son browsing in the nearby toy department, or ambling toward her from where she had been. But she did not.

She fought the surge of panic that every mother feels when she turns and finds her child suddenly lost from sight. The ripples on the surface of the nearby pond are all menace. The sounds of distant traffic suggest catastrophe and grief and guilt.

But she would not panic foolishly, this mother. She would retrace her steps. She would have the store announce her son's name, and that he should find a clerk and report himself. While store personnel stood ready, she would return to the place she had left her car. He would be waiting there, or he would come to her, or she would find him. She would not panic. She would find her son. Surely, she would find her son.

WASHINGTON, D.C.—FEBRUARY 13, 2006

At a Capitol Hill press conference, a reporter stood to ask a final question of John Walsh, leading proponent for the about-to-be-debated Adam Walsh Child Protection and Safety Act. Walsh, a private citizen, had become perhaps America's most recognizable crime fighter owing to his work as executive producer and host of the long-running television program *America's Most Wanted.* But also, in the wake of the 1981 kidnapping and murder of his son Adam, he and his wife, Revé, had dedicated much of their lives' energies to raising awareness of the problem and the plight of missing children in America.

As a result of the Walshes' work had come the passage of the 1982 Missing Children Act, the establishment of the National Center for Missing and Exploited Children in 1984, and the national AMBER Alert program of 2003. Walsh considered the new bill that was about to go before Congress the capstone of a life's work removing impediments to the recovery of the nearly 800,000 children who are reported missing in the United States each year.

"Mr. Walsh," the reporter began. "You've done much good work on behalf of children and families everywhere, and you've brought any number of heinous criminals to justice with your television show. But I'm wondering if it ever bothers you that you have been unable, in all these years, to find out who killed your own son?"

It was a question asked out of ignorance, the sort of thing that made several in the room wince. Walsh managed to respond without losing his composure, but following the incident, he and Revé contacted longtime associate and *America's Most Wanted* investigator Joe Matthews to set up a meeting that would prove to be momentous. As a veteran homicide detective for the Miami Beach Police Department, Matthews had supervised and conducted more than 20,000 criminal investigations and over 2,000 death and homicide investigations, and had obtained confessions and convictions in a number of high-profile cases, including Miami's infamous Baby Lollipops torture-murder, that of Washington State's spree killer Chad Daniel Roberts, and Canada's University of Waterloo serial rapist Christopher Meyer.

But more important, Matthews, a widely recognized polygraph expert, had been involved in the investigation of Adam Walsh's disappearance and murder from the very beginning, twenty-five years before. His skill and tireless efforts to bring mistakes and overlooked evidence to the attention of those in charge of that still-unresolved investigation had earned him the respect and the friendship of the Walshes over the years, and following his retirement from the Miami Beach force, Matthews had gone to work as a lead investigator for *America's Most Wanted*, where he was quickly credited with solving the program's first cold case investigation, the killing of a former high school wrestling champ by four football players at Lock Haven University, in Pennsylvania.

Matthews was well aware that for all the good work that the Walshes had accomplished over the years, there still existed a great void in their lives. Adam was gone, and though both they and he had expended vast resources and energy trying to do what the authorities had been unable to do, the person responsible had never been brought to justice. And for all the effrontery of the reporter's question, it was scarcely the first time it had been asked: the Walshes had been asking virtually the same thing of themselves—if only privately—nearly every day for a quarter century.

On this day, however, Matthews could see that something different had taken over the Walshes' demeanor. Perhaps it was the pain of such a jab coming in a context of seeming triumph with the passage of the Child Protection and Safety Act. Or perhaps the Walshes had simply heard one insensitive question too many. Whatever, Matthews thought as he waited for the Walshes' words, he'd walk through fire for John and Revé Walsh.

Normally, it was John who did most of the talking, but on this day, Revé took over before her husband could get started.

"Joe," she told Matthews in no uncertain terms, "I'm begging you. I know it's asking a lot, but I want you to go back through everything we've all tried to show the cops over the years. I want you to give it one last shot: put everything together and prove who killed our son, once and for all."

Matthews had made his decision before Revé was finished. He was honored that she'd even ask, he told her. He was an investigator through and through, and he had witnessed her suffering and that of her husband from the beginning of their ordeal. In truth, he had been aching for much of his adult life to do the very thing that she had just asked of him. He took her hands in his and nodded. He would give it his best shot, and he would start at once.

CHAPTER TWO

Blood of the Lamb

Q: Do you remember if she was a hitchhiker?

A: Yeah, I think she was.

Q: Did she have a name?

A: I wouldn't know.

Q: Didn't you ask her name when you picked her up?

A: I suppose so. I didn't pay much attention to stuff
like that.

—OTTIS TOOLE, TO AN INVESTIGATOR,
JACKSONVILLE COUNTY JAIL, DECEMBER 28, 1983

MIAMI BEACH, FLORIDA—JULY 31, 1981

When veteran Miami Beach PD homicide detective Joe Matthews got the call on Friday from captain of Hollywood detectives Steve Davis, asking that Matthews assist his department in the investigation of the disappearance of six-year-old Adam Walsh, Matthews was more than willing to join in. He was well aware of the anguish that had gripped the entire South Florida community since the boy had vanished earlier in the week. The reward offered for Adam's safe return had risen to $100,000, the highest ever for a missing child in the United States, and the case, which would be likened to the Lindbergh kidnapping, had attracted the attention of news media, not to mention cops, across the region.

Four days had passed since Adam had gone missing from the Sears store in Hollywood, and though twenty-five officers assigned to the Hollywood PD detective bureau had worked the case full-time, along with assistance from officers from Broward and other South Florida counties, what scant leads they'd uncovered had come to nothing. There was no reason to suspect that Adam had simply run away or wandered off; there were no disaffected family members who might be suspected of abducting him; nor had there been any ransom note or report of anything unusual spotted at the Sears store that day. In short, there had been nothing, and in the days long before AMBER Alerts, children's faces on milk cartons, and national databases that linked police departments in missing children cases, the Hollywood PD was up against a wall.

Furthermore, there was good reason for Captain Davis to contact Matthews. Matthews, thirty-five, had been employed by the City of Miami Beach since 1967, and had quickly risen through the ranks, promoted after only a year and a half as a patrolman to detective for the Criminal Investigations Division. In 1973, shortly after he married his wife, Ginny, he was promoted to the rank of detective sergeant. At about the same time, Matthews—always skilled at interrogation—had enrolled in a state-certified program for polygraph examiners, figuring the training would make him a better cop and, quite frankly, expand his prospects. He and Ginny had plans to start a family, and making do on a cop's salary was always a challenge.

By 1976 Matthews had become the chief polygraph examiner for the Miami Beach Police Department and had started his own state-certified school for polygraph examiners—a sideline that became more and more profitable as word of Matthews's skills as both an investigator and an instructor spread throughout the South Florida law enforcement community. The burly, avuncular Matthews was regarded as a tough but fair cop by his colleagues, and his meticulous style of interviewing subjects prior to the actual polygraph exam itself had proven to be most effective. As he was fond of reminding his students, "How can you know what kind of questions to ask if you don't know the person you are asking them of?"

Among those many students he had trained over the years was Steve Davis, who had even gone on to intern under Matthews at his Southern Institute of Polygraph. And while Davis considered himself an able polygraph examiner, along with others who performed the same duties within the Hollywood police department—many of them also trained by Matthews—in this case he wanted the best. Matthews was not only a top polygraph examiner, he was a highly regarded cop and investigator.

"We need you up here," Davis told Matthews, who needed little convincing. When he had heard the initial news bulletins late on the afternoon that Adam had disappeared, Matthews's initial reaction was one of sadness, mixed with some resignation. He was an experienced police officer, after all, and the world was a hard place. Maybe the Walsh boy had just wandered away and gotten lost. Hopefully, he hadn't fallen into one of the many canals that stitched the narrow habitable strip of South Florida land between the Everglades and the Atlantic. Hopefully, he would turn up safe somewhere.

But shortly after Matthews got home that evening, his feelings began to change. Ginny met him just inside the door, the kids' pj's tucked under her arm, wondering if he'd heard the news. He *had* heard, Matthews assured her.

"My God, Joe," she told him, then. "I was on my way to that same Sears this afternoon. But Joey got sick, and I had to turn around. It could have happened to us, that's what I keep thinking."

Matthews stopped, staring back at her, feeling goose bumps prickle even his thick skin. They lived in the unincorporated area known as Southwest Ranches, then a sparsely populated area of

Broward County a few miles from the fringes of real civilization and the Hollywood store where Adam had gone missing. The houses there sat on lots of an acre or more, and some neighbors still kept horses. The urban centers of Fort Lauderdale and Miami were nearby, and if you wanted a dose of the city, you could easily get it. But out here you could pretend you were still part of an old-time Florida, where foxes and raccoons and possums roamed, and if you were talking about predators, you meant the eagles and hawks and ospreys that still cut the skies overhead.

Matthews glanced into the family room, where his brood— four kids in five years—were raising their usual clamor in front of the TV set while Scooby-Doo hightailed it from a make-believe monster. His oldest son Joey was almost exactly the same age as Adam Walsh, born one day before him, on November 13, 1974. After Joey, there had come two more sons, Greg and Michael, and in 1979, just two weeks before Joey's fifth birthday, their daughter Christina was born. The things you take for granted, he found himself thinking, a wave of dread drifting over him.

It was a feeling that only increased over the course of the week, as reporters continued to chronicle the lack of results in the search for Adam Walsh. By the time Davis called to issue his plea, Matthews was more than primed to help. "Anything I can do," he assured Davis, who immediately put in a call to Emmit Miller, Miami Beach police chief, asking that his former instructor be loaned to HPD to conduct interviews and polygraph examinations.

"We need all the help we can get," an anxious Davis told Chief Miller, and the deal was done.

MIAMI BEACH, FLORIDA—AUGUST 5, 1981

In truth, the Miami Beach that Sergeant Matthews set out from to meet with his Hollywood PD counterparts the following Wednesday bore very little resemblance to the high-octane, pretty-peopled playground of today. Nor had it yet become the drug-fueled, money-laundering center of exotic crime mirrored in *Miami Vice*, where Crockett and Tubbs donned unstructured suits and chased swarthy miscreants in cigarette boats and Ferraris.

There was crime in Miami Beach to be sure, but it was still largely the old-fashioned variety that made its own kind of sense. From the 1930s, mob money had fueled the glittering beachfront resorts where big-name talent performed and movers and shakers cavorted, but much of that was about providing willing customers with what they craved: babes, booze, cards, and dice. Victimless crime, as it used to be called, and hardly a thing that outraged anyone, unless you happened to be standing behind a pulpit on Sunday morning. Besides, by 1981, most of the gambling action had moved on to Las Vegas and other climes, and the Eden Rocs, the Fontainebleaus, and their paler cousins up the Beach were already sliding toward irrelevance.

Residents of Miami Beach, as well as Americans just about anywhere, were aware of a trend toward more disturbing crimes. Truman Capote's depiction of the senseless 1959 murders of a Kansas farm family in his landmark *In Cold Blood* had opened the eyes of a nation to the possibility that dim-witted losers or small-time grifters might morph into homicidal maniacs at a moment's notice. Ten years later would come the stunning Manson Family murders in Los Angeles.

In the wake of the Clutter and Tate/LaBianca killings had come a number of ghouls to command the headlines, including David Berkowitz, the "Son of Sam," who terrorized New York City in 1976 and 1977, killing six persons and wounding seven more in a series of shootings that he said were ordered by a demon who possessed his neighbor's dog. Even more prolific was Ted Bundy, the law student turned killer of coeds and young women, at least thirty of them, including half a dozen in North Florida.

Not only had the nature of evil begun to divorce itself from any semblance of rational explanation, it seemed, but subsequent developments would suggest that the forces of good had lost their power to respond. In 1979, sixty-six Americans were taken hostage in Iran, and the mighty U.S.A., for all its bluster, appeared powerless to do anything about it. A vaunted military rescue operation failed miserably, and only the ouster of yet another president, it seemed, was enough to appease the kidnappers—not until 444 days had passed, and Ronald Reagan had replaced Jimmy Carter, were the last fifty-two hostages released.

There were other signs as well that fault lines had begun to split an orderly world. In December of 1980, apparent lunatic Mark David Chapman pumped four bullets into the back of Beatles singer John Lennon—perhaps the most beloved entertainer of his age—as he strolled arm in arm with Yoko Ono outside his Manhattan apartment. Chapman could offer no reason for the killing beyond the voice inside his head that told him, "Do it, do it, do it."

The attempt on Ronald Reagan's life by John Hinckley Jr. on the following March seemed positively rational in comparison—at least Hinckley claimed that he wanted to impress actress Jodie Foster. Nor did it compare to the events of May 13, 1981, when would-be Turkish assassin Mehmet Ali Ağca shot Pope John Paul II four times as he made an appearance in St. Peter's Square. Theories abound as to why Ağca did what he did—he has been described as everything from an addled opponent of all things capitalist to an agent of the Russian KGB to a brainwashed operative of a Muslim cabal. But what was certain was that someone had actually fired bullets into the body of the pope of the Catholic Church with the intent to kill.

And yet for all the impact such actions may have had upon the underlying psyche of a civilization, it remained in some ways a doggedly innocent age. When in late 1980 Calvin Klein presented CBS-TV with a jeans ad in which fifteen-year-old actress Brooke Shields dared to murmur, "You know what comes between me and my Calvins? Nothing," the network indignantly banned the spot.

And there were other concerns to divert the attention of a nation, as well. The first IBM personal computers were rolling off assembly lines, the wedding of Prince Charles and Diana Spencer was set for July 29, and thirty million tongues were wagging that Luke and Laura from television's *General Hospital* would soon follow suit.

So far as any national obsession with crime went, the burning question in most American minds for most of the previous year was, "Who shot J. R.?" The final episode of the highly successful television series *Dallas* had ended that spring with a cliffhanger in which an unknown assailant fired a bullet into the body of overbearing Texas kingpin J. R. Ewing. More viewers than in all previous television history—an estimated 83 million—watched J. R. go down, and, due to an ensuing Hollywood writers' strike, they would have to wait until late November to learn who pulled the trigger.

As for "ordinary" crime in Miami Beach, there was no shortage of it, not given what had recently taken place in Castro's Cuba, just ninety miles from Florida. In April of 1980, some 11,000 Cubans seeking to escape the clutches of the Communist regime sought refuge on the grounds of the Peruvian embassy in Havana, setting up a clamor that resounded in the world press and had the Cuban émigré community in South Florida seething.

Faced with yet another political and public relations nightmare while also loath to do anything that did not somehow redound to his own benefit, Castro hit on a solution that he considered genius. He would open the nearby port of Mariel, he announced, and allow any Cuban Americans with relatives who wanted to leave the island to come down and pick them up. The response of the Cuban community in South Florida was overwhelming. The ensuing Mariel Boatlift put just about every one of the area's seaworthy craft (and a number that were not) into service shuttling refugees across the narrow Florida Straits.

But the apparent gesture of mercy in fact came with a heavy price. In order to rid himself of undesirables who put a strain on his own social services infrastructure, Castro emptied his jails of criminals of every stripe and his mental institutions of the most deranged, shuffling these individuals into the desperate throngs that filled the docks at Mariel. In the month of May 1980 alone, almost 90,000 Cubans arrived in Miami, many of them without relatives, without education, without prospects . . . and many of them with long histories of violent and criminal acts. It was the beginning of the *Scarface* era in Miami, and the truly despicable of the Marielitos found easy pickings among the frail and the elderly in South Florida, and particularly in Miami Beach, which had long been a haven for retirees.

In fact, the incident that was often talked about when Joe Matthews's name came up among those in the know was one that had taken place at about this time in South Beach, long before it became a glamorous place.

For far less than the cost of a night's lodging in the Delano or the Carlyle today, a retiree in 1981 might have been able to lay down a month's rent for a room in any of the crumbling Art Deco relics that occupied the stretch of Ocean Drive from Fifth to Fifteenth. In those days, the tourists and the players were still staying well northward up the beach, and there were no buxom models or chiseled skateboarders to dodge on South Beach, no plethora of fern-draped sidewalk cafés to choose from, no daisy chain of Maseratis nosed to Lamborghinis nosed to Aston Martins clogging the streets, no $25 valet parking, no pricey boutiques selling furs for pets.

In the de facto retirement village of South Beach, you had your room, and your hot plate, and after some soup for supper, you could walker yourself to the elevator, jigger it down to the lobby, don your plastic nose protector and a pair of those wraparound sunglasses the size of windshield heat reflectors, and go out to join your fellow pensioners on the hotel porch. You'd sit there in an aluminum chair welded to the next and the next— maybe there'd be room for twenty cheek by jowl on either side of the lobby door—and you'd stare out at the lovely Atlantic through sunglasses dark enough to keep Dracula safe from dis- integration, hundreds of you on all those porches up and down Ocean Drive, like members of some strange white-beaked, dark- banded species waiting for the arrival of a ship on the darkening ocean, like you might be ready to step on board that ship and head off somewhere far, far away.

It was to one such establishment—the Shoreham—that Joe Matthews and his team had been called. Matthews was at the time still a young beat cop who had been selected as part of a crime-fighting task force formed by legendary Beach PD chief Rocky Pomerance. An informant in Chicago had passed along a tip that was relayed to the Miami Beach PD that a gang from Chicago that had knocked over some other hotels was headed south and had the Shoreham in its sights as a robbery target. It was the kind of crime that police departments were well equipped to fight, and accordingly a dozen or so cops were hid- den on the premises for the first couple of nights: they posed as guests and night clerks, jammed into closets and anterooms, itching for action, but as more and more evenings passed with- out incident, the size of the detail was trimmed.

Finally, only Matthews and two others were left to the assignment, and as yet more evenings passed uneventfully, his companions gradually became more focused on the nightly card game they set up in one of the anterooms off the lobby and the boozing that went along with it. Matthews was no teetotaler, but he was not a drunk, either. He'd have a drink or two, and play some cards, but invariably he'd be the last man standing by 3:00 or 4:00 a.m., left to keep an eye out on a deserted lobby while the others slept until sunup and time to go home.

He'd almost fallen asleep himself the night things turned all the way around. He heard the lobby door open about 4:15 a.m., and glanced through the curtains of the anteroom where he was stationed to see that three men wearing ski masks and carrying pistols had entered the lobby. Matthews gripped the shoulder of the partner slumped facedown on the table next to him. "Holy shit," he whispered. "They're here. Wake up."

The answer was a muttered curse, followed by a racketing snore. As for the third member of the team, he was fast asleep in another room. Meantime, one of the bandits already had a pistol at the back of the head of the night clerk—an actual civilian who had unluckily returned to the job—and was marching him toward the safe deposit boxes.

History suggested to Matthews what would happen next. The minute the boxes were open, the clerk was likely to be shot. If some bewildered pensioner stumbled onto the scene, whether drawn by the commotion or simply wandering into the lobby thinking he'd found the bathroom down the hall from his room, his fate was likely to be the same.

From the start, in fact, the stakeout team—Matthews among them—had been agreed as to strategy. It was a simpler time in law enforcement. These were bad people they'd been sent to deal with. The thugs would be given a chance to surrender, but if one of them tried anything stupid—and they might well be afforded the chance to—there'd be justice dispensed on the spot. "Whatever it takes" was the task force's watchword. Chief Pomerance had made that much clear.

However, any previous thoughts of strategy were gone from Matthews's mind now. It was him versus three. Even though he'd recently gone through the FBI's SWAT and sniper training academy in Quantico, he knew that a shoot-out would not work in his favor. At the same time, he was not going to hide out in an anteroom and hope that just this once, the gang would be content to empty a safe and leave a potential witness behind unharmed.

Matthews offered up an unspoken prayer, hoisted the shotgun leaning against the wall nearby, and eased silently out the door of the anteroom into the lobby. He carried about 185 pounds on his big-boned five-foot-ten frame, but he wasn't counting on his size to accomplish anything. Instead, he racked a shell into the chamber of the shotgun, a sound that rarely fails to gain a criminal's attention.

"If any of you move, you're dead," he called to the three, the Browning braced at his shoulder. At least *some* of you will be, he was thinking. "Put your guns down, *now*," he added. "And put your hands behind your heads."

Put down your guns and hold up your hands, Matthews heard the mocking echo of his own words in his head. Oh, sure, he thought, preparing himself for the fusillade to come next.

But amazingly, that is exactly what the three men did, and Matthews had handcuffed them all by the time anyone else came to.

It is the kind of story that cops love, and just one more reason why Steve Davis wanted Matthews's help on what was by far the most challenging case his department had ever faced. The Hollywood PD was considered one of the most efficiently run in Broward County, but as the days rolled by without any trace of Adam Walsh, and public scrutiny intensified, it was becoming clear that what was essentially a small-town force (the 1980 population of the city was just over 120,000) was in well over its head.

The department had a new building, a data-crunching computer paid for by federal funds, a Citizens' Crime Watch with more than 4,000 volunteers, and an active, visible chief in Sam D. Martin, proud of such accomplishments as Operation Reindeer, which had been successful in driving down the number of shopping mall robberies at holiday time. But the truth was that Hollywood, Florida, despite its proximity to the glamour towns of South Florida, was an outpost of Mom and Pop America. Drive a couple of miles inland from the beach, and you might as well be cruising the strip mall barrens of Dubuque or Des Moines.

Yet if the place was ordinary, it was becoming clear by the hour that the Adam Walsh case was anything but. According to FBI figures, somewhere between 750,000 and 800,000 children under the age of eighteen are reported missing in the United States each year—an average of more than 2,000 a day. Of these, the vast majority are runaways or young children who wander off and are quickly found. Another 250,000 or so turn out to have been taken by a feuding spouse or family member, or a friend involved in a family dispute. A very few missing children turn out to have met with some tragic accident.

Fewest of all are the victims of what statisticians call "stereotypical" kidnapping, where a child is taken by someone he does not know, or knows only slightly: someone who holds the child overnight, transports him more than fifty miles, demands a ransom or intends to keep the child forever, or—woe upon woe—someone who kills the child.

Only about one hundred children a year are the victims of such a kidnapping, making the odds of losing a child to illness or accident far greater. But parents have been programmed from the beginning of time to cope with the specter of a fatal illness or accident, no matter how tragic. Terrible as such losses are, they at least occur within the bounds of reason.

In contrast, the concept that another human being might have taken one's son or daughter is simply not part of the rational equation of parenthood—or at least it was not in 1981. Yet with every day that passed in the case of Adam's disappearance, the odds increased exponentially that no good end would come.

And still, for all that, and for all the assurances that Steve Davis had given Joe Matthews about how much they needed him on board, it didn't take Matthews long to discover that his association with the Hollywood PD was going to be something other than a honeymoon. Matthews was familiar with the spacious new headquarters building at 3250 Hollywood Boulevard, having been called there several times in the past to lecture on interrogation methods and polygraph examination techniques. But moments after he parked his unmarked Plymouth sedan and entered the building on this go-around, he encountered the first in what would be a long series of challenges to his involvement in the case.

Inside the building, Matthews reported to Lieutenant Dick Hynds, who worked under Steve Davis in supervising the detective bureau. All went smoothly enough at first. Hynds, whom Matthews had never met, was a heavyset old-timer who carried maybe 240 pounds on his six-foot frame—the kind of guy Central Casting would send over if you called and asked for "a cop." The two exchanged a few pleasantries, then Hynds walked him down a corridor to the desk of Detective Jack Hoffman, lead investigator on the Adam Walsh case.

Hynds explained to Hoffman that Matthews had come up from Miami Beach to lend a hand in interviewing and polygraph examinations. Hoffman glanced up impatiently from a report in front of him. He was a heavyset, dark-haired guy with a bushy mustache that accentuated the droop of his lips. He looked like a guy who disapproved of most things on general principle, Matthews thought.

"Why do we need somebody from Miami Beach?" Hoffman asked Hynds brusquely. He hadn't so much as glanced at Matthews. "We've got our own polygraph people."

"This is the guy who *trained* our people," Hynds offered, but Hoffman turned back to his report without a word.

Matthews thought it an unnecessary display of territory marking, but he'd been around a lot of cops. Some guys just seemed to think it necessary to protect their turf. Besides, he knew Hoffman was under considerable pressure, and after all, he'd come up from Miami Beach to help, not start trouble. He shrugged and followed Hynds out of the room without comment.

"Anyway, we want you to start with the father," Hynds told

Matthews as they walked back down the hall, and Matthews nodded. It was natural. Something goes wrong—a spouse is shot, a child goes missing—you begin by looking at the people closest to the situation. Law of averages.

Hynds suggested that they set up the polygraph exam for the day after tomorrow. Meantime, Matthews could familiarize himself with the case files and review what John Walsh seemed to know about his son's disappearance. On Friday, Matthews would go to work on Walsh himself.

HOLLYWOOD, FLORIDA—AUGUST 7, 1981

If they had in fact shown him everything, Matthews concluded after studying the files, then indeed the Hollywood PD did not have much to go on. According to her statement, Revé Walsh had run up and down the aisles of the Sears store for a few minutes after she'd returned and found her son gone, calling for Adam by his nickname, "Cooter, Cooter, where are you?"

Finally, she spotted a store security guard, seventeen-year-old Kathy Shaffer, and rushed to Shaffer to report that she had lost her child. Revé reached into her wallet and pulled out Adam's first-grade picture to show it to Shaffer. "Look, he's even wearing this same shirt," Revé said, pointing at the red-and-white-striped shirt she'd dressed him in that morning. Shaffer studied the photograph for what seemed a maddening amount of time, then finally shook her head.

"We can page him, though," Shaffer told Revé, who glanced at her watch. It was almost 12:45. She and Adam had entered the store almost forty-five minutes ago.

Revé waited nearby while Shaffer made a call, then listened as the announcement crackled over the store's PA system. "Adam Walsh, please report to the information desk. Adam Walsh, your mother is waiting for you."

"It was like I was drowning in a pool and couldn't reach

the edge," Revé would say, trying to describe how unreal her world had suddenly become. "I was trying to reach my child, but he couldn't hear me. I felt so helpless. I kept thinking that if I could just get everything to slow down for a minute, then I could catch my bearings and catch hold of everything. And then I could reach out and pull Adam back."

The announcements were repeated again at 1:00 p.m. and every fifteen minutes thereafter, but Adam did not appear. Revé questioned every store employee she could find, but no one remembered seeing Adam, and worse yet, none seemed too concerned. By 1:55, two hours after Adam's disappearance, Revé was nearing hysteria. Using a Sears phone, she called the Hollywood police to report that her son was missing. Then, fighting back tears, she called her husband John at work and told him what had happened.

By the time John Walsh arrived at the mall, it was almost 3:00 p.m., and a cluster of Hollywood police cruisers were nosed up to the curb outside the garden entrance to the Sears store, their flashers whirling. He parked quickly and ran inside to find a distraught Revé speaking intently with a policeman. When she turned, he saw the desperation in her face. As he put it, "For the first time in my life, I understood what real fear was."

Still, Walsh did his best to calm Revé, and the two of them worked painstakingly to describe their son to the investigating officers, who had already put out word of a child gone missing at the Sears Mall. Local news station WINZ broadcast an announcement of Adam's disappearance, and Miami television stations interrupted programming to run Adam's photograph and a plea for any information. Friends and neighbors were standing by at the Walsh house little more than a mile from the store—they'd call if Adam wandered home.

Police were sympathetic, but there was little that they could do except broadcast the alarm. As the day wore on and the shadows lengthened, one cop pointed out the location of the police station, ironically located just a short walk across the mall's vast parking lot. "We're right over there," he told the Walshes, as if the statement meant something.

As the hours passed and the store began to prepare for closing, the reality of Adam's disappearance heightened for the Walshes. It was almost as if as long as the lights in the aisles burned brightly, Adam might somehow come around the corner of one of the aisles, smiling, with his arms outstretched. He'd just been hiding, nothing bad had happened. But once the store closed, and all was dark, what then?

John rushed home and returned to the lot where Revé waited by the family car. He'd brought blankets and some of Adam's favorite books and toys. Together they made up a little bed in the big backseat of the family car, a converted Checker taxi. Revé folded Adam's favorite blue blanket up to make a pillow. They left the doors unlocked and left a note on the dashboard that could be read through the window: "Adam, stay in the car. Mommy and Daddy are looking for you."

And finally, some time after the lights of Sears had blinked out and the parking lot had emptied except for the hulking shadow of the Checker, the two of them got in John's car and drove home.

Any thought of rest, however, was impossible. Shortly after they'd pulled into the drive and consulted briefly with the family and friends who had gathered, Revé mounted her bicycle and was pedaling up and down the streets of their suburban neighborhood, calling her son's name. She returned to circle the shuttered Sears store, peering through the darkened windows for any sign of Adam, and even made her way up a set of fire stairs to the roof, where she called for him down the building's ventilator shafts.

As Revé searched, John joined with a team of friends and neighbors to form a human chain that swept the nearby Hollywood Golf Course. A group of Crime Watch volunteers organized a walking search of the city, aided by a police helicopter that swept the streets with its spotlight.

At one point late in the night, John Walsh hailed a cruiser driving through his neighborhood. "How's the hunt going?"

The patrolman behind the wheel was a rookie named Mark Smith, who pointed to a photo of Adam pinned to his visor. "We're all looking for him," Smith said. "Don't worry."

But still there was nothing. By morning, the news had hit the local papers, with the local *Hollywood Sun-Tattler* running a front-page banner: "Massive Search Launched for Boy, 6—Adam Walsh Disappeared from Sears Monday Afternoon." A piece in the *Miami News* quoted Hollywood police as saying that while six-year-old Adam Walsh had indeed gone missing, "kidnapping is not suspected." And in fact, there was little concrete reason at that moment to believe that an abduction had taken place. There was no ransom note, no disgruntled parent held at arm's length by divorce, none of the "logical" reasons for a child to be taken.

John Walsh, however, could not shake the feeling that someone who had recently lost a child to some tragic circumstance might have taken his son. Yet even that scenario was preferable to the most logical explanation for many a missing child case in South Florida. The spidery network of drainage canals that intersect the narrow strip of habitable land between the Everglades and the Atlantic—the crackpot work of developers such as Henry Flagler and Napoleon Bonaparte Broward—had claimed more than their fair share of children over the years. It is hard to drive a mile in South Florida without encountering one of the deeply chiseled, rock-walled channels meant to turn the Everglades into homesites, few of them fenced, many of them abutting parks, bike paths, and heavily traveled thoroughfares. If Adam had tumbled into one of those canals . . . well, it was a prospect John Walsh did not want to contemplate.

And despite the efforts of the local police and news media, there was the distressing possibility that Adam and his abductor were long gone from the area. In 1981, there were none of the regional and national alert systems and shared databases that the public and the law enforcement community take for granted today. Despite the fact that hundreds of thousands of children went missing each year, the world had simply not recognized the need for such measures. Most kids "showed up," right? Such disappearances were ordinarily treated by law enforcement as local matters.

But by now it seemed to the Walshes that Adam was not simply going to "show up." And if he had indeed been taken, and his abductor had slipped them outside the local network of cops and media alarum, who would even notice?

To try and cover such bases, the Walshes designed a poster offering a reward of $5,000—no questions asked—for Adam's safe return. It featured a photograph taken only a week before— a gap-toothed little boy in a baseball cap, holding a bat—and assured anyone who might have taken Adam, "DO NOT FEAR REVENGE! We will not prosecute. We only want our son." They printed 150,000 of the posters, and they did a thing unheard of at the time: through friends with connections to Delta Airlines, copies were given to every passenger who passed through the airline's busy Atlanta hub. Copies, including those translated into Spanish, were distributed on every outgoing flight at the Fort Lauderdale airport. Eastern Airlines followed suit, and soon the posters were being issued to their passengers at every airport in the United States.

By Wednesday, forty-eight hours after Adam's disappearance, it seemed almost certain there would be no simple resolution to the case. "Probes Yield No Clues to Missing Boy," the headlines read. "Reward Rises as Police Probe Any, Every Clue."

Fred Barbetta, public information officer for the Hollywood PD, assured reporters that the cops had spared no effort. "We've got the whole Detective Bureau on this one," he told reporters, "the whole patrol, everybody." But then he added a grimmer assessment, one that reflected what many inside the department had come to think: "It's time we hit the waterways hard. If he's in the water, this is when he'd come up." As a result, those same volunteers who'd scoured the streets and combed the parks and playgrounds and golf courses began to walk the banks of the dark canals.

On Thursday, lead detective Hoffman made his first public statement on the case, telling reporters that Adam's disappearance might possibly have been an abduction after all. "This is not the type of child to just walk off," he explained. He'd had considerable discussion with the parents, and they had convinced him that Adam was a well-behaved and happy little boy. "But we don't have any clues whatsoever what the motive would be. It's extremely frustrating," Hoffman added. "We've got no clues, no leads, no evidence and no motives." Hoffman reiterated his department's plea for anyone who might have witnessed anything out of the ordinary that day at the Sears Mall to come forward.

Meanwhile, certainly no one had given up the search. Twenty-two Hollywood police officers had volunteered their unpaid overtime to keep looking for Adam. Influenced by the Hollywood PIO's grisly reminder that gases inside a decomposing body would by now have sent it floating to the surface of the water, the Florida Game and Fresh Water Fish Commission donated one of their helicopters for use in searching area waterways. Seven wildlife officers volunteered their time to conduct a ground search in the nearby Florida Everglades.

Revé, desperate for anything that might help, agreed to undergo hypnosis, in the hopes that she might have blocked some detail, however small, of her activities that Monday. But the account she gave of her activities under hypnosis was depressingly similar to that of her conscious recollections. Her memory of the timing of events matched to the minute, and she had seen nothing out of the ordinary and no one suspicious on her way into the store that day.

Meantime, the press had set up camp outside the Walshes' more-than-modest Hollywood home, eagerly trumpeting any tidbit they picked up off their police frequency scanners. They had taken to describing John Walsh as a "marketing executive" in their stories, and somehow the converted Checker cab had become a "custom car." While the reward was bumped up to $25,000 and ultimately $100,000 through the donations of friends, the Walshes had begun to fear that they were being painted as millionaires, the type of people who might be targeted for a colossal ransom.

And then, late on Thursday, came a phone call that finally gave Hollywood Police some reason to hope. A woman named Marilyn Pottenberg phoned, explaining that her ten-year-old son Timothy told her that he had noticed something suspicious during their visit to the Sears store the afternoon that Adam Walsh disappeared. She herself had not witnessed it, Mrs. Pottenberg said, but her son told her that he had seen Adam—or someone who looked like Adam—being pulled into a dark blue van in the parking lot. Mrs. Pottenberg was not eager to have her son interviewed by police, because he suffered from severe migraine headaches. She would have to speak with Timothy's doctor before she could allow that. She would get back to them.

Though there were certain inconsistencies in the tip, including the suggestion that Timothy had witnessed this event long after the time that Revé Walsh had raised the alarm for her missing son, Lieutenant Hynds appeared before reporters on Saturday, August 1, to announce that his force was following up on "the first solid lead" they had uncovered to date—and he put out the call to anyone in the community who might have seen such a suspicious vehicle.

The local Crime Stoppers staged a reenactment of an Adam look-alike being snatched through the doors of a blue van by a white male perpetrator, and the footage was aired on every local television station. Tips flooded in from everywhere, and hundreds of vans of every shade of blue were stopped and searched by cops in Palm Beach, Broward, and Dade counties. Florida highway troopers were doing the same across the entire state.

But by the following Tuesday, eight days after Adam had disappeared, even Lieutenant Hynds was backpedaling. He'd come to have "some misgivings" about the veracity of the Pottenberg tip, he told the press. And, too, he was a bit concerned about inconveniencing innocent citizens, some of whom had been stopped and searched twice.

So this was where *he* had come in, Joe Matthews thought, dropping the last of the case files on his desk. Beyond the "blue van" lead, which seemed about as consequential to him as a sighting of the Loch Ness Monster, precious little had been developed over ten days and thousands of man-hours of police work. Furthermore, during the time that he had spent at Hollywood police headquarters, he'd noticed a few disconcerting things about the way the investigation was being handled in the offices around him.

While Matthews sat at a vacant desk, poring over the files that were rather grudgingly parceled out to him, the phones at other desks were ringing constantly. While some of the detectives seemed organized, others assigned to the case would answer incoming calls randomly, jot information given by tipsters on scraps of paper or napkins or whatever might be handy, then hurry out on unrelated assignments without bothering to log their calls.

Desks were shared, files piled and unpiled, scraps of paper sent fluttering, napkins balled and tossed and swept. To Matthews, it seemed impossibly chaotic. It wasn't that the detectives seemed incompetent or unconcerned—there simply seemed to be no one in charge.

In his own department, all calls pertaining to a specific investigation went through one central logging station, and each lead, however lunatic or promising on the face of it, was assigned to someone for follow-up. After the leads were checked, reports were filed, and someone with authority over the case regularly reviewed the status of each and every inquiry, no matter how unimportant it might appear. Such organization seemed to Matthews the first principle of effective investigation technique, but when he mentioned the seeming disarray to Hoffman, he got only a raised eyebrow in return. If Hoffman had anything to say about it, Matthews wouldn't be there to begin with, he was reminded.

Matthews was hardly surprised at Hoffman's response, but he couldn't have stopped himself from making his point. Ten days gone by and not a scrap of worthwhile information turned up, how could he keep his mouth shut? He even walked down the hallway to repeat his concerns to Lieutenant Hynds. Hynds gave him a look obviously meant to remind Matthews who was in charge. "I'll look into it," he told Matthews.

Matthew got the picture. He'd stick to what he could do, he thought, what he'd been authorized to do. And he would begin with the father of the missing boy.

Matthews had formed no impression as to any involvement that John Walsh might have had in the crime that he'd been called to help investigate. Impressions only got in the way. What Matthews relied upon was his technique.

Before conducting a polygraph exam, any competent expert performs something of a pre-exam interview with a subject, but in Matthews's case those interviews were anything but perfunctory. Though he has thought about the matter, he is not exactly certain where his ability to connect with people comes from, though he does recall that as a child growing up in a devout Catholic household, he'd thought he was going to become a priest. "When it got closer to the time to go away to the seminary, though, I wasn't so sure. My mother knew I was upset and sat me down one day to tell me it was okay if I didn't want to go. I didn't have to be a priest just to please her, she told me." He shrugs. "It was a big relief to me at the time. But sometimes I think being a cop is almost the same thing."

In any event, when his subject on the day of August 7, 1981, sat down in the examining room, Matthews started by asking, "Tell me a little about yourself, John." When Walsh began by telling Matthews where he'd gone to college and what his major had been, Matthews held up a hand. "No, I mean, tell me about how you grew up. About your mother and father. Like if I asked you to rate them on a scale of one to ten, with ten being tops, and why. That kind of thing."

On that day, "that kind of thing" went on for almost seven hours. Prompted by Matthews, Walsh said that if ten were tops, then his father, a hardworking war hero he had idolized, was probably a twelve in his eyes. Walsh and his mother had what he considered a normal relationship. There were typical mother-son issues between them, but he loved her, and she had always been supportive of him. Give her an eight.

Matthews and Walsh did get around to a discussion of college, though it took a while. He was an English major at the University of Buffalo in New York when he met Revé, though he'd been stunned to discover she was still in high school at the time. Even though she was five years younger than he was, he'd found her so poised, and so intelligent. From the moment they met there had been no one else for him, Walsh told Matthews. They'd been married for ten years, since July 1971.

Walsh also told Matthews a story from his days as a pool manager and lifeguard at the Diplomat Hotel out on Hollywood Beach. He was keeping watch at the pool one afternoon when he saw a group of kids rushing toward him from the nearby jetty. Frantic, they told him that one of their friends was in trouble out by the jetty's end, where a massive discharge pipe emptied runoff water into the ocean. They'd been playing near the mouth of the pipe when the tide shifted in and trapped their pal, lodging him in a crevice against the rocks. The boys had tried, but they couldn't get him out. The force of the incoming tide was just too strong.

John ran out to the end of the jetty and scrambled down the

rocks to find matters just as the boys said. Indeed there was a kid lodged between the rocks and the mouth of the pipe, the waters rising inexorably toward his chin. And as if it could be worse, he realized that he knew this child. It was John Monahan Jr., son of the Diplomat's chief executive, trapped there in the rising waters. He'd given the boy a series of scuba lessons earlier that summer.

He managed to get young John calmed somewhat, then tried pulling him out of the crevice by the arms, but it wasn't working. The water was close to the boy's chin when John called to the kids watching from the top of the jetty for help, but they couldn't understand what he wanted.

"You've got to hang on," he said, turning to young Monahan. "I'm coming right back." Then he bounded up the rocks and back to the pool storage shack, where the diving equipment was stored. He kicked the door open, found a tank, mask, and regulator, and raced back along the jetty to Monahan. "We're going to do it just like we did it in the pool a hundred times," he assured the boy, helping him into the gear as the waters rose over his head.

Once the boy had been reassured and was breathing in a passable way, Walsh slipped under the water and put his arms around Monahan's chest. He pushed hard with his feet, levering against the rocks, and suddenly, as if a cork had popped from a bottle, the boy was free.

Needless to say, the incident made John Walsh far more than a trusted employee at the Diplomat. When Walsh and Revé got married, Monahan's father insisted on paying for a honeymoon trip to Europe for the couple, and the Walshes and the Monahans had remained friends ever since.

It was a captivating story, but it was the sort of thing that Matthews encouraged for other reasons. "You get someone talking about emotional things they haven't thought about in ten or twenty years, you establish a good baseline," he says. "When you finally get around to asking about some crime they may or may not have been involved in just the other day, you can judge any little changes in body language, in rate of speech or eagerness to respond and so on, and know you may be onto something."

As for the polygraph instrument itself, Matthews says, "It's not infallible. It's just a tool that helps validate the information that is gathered during the interview. The polygraph can indicate deception, but only a confession establishes guilt."

At the end of his time with Walsh, and following the administration of the polygraph exam itself, Matthews felt he had his unequivocal answer, however. "It is the examiner's opinion that Mr. Walsh was not criminally involved nor has he guilty knowledge as to who is responsible for the abduction of his son Adam."

On the other hand, Matthews did come across one item of interest during his interview, one that would affect the investigation irrevocably. As they talked, Walsh brought up a name that had surfaced nowhere else in the course of the investigation: it was that of Jimmy Campbell, a man Walsh identified as Adam's godfather.

Campbell was a younger man whom Walsh had gotten to know at the Diplomat Hotel in his lifeguarding days. Campbell was a pool boy, a decent, hardworking kid who'd never had much of a home life or any chance for a college education, and Walsh had always liked him and felt sorry for him— "Dudley Do-Right," he nicknamed him. When the Walshes started to move up in the world and he and Revé bought a house, Walsh and his wife invited Campbell to live in one of the spare rooms. He was to help out around the place and get himself into the community college. As long as he stayed in school, he could stay with the Walshes, but if Campbell quit school or flunked out, he'd have to leave. That was the deal. Unfortunately, Jimmy *had* dropped out of school a few months ago, Walsh told Matthews during their interview. And Walsh had been true to his word.

"So where is this Jimmy Campbell now?" Matthews asked, casually enough, after their exam had ended.

"Dudley?" Walsh shrugged, clearly still disappointed with his former ward. "He's out there helping with the search."

Matthews took another look at Hoffman's list of subjects to be examined, which Hynds had passed along. No Jimmy Campbell among them. A guy living in the Walsh house until a few months ago, intimately connected to the family, and he's not on the list? He glanced back at Walsh.

"You got this Campbell's phone number?"

Walsh was puzzled, but he was already reaching into his pocket for his address book. Matthews jotted down the information, and by 9:00 p.m. that evening, Jimmy Campbell was in the examining room at Hollywood PD, and Joe Matthews was hard at work on his next subject.

HOLLYWOOD, FLORIDA—AUGUST 8, 1981

In the wee hours of Saturday morning Matthews finished his work with Jimmy Campbell. He was tired, and what he had learned during his interview with Campbell had wearied him even more. He completed his notes on the examination and took a walk down the hall to Detective Hoffman's desk.

"Yeah?" Hoffman asked in his normal surly fashion when Matthews approached.

"I finished with John Walsh," Matthews said.

"It took you long enough," Hoffman said, with a glance at his watch. "So what's the story?"

Matthews shook his head. "He's clean. No involvement, no guilty knowledge."

Hoffman said nothing, but he seemed anything but pleased. "So who's next?"

"I already did 'next.' A guy named Jimmy Campbell."

Hoffman stared back, surprised. "That name's not on the list."

"I know," Matthews said, and then began to explain why he

had called Campbell in and what he had learned during the interview.

When he finished, Hoffman was beside himself with excitement. "That's it. There's our fucking guy," he said, halfway out of his seat.

Matthews held up his hand. "What are you talking about? You're not even listening to me." He pointed to his notes, where everything of real importance was spelled out:

The following are the relevant questions asked of Mr. Campbell during his polygraph examination:

Concerning Adam's disappearance, do you intend to answer all my questions truthfully?

Answer: Yes.

Do you know who took Adam?

Answer: No.

Do you know where Adam is now?

Answer: No.

Did you conspire with anyone to cause Adam's disappearance?

Answer: No.

Are you withholding information from the police concerning Adam's disappearance?

Answer: No.

Do you suspect anyone of taking Adam?

Answer: No.

Do you know who took Adam?

Answer: No.

Did you take Adam?

Answer: No.

"I worked him every which way. He's not involved," Matthews assured Hoffman.

"Bullshit," Hoffman responded, shaking Matthews's report

between them. "You tell me the guy was living in the house, doing what you say he was, and he's not involved in the crime somehow?"

Matthews sighed. He knew what he'd written down, what Hoffman was so worked up about. In fact, he had realized very early on in his interview with Campbell that the young man was holding something back, and it had not taken Matthews long to draw his secret out.

However, as with John Walsh, Matthews had gone to considerable lengths to determine just who he was dealing with before he got around to any pointed questions concerning the here and now. It was quickly apparent that Jimmy Campbell's childhood had been an unfortunate one: he had never received much affection from his own parents, and he might well have taken that deprivation out on the world in turn, just as many of the miscreants Matthews dealt with on a daily basis had. Instead, Campbell turned out sweet and gentle, one of the rare ones who understood just how important a little kindness could be. It was the less common response to a lousy upbringing, but it happened, just as some abused animals come crawling for affection instead of trying to tear your face off. Sometimes, Matthews thought, you catch a break.

Campbell loved John and Revé for their kindness and generosity, and he loved being with a family who cared about each other and who clearly cared for him. With John often away on business—his company was expanding, with a major resort hotel in the Bahamas under construction, among other things—Jimmy was happy to help out around the house, doing the heavy lifting when John was away, filling in when Adam needed pointers with baseball, doing anything he could do to repay the Walshes and show his appreciation.

No way had he intended this, Campbell explained to Matthews, but over time his affection for Revé had gradually turned to something else. Obviously, she was attractive and smart and warm . . . and quite simply, he fell in love with her. And one night while John was away on an extended trip, well, something happened that shouldn't have.

No way he could have stopped himself, Jimmy admitted. He was way too smitten for that. But however much he was attracted to Revé and however much affection she felt toward him, they realized in the aftermath that what they had done was wrong. Understandable, maybe—everyone is human—but nonetheless it was wrong.

Campbell could hardly live with himself for betraying John, his old friend and benefactor, he told Matthews. No way he could stay on in the Walsh house, that much was certain. And soon he had moved out.

All this Matthews had included in his report, of course, the good, the bad, and the ugly. Unfortunately, however, Jack Hoffman was fixated upon the ugly.

"It's as clear as day," Hoffman told Matthews excitedly, still brandishing the report. "Campbell's banging the wife, Walsh finds out, throws his ass out, and the guy snatches the kid to get back at him."

"Come on, Jack," Matthews protested, but the beleaguered detective was having none of it. Almost two weeks without a thing to go on, and finally this bombshell dropped in his lap.

Hoffman snapped his fingers then, as another thought occurred to him. "Maybe Campbell still had the hots for Mrs. Walsh, and he thought getting rid of the kid would help clear the way."

"You're not listening to me," Matthews said, trying to counter Hoffman's belligerence. "We're not writing a fucking novel here, we're conducting an examination. He's got a solid alibi for the day Adam Walsh went missing. And his polygraph test is absolutely conclusive. He and Revé might have made a *big* mistake. But as to Adam's disappearance, there is no deception. Look at what I'm telling you. *Read*."

Hoffman shook his head. "He beat the test somehow, that's all. I want a follow-up exam."

Matthews stared back at Hoffman for a moment. He should have been prepared for this. Clearly, Hoffman and the department as a whole were desperate. Earlier, when Matthews had asked Hoffman why the department hadn't announced that they no longer believed in the "blue van" theory, Hoffman had simply shrugged. "Hey, that's all we have to give the public," the detective told him. "We have to keep something out there so they'll stay interested in the case."

Matthews sighed inwardly, trying to put himself in Hoffman's shoes. "Jack," he said patiently, "there is no need for a follow-up examination. There is no doubt here."

Hoffman seemed about to go off at that, but he caught himself and mustered a conciliatory gaze. "Listen," he said. "I'll make a deal with you. You do a follow-up with Campbell, and if he passes, I'll drop him as a suspect. You have my word."

It was a waste of time, Matthews thought, but if it would put the matter to an end, he supposed he could do it. "Okay," he told Hoffman. "I'll call him back in."

"You do that," Hoffman said, satisfied. "Meantime, I'll check out this so-called alibi of his."

Thus, a weary Matthews reluctantly called Campbell, who agreed to appear at Hollywood PD at 10:00 a.m. on Monday for a follow-up exam. And later that Saturday, Hoffman took another detective with him to the Gold Strand Motel on Collins Avenue in far north Dade County, where Campbell had been running a boat rental concession for about seven months.

At the Gold Strand, Hoffman spoke with the hotel manager, Carroll Shannon, who confirmed that Campbell indeed worked there, but as to his whereabouts on the Monday that Adam Walsh disappeared, she had no idea. Maybe they should talk to Louis Munoz, her assistant pool manager. When Hoffman and his partner found Munoz, he remembered the day well. Munoz told them that Jimmy Campbell had arrived at about ten thirty that morning, excited about getting his sailboats cleaned up for a TV commercial that would be filmed at the hotel later in the afternoon. He noticed Jimmy puttering about throughout the day, Munoz said. When Joe Walsh, John's brother, came by looking for Jimmy at around three thirty, he was out on the ocean on one of his boats.

From the Gold Strand, Hoffman and his partner went to Jimmy Campbell's home, where they interviewed him regarding his association with the Walsh family and his whereabouts on July 27, the day Adam disappeared. As he had told Matthews, Campbell explained that he had known John Walsh for nine years and that he had lived with the family for about four years. He did various chores around the place, and sometimes babysat for Adam, whom he had come to love. He took the boy on outings to the beach, the zoo, and baseball games. He'd even served as Adam's T-ball coach this past year.

He'd been at work the day of Adam's disappearance, leaving only briefly to go to the nearby Thunderbird Motel boat concession to see if he could borrow two clean sails for his upcoming shoot, but the person in charge wasn't around, so he returned to the Golden Strand. As to who might have been responsible for Adam's disappearance, Campbell told the detectives that he had not the slightest idea. Hoffman took it all down in the form of notes, for some reason failing to record the interview as he had all the others he had conducted during his investigation. At the end of the interview, Hoffman noted that he asked the subject to voluntarily submit to a polygraph examination, as if Matthews hadn't already conducted one. It would be a long time before the reason for that odd statement—and Hoffman's failure to record his interview—came to light.

HOLLYWOOD, FLORIDA—AUGUST 10, 1981
On Monday, Joe Matthews was back at Hollywood police headquarters bright and early, preparing to reexamine Jimmy Camp-

bell. Matthews was convinced it was a waste of time, but if it might somehow put Hoffman's suspicions concerning Campbell to rest, then he would do it.

When the appointed hour of 10:00 a.m. came and went without Jimmy Campbell's appearance, however, Matthews became concerned. By 11:00, he decided to walk down to Hoffman's desk and let the detective know that Campbell was a no-show. Maybe the kid was scared, he thought. Maybe he'd overslept. But he wasn't involved in Adam's disappearance. That much he was sure of.

Hoffman, however, was not at his desk. When Matthews asked the detective bureau's secretary where Hoffman was, she told him Hoffman was in the interview room. He and his partner Ron Hickman had been grilling a suspect since seven that morning. What suspect? Matthews wondered. He hadn't heard anything about a suspect.

"Some guy named Campbell," was the secretary's answer.

Matthews couldn't believe it. He hurried down to the interrogation room—where the "Interview in Progress" sign had been left unlighted, he noted—and yanked open the door. Some "interview," he was thinking. He had heard Hoffman screaming, "You lying piece of shit," all the way down the hall. Sure enough, inside the room, he found an ashen Jimmy Campbell on the other side of a table from a livid Hoffman and Hickman.

"What the fuck are you guys doing?" Matthews asked.

"We're interviewing a suspect," Hoffman managed. His bravado seemed to have faltered. Even Hickman was avoiding Matthews's gaze.

"The hell you are," Matthews replied. "He's supposed to be with me right now. I can't fucking believe it," and with that he pulled Campbell from the room and back to his own desk. There wasn't even a murmur of protest from Hoffman and Hickman.

"Why are they treating me so rough?" Campbell asked when

they were finally settled. "They seem to think I'm responsible for Adam being missing. They're making all kinds of accusations." Matthews did his best to get Campbell calmed down so that he could be productively examined, all the while thinking that it was just one more screwup on the part of Hoffman. No way on earth could you accuse a suspect of a crime minutes before administering a polygraph exam and expect to get anything usable out of it. Hoffman simply seemed oblivious to standard police procedures.

After a bit of time in Matthews's presence, Campbell finally began to breathe again. "I know I've got to calm down," he told Matthews. "I've got to calm down and convince myself not to let the barbarians get to me." Still, as he confided to Matthews, it was more than difficult to be accused of doing harm to a child whom he loved. "I *do* take it personally. It's very upsetting."

To get Campbell relaxed, Matthews took him out to lunch, then brought him back to the station, where they went back over the events they'd discussed two nights earlier. Finally, early that evening, Matthews deemed Campbell ready, and he began the testing once again.

They were nearing the conclusion of this second exam when the door to the room flew open and Matthews saw an obviously agitated assistant chief of police Leroy Hessler beckoning him outside. Matthews told Campbell to hold on for a moment and went to join Hessler in the hallway.

"We just got a call," Hessler told Matthews, grimly. "They found a severed head in a drainage ditch beside the turnpike up in Indian River County. They think it's the boy's."

He pointed at the door to the interview room where Campbell sat, oblivious. "We know he did it," Hessler said to Matthews. "And I want a confession."

Matthews paid little attention to Hessler's demands, but at the same time he was numbed by the information that Hessler had delivered. Statistics might dictate that fewer than one hundred children are kidnapped and murdered in a year, but reassuring statistics are little comfort when you're one of the exceptions. As for Hessler's cockeyed demands that he extract a confession from Jimmy Campbell come hell or high water, Matthews considered any number of outraged responses, most of which would have accomplished little good.

"I'm in the middle of an examination," he told Hessler finally, turning away. "I'll bring my report down as soon as we're finished in there."

Back inside the room, Matthews apologized to Campbell for the interruption and managed to complete his examination, which indicated once again that his subject—despite everything he had been subjected to—clearly and positively had no idea of what might have happened to Adam Walsh. Matthews thanked Campbell for his cooperation and told him to go on home. He sat alone then for a moment, wondering if it was true—that the water had claimed Adam Walsh after all, if scarcely in a way that anyone might have imagined. Tragedy didn't come any grimmer than that, he thought. Then he went to track down Hoffman.

He found the lead investigator in a back office where a crowd of somber-looking detectives had gathered, along with Assistant Chief Hessler. In the two hours that had passed since Hessler burst into Matthews's examination room, the news had been confirmed. With the Walshes off in New York City to be interviewed about the search for Adam on *Good Morning America*, family friend John Monahan had been summoned by Indian River authorities to see if he could make an identification and confirm what dental records seemed to suggest.

Coincidentally, the canal where the gruesome find had been made bordered an orange grove recently treated by pesticides. The runoff had so drenched the canal with chemicals that nothing was alive to disturb the flesh on the severed head, despite all the time that had passed. There was not a doubt in the witness's mind.

In the back office of the Hollywood PD, about a hundred miles south of where Monahan had made his identification, Hessler turned to Matthews and jabbed a finger angrily. "You don't have the balls to call this Campbell deceptive."

Matthews was astonished. No way on earth had Jimmy Campbell murdered Adam Walsh, then hacked off his head and dumped it in an upstate canal. Every fiber in his cop's body was certain of it.

Jimmy Campbell had nothing to do with the crime and there was no way Matthews would be bullied into saying otherwise. Everyone else in the crowded room was quiet, looking at him expectantly. In other offices down the hall, phones rang, file doors creaked and slammed, voices rose and fell, all the hum-drum sounds of daily cop business. In this room, Matthews thought, "ordinary" had lost its meaning, "procedure" had taken a hike.

Finally, Matthews spoke. "I'm nobody's whore," he told Hessler. "I call it the way I see it."

Hessler regarded him for a moment, his face a mask of rage. Matthews wondered for a moment if the man might be about to take a swing at him, but the moment passed, and Hessler turned to take Hoffman by the arm, guiding him quickly out of the room. As the two disappeared down the hallway, Hessler fired his parting shot. "This one you called wrong, Matthews."

CHAPTER THREE

World of Hurt

Q: How many killings would you say you've been
involved in?

A: I don't know. Maybe a couple hundred.

Q: Would you say more of those were women or more
were men?

A: A little bit of both.

Q: And you say you did these killings because it gave
you a high?

A: That's right.

Q: And how long did that feeling last?

A: Maybe a week, maybe a month.

Q: And when the feeling went away?

A: Then you go out and do it again.

—OTTIS TOOLE, WITH TEXAS RANGERS,
MARCH 24, 1984

JACKSONVILLE, FLORIDA—MAY 16, 1981
If Ottis Toole had ever felt much sense of control over his life,
the sensation was a fleeting one. He had an IQ of 75, considered the borderline for retardation in the adult population, just

above the average intellect of a twelve-year-old child. According to the literature, adults in this category are considered "slow and simple," and while they are capable of gainful employment, supervision must be constant. Such individuals are only marginally capable of coping in an adult world, and in the language of the Stanford-Binet Intelligence Scales, "need help from friends or family to manage life's complications."

In Toole's case, about the only such help he ever received came from his mother, Sarah. He'd been born to her in March 1947, but he'd never known his father. A stepfather named Robert Harley arrived when Toole was ten, but he had never bonded with the man, who had alcohol problems. Perhaps the fact that Toole was "slow" helped keep them apart. Or it could have been the seizures that he had suffered since the day when a neighbor kid chucked a rock against Toole's skull, intending to "kill the retard."

He'd managed to struggle through seven years of special education classes and had even gotten to the point of being able to read and write, and also, to suffer when other kids ridiculed him. He was sexually molested by the husband of a neighbor when he was six, and once, during the several times he ran away from home, was picked up by cops who noticed that he had dressed himself as a girl. Gradually, he came to think of himself as a homosexual, but he wasn't entirely sure. He had intimate relations with women as well, and even tried marriage, thinking it might help "change" him. The experiment hit its first serious obstacle after four days when Toole disappeared, and one of his older sisters informed his new bride that Toole was "queer as a three-dollar bill."

Life had obviously been a continual struggle for Toole, but there was one constant, one source of comfort in his mind, and that was his certainty that his mother loved him. She herself suffered from bouts of mental illness, but when it came to Ottis, the youngest of her nine children, she seemed to understand that she was the only force standing between her son and an unimaginable bleak emptiness.

If indeed it was the love of Sarah Toole that enabled Ottis to cope, it was a tenuous form of coping by any standards. He'd been booked at seventeen for loitering, and for petty larceny the year after. In 1968, at the age of twenty-one, he was arrested for vagrancy and a few months later for prowling. The next year he was again charged with vagrancy. In 1972, he was apprehended while carrying a concealed weapon, a four-inch hunting knife. He'd been arrested for loitering in a bus station in 1975, for lewd and lascivious behavior in an adult theater in 1976, and later that year for public intoxication. In 1977, he was arrested for making obscene phone calls, window-peeping, cross-dressing, and exposing himself in public.

Yet Toole had still managed to weather all this, to make his way through a sad facsimile of life, because—in his mind, at least—he had his mother, and she loved him, right up to the last day of her life, which was May 16, 1981. And that is when things truly began to fall apart.

At the time of his mother's death, Toole, then thirty-four, was living at home with her and his stepfather, Robert Harley, and the three young children of his sister Druscilla: Frieda, Frank, and Sarah Powell. Also living in the home at 708 Day Avenue was Toole's lover, Henry Lee Lucas, forty-five, a slightly built, glass-eyed drifter he had met at a Jacksonville soup kitchen three years earlier. While photographs taken of Lucas around the time depict him as marginally presentable, it is difficult to imagine what he might have found attractive in the gangly, slump-shouldered, gap-toothed Toole, who generally sported several days' growth of grizzled facial hair, his sandy hair thinning and generally unkempt, his clothing characteristically rumpled and rank from days of wear.

Still, indifference to style and hygiene are not always barriers to love, nor to gainful employment. In fact, Toole was working as a laborer for a man named John Reaves, who owned a couple of roofing businesses in Jacksonville. Toole took his mother's death hard, Reaves recalls. He'd go out to the Evergreen Cemetery where she had been buried and lie down on her grave. To Toole, the ground above her coffin seemed inexplicably warm, and he was convinced that at times he could feel it move beneath his body.

Toole, who was becoming more despondent by the day, confided that he began to hear voices suggesting that he should kill himself and "go to rest" with his mother. Sometime he heard the voices in his sleep, and other times he was wide awake. It could have been his mind, he thought. Or it could have been the devil.

Not surprisingly, Toole's appearances at Reaves Roofing company became less and less frequent, and on Friday, June 5, 1981, they ceased altogether. Meantime, Robert Harley reported the theft of several items, including jewelry and furniture, from the house he had shared with Toole's mother. He suspected Toole and Lucas, but he had no idea where the two of them might have gone. Harley was alone in the house now, since Toole's older brother Howard had agreed to take custody of the younger children. And then, on June 23, 1981, while Harley was away, the home at 708 Day Avenue was set ablaze, an apparent case of arson.

Police might have talked to Ottis Toole and Henry Lee Lucas about the thefts and the fire, but the two were nowhere to be found. As it turned out, they had borrowed a Ford pickup truck from Toole's sister-in-law Georgia, telling her they were going to haul a load of scrap iron to the Jacksonville dump. In truth, they were on their way up the East Coast to Maryland, intending to make "a fresh start," and taking with them Ottis's twelve-year-old nephew Frank and his 13-year-old niece Frieda "Becky" Powell.

On July 8, the truck was found abandoned in Wellington, Delaware, and police contacted Georgia, telling her she had thirty days to reclaim it before it would be sold at auction. Georgia quickly filed a report with the Jacksonville sheriff, accusing Ottis Toole and Henry Lee Lucas of the theft of her truck, and on July 22, 1981, after an APB was issued, Maryland state troopers spotted Henry Lee Lucas in the town of Pikesville. Lucas was arrested on charges of unauthorized use of a motor vehicle and taken immediately to jail. The children, who were with him at the time, were placed in the hands of Child Protective Services to be sent back to Florida.

Toole, meantime, was not involved, because he had wandered off from the others during a hard night of drinking the night before in Newport News, Virginia. Convinced that Lucas (an admitted bisexual) had fallen in love with thirteen-year-old Frieda and run off without him, Toole swallowed an overdose of sleeping pills and collapsed on the streets.

When he awakened in the Riverside Hospital in Newport News on July 23, Toole was willing to talk with doctors concerning his depression over the death of his mother, but he denied that he had attempted suicide. He said that he had been drifting around the country, sleeping on the streets, and now wanted only to return to Jacksonville, where there was a job waiting for him with a roofing company. Adjudged no threat to himself or to others, he was discharged from the hospital, and on the afternoon of July 24, Ottis Toole was given a check by the Newport News Salvation Army, made out payable to the Greyhound Bus Company in the amount of $71.93.

Toole walked the two miles from Salvation Army headquarters to the Greyhound station, where he exchanged the check for a one-way ticket to Jacksonville, and at 6:30 p.m. he was on board. It would take somewhere between sixteen and twenty hours for the bus to make its way from Virginia to Florida, and as every mile clicked by, Ottis Toole thought of his mother, and of the lover who had betrayed him, and listened to the voices in his head.

JACKSONVILLE, FLORIDA—JULY 25, 1981

It was around eleven on Saturday morning when Ottis Toole stepped off his bus at the Greyhound terminal in Jacksonville.

Some individuals might have been exhausted by a twenty-hour bus ride across five states, but Toole was not. Compared to sleeping on the seat of a pickup truck carrying four passengers, or on a sidewalk, or in a jail cell, or in a hospital psychiatric ward with lunatics screaming and doctors and nurses poking and prodding, to Toole all those hours in the broad reclining seat of a Greyhound bus was an interlude in paradise.

He stretched, undaunted by the humid blanket of Florida summer heat, and began the seven-mile walk to Reaves Roofing, the company owned by John Reaves Sr. There wouldn't be anyone there on a Saturday morning, but that was fine by Toole. Despite what he'd told the doctors and the people at the Salvation Army in Newport News, he had no intention of going back to work firing up tar pots and hoisting heavy rolls of one-ply asphalt up to scalding rooftops. There were easier ways to make money and better places than Jacksonville to do it in.

It took him about two hours to reach Reaves Roofing. As he expected, the compound was deserted, and his key to the gate still worked. There by the gas pumps, just where it was the last time he'd been in the yard, sat the black-over-white '71 Cadillac he'd purchased back in January from Faye Reaves McNett, the aunt of his boss.

Technically, the car was no longer his, since he'd long since fallen behind on the weekly payments of $25 he'd agreed to make. He'd returned the car to McNett some months ago, but she stored it in the company compound, and Toole, using the spare keys he had for the place and those he had made for the car, had "borrowed" the Caddy on more than one occasion since.

Toole filled the Caddy with gas from the company tanks, locked the gate behind him, and drove the few miles to what was left of his mother's house. He'd forgotten something that day that he'd set the place on fire, but he was fairly certain it was still there.

He kept a number of tools in the Caddy, and it did not take

him long to unearth the coffee tin full of cash that constituted his "bank," buried underneath the still-standing front porch. Toole stuffed $300 worth of bills in his pocket, tossed the can into the charred rubble of the house, and set out on the five-hour drive down I-95 to South Florida.

It was his intention to hit the gay parks up and down Biscayne Boulevard in Miami, where he could fatten his bankroll by anywhere from $20 to $50 a trick, and even more by jack-rolling the defenseless among his clientele. But by the time he passed through Fort Lauderdale, a half hour north of his target, it seemed a bit early for such goings-on.

Still, he thought, there were ways he might amuse himself in the meantime. Accordingly, at the Hollywood Exit, he swung the Cadillac off I-95 and cruised along the boulevard until he spotted a Kmart up ahead. Toole pulled into the crowded lot, nodding with satisfaction at all the cars. He didn't need to buy a single thing, it was true, but there were other attractions at a place like this.

Arlene Mayer remembers that it was about seven in the evening when she and her husband, Wayne, arrived at the Hollywood Kmart. They had their twelve-year-old daughter Heidi in tow and were set on picking up a few things for the house. If Heidi kept her promise to be good, she might get that toy Arlene had been promising.

Wayne had just gotten off work, and since he considered himself too dirty to be seen, he told Arlene that he would just relax in the car while she and Heidi did the shopping. It presented no problem for Arlene. She reminded Heidi that she had better be good, and the two set out for the store.

As they walked past what Arlene remembers as a "large white car," they noticed the driver's door swinging open. He was white, in his mid-thirties, and was odd-looking to both of them, "like a bum." Most distressing was the fact that Arlene could hear his footsteps dogging the two of them all the way across the parking lot. Why had she been so accommodating when Wayne said he wanted to sit tight? she wondered.

As they neared the building, the man hurried past them and approached a bank of pay phones by the entrance. He lifted the receiver of one of the phones and mimed dropping coins into the slot, Arlene recalls, even though it was obvious he had no money in his hand. The two of them were happy to get past this creep and into the safety of the brightly lit store.

They grabbed a shopping cart just inside the entrance, and to appease her daughter, Arlene took them straight to the toy department. "Go ahead and look around," she told Heidi, then pointed to the nearby housewares section. "I'm running right over there for something. You keep the cart. I'll be right back."

Heidi was understandably delighted to be left alone in wonderland. But the moment her mother had disappeared and she turned her cart to head for the section where the dolls were stacked, she stopped short. Blocking the aisle before her was the man who'd followed them through the parking lot. In the bright Kmart lights, he looked like something out of a slasher film. Several days' growth of beard pocked his cheeks, his hair was unkempt, one eye wandered aimlessly, and a lunatic smile exposed a set of yellowing teeth. Heidi could feel the wash of this man's fetid breath and smell his ripe body odor from several feet away.

"Why don't I give you a ride in that shopping cart?" he asked in a tone that was meant to be enticing.

Heidi had the good sense to scream.

Toole was gone long before store security came looking for him. By the time the girl was able to stop crying and make herself understood to her mother, he had ambled away, into the shadows of the parking lot. As soon as things calmed down, he'd get into his Cadillac and drive away, just another departing Kmart shopper.

He would head on down to Miami now and spend the night

as he had intended. And once that was over, he would find a place to park the Caddy, somewhere that he could sleep in peace. And tomorrow or the next day, he could try some shopping again.

That little girl he'd followed into the Kmart was about the same age as his niece Becky Powell, who'd dumped him and ran off with Henry Lee. This one hadn't seemed too fond of him either, but that was okay. There were lots of young ones to talk to, and he knew that, eventually, he would find one who would listen. In these parts, there seemed no end of promising malls.

HOLLYWOOD, FLORIDA—JULY 27, 1981

Bill Mistler, owner of a local pest control company, is certain of what he saw outside the Sears store in Hollywood on the fateful Monday afternoon that the Walsh boy disappeared. Mistler was on his way to Sears to pick up some supplies for a camping trip he'd planned for his family the next day, and while he was waiting for an old lady to work her way into a parking space at the curb by the store entrance, he noticed a white Cadillac with a black top coming toward him from the opposite direction.

The Cadillac, which seemed to have a bunch of long-handled gardening tools in the backseat, stopped in the driving lane opposite, and Mistler watched as an odd-looking man with reddish brown hair and a wandering eye got out and started toward the store.

As Mistler waited, the man, who was wearing a filthy T-shirt, approached a neatly dressed boy of about five who was standing on the sidewalk by the curb. Nearby were a woman and another young boy and girl. Mistler assumed it was a mother and her three children at first, but when the odd-looking guy from the Cadillac bent down and began talking to the younger boy, the mother seemed to take no notice. After a moment, in fact, the woman gathered her two children and walked away.

Mistler looked again at the shabbily dressed man and the little boy. Though it seemed impossible that the two belonged together, the child did not seem afraid. After a moment, the man stood and took the boy's arm and the two walked together toward the Cadillac. The man helped the boy into the front seat through the driver's door, then got in after him.

By this time, another parking space had opened up, and Mistler pulled his truck in. As the Cadillac drove past, Mistler noticed that someone had left quite a dent in the right side of the car's rear bumper. And, to his everlasting dismay, that is the last that he thought of it all for a very long time. He simply did what anyone might have done: he went into the Sears store, did the shopping for his trip, and forgot all about what he had seen.

"I told the little cocksucker I had some candy and toys," Toole confided later. The moment the boy was in the car, he locked all the doors and windows. The boy wondered about that, but Toole explained that it would make them safe. They would just have to drive a ways to where the candy was.

He made a quick right out of the parking lot, and inside ten minutes they were headed north on Florida's Turnpike. He had to stop at a tollbooth to pick up a ticket, and by now the boy was raising all kinds of hell, trying to get the attention of the clerk. Toole gave the clerk a weary smile—"Kids."

As they rolled on out of the toll chute, Toole gave the boy a healthy backhand across the face, which only seemed to set him off further. The kid was really getting on his nerves now, so Toole landed a few more punches to the boy's stomach and face. "I'm pretty sure I knocked that kid out," he remembers. In any case, the car was now quiet.

Toole drove in silence for a while, the Caddy's big V8 chewing up the miles. He'd intended to take the kid slumped on the seat beside him back up to Jacksonville where they could live together and be friends, but obviously, that wasn't going to work. The problem was, what to do next?

Toole was no dummy, after all. This kid was very young, but

he also seemed pretty smart. Smart enough to identify Toole if he just let him go.

All in all, there didn't seem to be much choice. He'd driven quite a ways up the turnpike by the time he made his decision, and the busy sprawl of South Florida was far behind him. The brightly lit malls had disappeared, the glittery beachside hotels that loomed like giant, overdecorated Cadillacs were gone, the whole miragelike tropical landscape that seemed to offer up anything a person might want was vanished like a fever dream.

He was alone with an unconscious little boy on the broad seat beside him, and now they were driving through flatlands that seemed to stretch forever, plains dotted here and there by hardwood hammocks or clusters of palmetto scrub, vistas that might have evoked the Serengeti Plains had there been anyone around to know what Africa was.

Prehistoric. Elemental. A man could distinguish crazy dreams from cold, hard reality in a place like this.

Finally, from the corner of his eye, Toole spotted an unmarked service road leading off the turnpike. He'd overshot the unpaved exit, and had to pull to the side of the turnpike and back up to get to it, but that made it perfect for his purposes. It was a rough road, winding through a thick tangle of Australian pines and Brazilian holly, but the jolting did not wake the boy.

Just as well, Toole thought. He didn't want to have to hurt anyone. When he reached a fork in the road and was sure that they were out of sight of the turnpike, he stopped and switched off the Caddy's engine. He got out and went around to the passenger's door, opened it, and lifted up the unconscious little boy. It was so quiet here that the distant traffic was like a gentle surf, the pinging of the cooling Caddy's hood keeping time. He carried the boy to an open space he had spotted in the forsaken tangle of trees and brush and laid him facedown in the sandy dirt.

Toole walked back to his car and stood surveying his tools,

ignoring the cloud of bloodsucking mosquitoes that had already homed in on him. There was a machete in the backseat that he supposed he could use, and a bayonet that he kept hidden under the front seat. That ought to be enough to manage it. He reached for what he needed, and then he went to do his work.

VERO BEACH, FLORIDA—AUGUST 10, 1981

At 8:45 p.m. on a Monday evening two weeks after Adam Walsh went missing, Indian River County medical examiner Franklin H. Cox received a phone call from the sheriff's office informing him of a gruesome find in a canal near the turnpike about twenty miles west of his office in the town of Vero Beach. Cox was no stranger to the aftermath of violence, for even a sleepy beachside hamlet like Vero Beach has its share of bloody family disputes and garden-variety shootouts at convenience stores, but it is safe to say that the call he received that evening, informing him that fishermen had found the decapitated head of a young boy floating in the water, was the first of its kind.

The severed head was transported to the autopsy room at Indian River Memorial Hospital in Vero Beach, and at 2:00 a.m., Cox met police there to perform a preliminary examination of the remains. Don Coleman and Sid Dubose, homicide detectives from Indian River County, were present, along with three detectives dispatched from Jack Hoffman's team at Hollywood PD, 136 miles to the south.

Cox described his findings in the dispassionate language of his profession, noting "extensive cutting and chopping wounds . . . posteriorly from ear to ear" as well as cuts to the ears and occipital bones. One of the cervical vertebra was exposed at the base of the skull, "transversely sectioned," Cox recorded. There were no ragged tissues anywhere—just the clean, sharp edges that might be expected when a head is cleaved from its body with a heavy weapon.

Cox observed that the eyes in the head were bulging, but that was likely a postmortem phenomenon, a result of the gas that had formed in the decomposing tissues of the brain and sent the organ rising to the surface of the canal. As Cox also took the time to mention, "Extensive putrefaction with a foul-smelling odor [was] present."

Cox completed his work with an examination of the teeth. He found the upper right incisor missing, where a new tooth had been erupting through the gum to take its place. All the other teeth were whole, though there looked to be an amalgam filling in the last left molar, an observation that Cox confirmed with X-rays. With that, Cox concluded his examination. All he could do then was wait.

At about 11:00 a.m. on Tuesday, Lieutenant Dick Hynds, the supervisor of detectives who had introduced Joe Matthews around Hollywood PD less than a week before, arrived in Vero Beach, accompanied by John Monahan, the man whose own son John Walsh had saved that long-ago day at the Diplomat Hotel. Hynds brought with him Adam Walsh's records and X-rays from Hollywood dentist Marshall Berger, which showed an amalgam filling "on the buccal side of the last lower left deciduous molar." The filling was identical to that which Cox had discovered.

If there remained any doubt as to the identity of the remains, Monahan quickly took care of it. He took one look at the face—he *could* be wrong, he told himself—then asked the medical examiner to part the lips. When he saw the missing incisor and the tooth that had been coming in to replace it, his hopes vanished. He closed his eyes briefly, then turned to Hynds and Cox. "That's him," Monahan said. "That's Adam Walsh."

Earlier that morning, John Walsh awakened in his bed at the St. Moritz Hotel in New York City, groping over a still-sleeping Revé for the ringing phone. As he lifted the receiver, he glanced at the bedside clock: 6:00 a.m.

Walsh was so groggy he couldn't even be sure who the caller was, but when he finally made his purpose clear, Walsh snapped awake.

Some remains had been found, the voice on the other end was telling him—it was a cop, wasn't it?—but Walsh was not to be concerned, since the discovery had been made such a distance from Hollywood. They suspected it was a missing ten-year-old boy from the Tampa area. They just needed the name of the Walsh family dentist—they'd get the records and rule out any chance that it was Adam. Meantime, Walsh should not be worried.

Not be worried? Walsh thought, as he gave the caller the information. He hung up the phone, trying to process what he had just heard, trying to decide whether or not to wake Revé and share the news.

As he pondered, the phone rang again, and Walsh snatched it up. This time it was a producer from *Good Morning America*. Word had already reached the network that a severed head had been found in a canal in Florida. The producer wanted to offer the Walshes a chance to cancel their appearance on the show in case the remains turned out to be Adam's.

But Walsh wasn't canceling anything. Despite the dread that he was feeling, he couldn't be certain what this discovery in Florida might mean, and the opportunity to appear on national television to publicize Adam's disappearance was one in a million. He had brought along photographs of other desperate parents' missing children as well; no way could he cancel the appearance.

"What else can I do?" he told the producer, willing away his dread. Even if it was Adam who'd been found, he said, "I still have to give it a shot for all the other kids."

The producer understood. This was the Walshes' call. The car would be at the hotel to pick them up, as scheduled.

By the time Revé woke, Walsh had made the decision to keep the phone calls to himself. No point in worrying her, he told himself. And besides, to talk about the calls only made the possibility that Adam had been harmed seem all the more real.

The interview, with *Good Morning America* coanchor David Hartman, went on for seven full minutes, without a hitch. The Walshes described their plight in touching detail, and Adam's photograph and description were broadcast to millions of viewers around the country. John got the opportunity to work in photos of the other missing children as well. It was the first time that national network news had ever broadcast such a story on the helpless situations parents of missing children often found themselves in, and for all that the Walshes were cheered.

At the end of the piece, however, Hartman asked about the chilling report that remains of a young boy had been discovered in a canal near Vero Beach. Walsh stole a quick look at Revé. She was quiet and composed, but he knew his wife well enough—she'd been blindsided by the news.

Walsh quickly told Hartman that he'd been reassured the discovery had nothing to do with Adam. And in any case, the news only underscored the importance of their appearance on the show. There were terrible things that were going on all the time, and no one was hearing about them. It was vitally important to get the word out quickly, everywhere, when a child went missing.

By the time the segment was over, Revé seemed to have put aside the disturbing news Hartman had divulged, and John was relieved that his sister Jane and a few others were there to help. "I have to run up to the room to make a couple of calls," he told them, as the car delivered them back to the St. Moritz. He promised to meet them just down the street at the Plaza for something to eat in just a few minutes.

Back in his room, John checked for messages and was relieved to find there were none. Still, he could not shake the ominous feeling that the 6:00 a.m. call had instilled in him. A child's head found severed and floating in a canal. Unthinkable. Surely such a thing could not have happened to his Adam. Besides, the voice on the other end of the telephone line had told him not to worry. But how long could he live with such uncertainty? One moment he was composed, the next he found himself fighting to draw a breath.

He glanced at his watch—11:35 a.m.—and that was when the phone rang again. "Give it to me straight," he told the caller. And that is what he got. *Hollywood Sun-Tattler* reporter Charlie Brennan, who'd accompanied John and Revé on their trip to New York, was in the room and later described Walsh as he hung up the phone: "A man with a large part of his heart now stolen."

Revé Walsh was sitting with her sister-in-law at the bar of the Plaza Hotel when a young man with a carefully masked expression came to whisper something in Jane's ear. Jane's expression did not waver, but in Revé's mind, all the pieces fell immediately into place.

All Jane would say was that John was waiting for her back at the hotel. But Revé knew. No one had to tell her. She was Adam's mother.

On the way back to the St. Moritz, it was Revé who squeezed Jane's hand and told her it would be all right. And when John opened the door to their room and said simply, "Our baby's dead," Revé could only reach out for his waiting arms and hold on and tell him that yes, she knew.

Shortly after noon on Tuesday, and at the urging of Hollywood authorities, medical examiner Cox phoned Dr. Ron Wright, his counterpart in Ft. Lauderdale, to pass along the results of his preliminary examination. As chief medical examiner in the county where the investigation of Adam's disappearance was centered, Wright was the natural choice to complete the autopsy. Accordingly, Cox had the remains packed in ice and handed them over to Ronald Young, one of the Hollywood detectives present at Cox's exam, who quickly boarded a helicopter for Broward County.

By 4:00 p.m., Dr. Wright had begun his own examination, quickly determining that the brain matter inside the skull had liquefied, which suggested that death had occurred at least ten days or more prior to discovery. Among other findings, Wright reported that the victim had received repeated blows to the face and had suffered a fractured nose. Given the presence of burst blood vessels in the eyes, Wright theorized that the victim had been strangled and, at the time of the decapitation, was likely dead. He noted the likely cause of death as "asphyxiation," which put a slightly finer point on medical examiner Cox's preliminary notation of "homicide."

As to the decapitation itself, Wright said that it had taken place with the victim lying facedown, that the assailant had been right-handed, that the person had employed a machete or cleaver with a blade five inches or more in length, and would necessarily have needed two hands on the weapon's handle in order to exert the required force.

Meanwhile, search and dive teams had been dispatched to the canal where Adam's head had been discovered, but the failure to find the slightest bit of evidence led authorities to believe that the crime had taken place elsewhere, with the head discarded in the canal at a later time. Law enforcement officials in four neighboring counties searched other canals and fields for the body. Florida Highway Patrol officers combed both sides of Florida's Turnpike between Miami and Orlando looking for clothing or other clues, and game wardens in the vast swampy regions west of the turnpike redoubled their own efforts.

By Wednesday, the story was front-page news across South Florida: "Adam Walsh Found Dead—Discovered in Vero Canal." "Sixteen Days of Agony Grow into Horrid, Tragic Climax." "As Parents Pleaded, Police Suspected the Worst." Broward County medical examiner Wright told the Associated Press that indeed Adam had been dead for at least ten days before his head was found, and Hollywood supervisor of detectives Hynds warned that a dangerous psychopath was on the loose: "No one else could have done it," Hynds said.

The Walshes returned to South Florida on Tuesday evening and, after spending the following day fending off an onslaught from the media, held a private wake for their son at a local funeral home. On Saturday, Adam's funeral took place at St. Maurice's Catholic Church in Hollywood, with more than one thousand people in attendance.

Father Michael Conboy, John Walsh's cousin and a pastor at an upstate New York parish, delivered the eulogy. "We'll see you again, Cooter," Conboy said. "We promise."

The words were spoken as John, wearing a gray suit and tie, and Revé, in a muted print dress and dark-banded straw hat, stood somberly by an empty coffin. Adam's remains were being held by police. It was a necessary step, authorities explained. Should there be a confession, they would then be able to match the statement against the evidence.

Also in accordance with standard police procedure, Hollywood PD stationed a photographer to take surveillance photos of the attendees. It was not unknown for a stranger to turn up among the mourners of a loved one, and sometimes that stranger—drawn by the stir—turned out to be the reason for it all. Or to put it another way, sometimes the cops plain got lucky.

It was in this way, then, that the search for a missing little boy was transformed to a search for the person responsible for his death. The former undertaking, however grueling, had been fueled in part by a certain measure of hopefulness; but success in the latter would depend much more on grim resolve. In the end, it would turn out to be an extraordinarily long and arduous undertaking, and where luck figured in, almost all of it was bad.

CHAPTER FOUR

Through the Boneyard

Q: I know it's been four years . . .

A: Yeah, sometimes I can't keep it all straight in my mind.

Q: If I show you some pictures, maybe it'll help you remember.

A: Maybe.

Q: How about this one looking down into the culvert where we found the body. Do you remember stopping and throwing her down into the culvert?

A: Not really.

Q: How about this one? It's a little closer. You can see she's wearing only orange socks.

A: Yeah, I remember, now.

Q: But you don't remember what you did with the rest of her clothes?

A: Lots of times I'd just take the clothes and drive a piece and throw them down on the road a little ways from the body. Other times I'd leave them right there. I just don't remember about this one.

—OTTIS TOOLE TO DETECTIVES, JACKSONVILLE
COUNTY JAIL, DECEMBER 28, 1983

HOLLYWOOD, FLORIDA—AUGUST 13, 1981

The day after the news of Adam's death broke, Hollywood detectives received a report from Dr. Mark Reisner, a psychologist sometimes employed by the Los Angeles Police Department, who offered an unsolicited profile of the type of individual "capable of abducting, murdering and decapitating Adam Walsh." According to Reisner, who based his report on a match of the known details of the case against data compiled on known psychopathic behavior, Adam's killer was almost certainly male, somewhere between nineteen and thirty-five, though most probably in his early twenties.

Because such behavior is not generally interracial in nature, Reisner theorized that the perpetrator was either Caucasian or Latin. The nature of the crime also indicated the possession of a "borderline" psychopathic/psychotic personality with a powerful homosexual conflict ultimately expressed in rage and violence. Although the person was very likely a loner, liked by few, he would nonetheless be motivated to brag about the actions he had taken in order to validate his sense of self-worth. However, Reisner said, it was unlikely that he would exhibit any sense of remorse or guilt, or offer a formal confession to the abduction or murder.

The individual would likely have gained little formal education, Reisner noted, and probably came from a lower socioeconomic background, with a work history involving manual labor and jobs requiring minimal skills. Because such an individual would not have progressed in any meaningful social or psychological way himself, he would be likely to identify with and be attracted to children. He might even have sought work that placed him in the company of children, with whom he could more easily develop bonds than with adults, either male or female.

Almost certainly, Reisner said, this individual had abducted or attempted to abduct other children in the past. And Reisner was equally certain that he had sexually assaulted other children and had very likely been arrested and imprisoned for such acts. Perhaps most distressing was one of Reisner's final observations, that the decapitation and disposal of the head indicated that there had been sexual contact with the boy—the perpetrator ridding himself of the principal locus of the shame, as it were.

While all this might have proven of interest to investigators, there was little that matched up with any of the individuals in the known orbit of the Walsh family's lives. Certainly, Reisner's profile dovetailed with Lieutenant Hynd's statement that only a psychopath could have done what was done to Adam, but as to the identity of that individual or suggestions as to how he might be found, there was not much to go on.

On Tuesday, August 18, lead detective Hoffman called Revé Walsh to Hollywood PD headquarters, where he and partner Hickman led her through a painstaking re-creation of her activities on the day that Adam disappeared. Her account was virtually identical to that which she had provided before, however, leaving the detectives stymied. By August 27, the baffled department issued a statement to the press that the investigation had been scaled back to three detectives. As Detective Hoffman explained, "It can't go on forever. The manpower is needed in other places."

On August 28, Hoffman met with Adam Walsh's first-grade teacher, Christine Bernard, who assured the detective that Adam was a good student, but a shy and somewhat timid boy who had never wandered off during recess or school outings. Following that interview, Hoffman returned to the Sears store to interview the clerk who had waited on Revé Walsh the day of Adam's disappearance. The clerk recalled Revé, obviously, and remembered her returning in distress to the lamp department looking for Adam, but she had nothing useful to add. On the following day, a UP story carried a statement that seemed provocative enough: an investigator with the Broward County medical examiner's office told reporters that they knew what kind of weapon had been used to decapitate Adam Walsh but were keeping the information secret so that they could discount the claims of "wackos who want to claim responsibility."

There appeared to be no surplus of such wackos lining up, however. Hollywood PD public information officer Fred Barbetta admitted to reporters that the investigation seemed to have hit a dead end. "We have nothing to go on," he said. "Nothing whatsoever."

The only solid lead that had come their way—the supposed sighting of Adam being dragged into a blue Ford van—had resulted in nothing but frustration for officers and area drivers alike. Police had checked a list of nearly seven thousand such vehicles sold in South Florida over the past three years, Barbetta said, but nothing had come of it. Though twenty-five detectives had originally been assigned to the case, only Hoffman and Hickman now remained, and scarcely a month had gone by.

On September 2, Detective Hoffman for the first time interviewed Sears security guard Kathy Shaffer, the first person at the store to whom Revé had gone for help when she discovered Adam missing. Though Shaffer had told Revé that she had not seen her son that day, her story to Detective Hoffman was somewhat different. She said that in fact she had witnessed a bit of a disturbance at the Atari PlayStation display at around 12:30 on the day of the disappearance. Two white male children and two black male children appeared to be arguing over the game, and as she approached them to see what was going on, one of the black kids slapped one of the white kids, a child whom she judged to be ten or so. One of the black children spoke impertinently to Shaffer, she said, and she told them all to leave the store.

The two black children left via the south doors, Shaffer told Hoffman, and the two white children left through the north doors. When the detective asked her to describe the second white child, Shaffer said that he was probably about seven, and had been wearing green shorts and a white shirt. At that point, Hoffman produced several photographs of Adam and asked if that was the boy she was talking about. Shaffer studied the photographs and then glanced up at Hoffman. She simply was not sure, she told him, and with that, Hoffman concluded their interview.

Two days later, on September 4, Hoffman's partner Hickman reinterviewed Marilyn Pottenberg, mother of the young boy who reported seeing Adam being dragged into "a blue van." With Mrs. Pottenberg and her son Timothy on that day was Timothy's grandmother Carolyn Hudson, and the two women pieced together the details of their shopping trip to Sears on the day of the abduction. They had arrived at the store about 11:45 a.m., they recalled, and left to have lunch at about 12:35 p.m. As they were leaving the store, Hudson recalls, they heard the page for a missing child. They all had lunch together, and at about 1:25, nearly an hour later, as they were walking through the parking lot toward their car, Timothy witnessed the incident with "the blue van."

If Hickman sighed as he recorded the details given him by Mrs. Pottenberg and her mother, he doesn't say so in his notes. But the information he'd just been given was the death knell for the "blue van" theory. Who knows what Timothy Pottenberg had actually seen that day? But it certainly wasn't Adam Walsh being dragged into a van, not almost an hour after his mother had begun her frantic search for him. "It appears that the incident that Timothy Pottenberg witnessed is unrelated to the Adam Walsh abduction," Hickman concluded.

With that lead gone, Hollywood PD was reduced to grasping at straws. Joe Matthews was asked to schedule a polygraph examination with Revé Walsh, to confirm that her unwavering account of Adam's disappearance could be trusted, and Matthews arranged it for Thursday, September 10, at police head-quarters.

At about nine on the morning of September 10, as Matthews traveled down Flamingo Road in western Broward County, on his way to meet with Revé, he found himself stuck behind a sedan traveling maybe fifteen miles an hour. Matthews pulled into the opposite lane to pass, but realized that the wise-guy driver on his right had suddenly sped up. Worse yet, a dump truck was now approaching from the opposite direction, and the driver he was trying to pass showed no signs of letting him by. Trapped now, Matthews floored his Plymouth and managed to squeeze past, only an instant before the roaring dump truck could pulverize him.

A bullet dodged, he was thinking, but then the real nightmare began.

What happened next was a blur. His wheels dropped off the pavement, digging into the gravel shoulder, and in the next instant the Plymouth was airborne. To anyone watching, it would have seemed like a spectacular scene from a car chase in an action film. The Plymouth soared out over the broad drainage canal that paralleled the highway, twisted over, then pancaked top-down onto the water's surface.

The impact rendered Matthews momentarily unconscious. When he came to, he found himself under several feet of water, still behind the wheel, the Plymouth sinking steadily toward the canal's muddy bottom. People and their vehicles ended up in these canals on an almost daily basis, and helicopter shots of bystanders gaping as cars and vans—often bearing their unfortunate passengers—were winched out were a staple of South Florida television news. Matthews had seen it a hundred times and had always marveled at the spectacular misfortune of the victims.

He'd rather go head-on into a bridge piling than sink to a watery grave, but somehow he had ended up in just that place, and goddamn Napoleon Bonaparte Broward anyway for thinking he had the right to drain the Everglades just so he could line his pockets. . . .

It's the sort of thinking that passes in a millisecond during a crash. In the next moment, Matthews had already forgotten about bad luck and greed, one hand groping for the door lever, the other flailing about for the precious possession beside him. He snatched his polygraph instrument by its case handle, managed to wrench his door open, then kicked himself free of the sinking car and burst to the surface of the murky water, gasping. Already, there was a highway patrolman clambering down the steep bank to help him out.

The cop took the case and helped Matthews up the rocky, debris-laden slope. At the top he regarded Matthews for a moment, then reached into the trunk of his cruiser and handed him a towel. "You better hold this on your head until the ambulance gets here," he said.

Matthews stared back at the cop, uncomprehending. "Why would I need to do that?"

"Just hold it right here," the cop said, pressing the towel to Matthews's head.

At the hospital, several hundred stitches to his laid-open skull later, Matthews gradually came to realize how badly he'd been hurt. Furthermore, he recalled, he'd been on his way to an important appointment, and managed to convince his doctors that he had to make a phone call. Only after he'd spoken to someone at Hollywood PD, then managed to reach his brother to tell him what had happened, did he give in to the doctors and the sedatives.

When he woke the next day, there was something nagging at Matthews, but he was still groggy from the concussion he'd suffered, and a severely dislocated shoulder was causing him immense pain. He simply couldn't put his finger on what was gnawing at him.

Not until he was released and on his way home several days later did he remember once again the polygraph exam that he had scheduled with Revé Walsh. The moment he made his way through the door of his house, he called Jack Hoffman at Hollywood PD. "I'm sorry about the exam, but I had a pretty bad accident—," Matthews began, but Hoffman cut him off.

"Yeah, we heard," the detective said. "Don't worry. We got somebody else to do it."

"Really?" Matthews said, taken aback. Matthews wasn't even sure how Hoffman knew he'd been hurt, for he had no recollection of making the call to Hollywood PD from the hospital. And while he couldn't blame Hoffman for going ahead without him, it was still a bit disconcerting—it would have been better for consistency's sake to have the same person conducting all the polygraph exams. What Hoffman said next, however, took him completely by surprise.

"Fact is, I'm glad you called," Hoffman continued. "I wanted to let you know we won't be needing you any longer."

Matthews felt his jaw sag as Hoffman continued. The investigation was winding down, the detective explained. If the need for any other testing arose, the department could take care of it themselves. Matthews could go on back to Miami Beach.

Matthews stared at the phone, as the connection broke, incensed at Hoffman and dismayed at the prospects for the investigation. From the beginning, he had pegged Hoffman as a turf-protecting blowhard if there ever was one, but he had dealt with those types before. What was truly disheartening was the response he'd received from Lieutenant Hynds when he'd tried to point out how the investigation seemed to be going awry.

From the moment that Hynds had put him off, he'd sensed that he was battling a prevailing current of face-saving at Hollywood PD, but what could he do besides perform the job he'd been called in for and hope that his results would have some effect? And, he supposed, his efforts had achieved something. If not for his work, it was possible that a hapless Jimmy Campbell could be in custody right now, desperately trying to proclaim his innocence.

There was plenty on his own plate. He had a full-time job in Miami Beach, and he was being called in as an outside polygraph expert on a regular basis by other agencies as well, including Canada's Crown Counsel, the equivalent to the office of the U.S. attorney general. Also, there was his thriving technical school, the Southern Institute of Polygraph, to manage. In the end, Matthews could only wish Hollywood PD well, offer his help on the Walsh case at any time, and, for the time being, anyway, go back to work.

As Hoffman had suggested to Matthews, it seemed the beginning of the end of any serious search for Adam's killer at Hollywood PD. When Revé Walsh showed up for her scheduled examination with Matthews, she was questioned briefly about her activities on the day that Adam was taken. She was told that her polygraph would have to be rescheduled, and on the following Monday, September 14, an examiner from the Broward County State Attorney's Office conducted the exam. Once again, Revé recounted the events of the day that her son disappeared, and the examiner confirmed that she had passed—there were no signs of deception anywhere in her account.

A few days later, detectives returned to the Sears store to reinterview the employees who had been working the day of Adam's kidnapping, but the results were fruitless. On September 22, there was a brief flurry of excitement when a St. Lucie County Sheriff's Department detective phoned Hoffman to relay a tip that a Fort Pierce woman named Mary Green was involved in the kidnapping of Adam Walsh. According to the tipster, Green had knowledge as to who had actually killed the boy.

It took Hoffman and Hickman a few days, but on September 30, the two traveled to Fort Pierce in St. Lucie County, just south of the spot where Adam's severed head was pulled from the canal. They spoke with St. Lucie County detectives and then interviewed Mary Green and her live-in lover J. A. Childress, whom local authorities identified as the source of the tip.

Green admitted to the detectives that she was a chronic alcoholic—in fact she had spent a couple of nights in the Fort Pierce detox center shortly before the time of Adam's disappearance. Like everyone else, she had heard all about the crime, but she certainly had no involvement in the matter, nor did she know anyone who did. She explained to Hoffman and Hickman that Childress, the man who had turned her in, was also a drunk and prone to all sorts of deception. He was upset with her at the time, and simply decided to tell people she'd been involved in the kidnapping.

Though by now it seemed a waste of time, Hoffman and Hickman arranged for the St. Lucie County Sheriff's Department to administer a polygraph examination to Green. When the examiner was finished, what already seemed apparent to the detectives was confirmed. Mary Green might be a hapless loser, but she had nothing to do with the kidnapping and murder of Adam Walsh.

It was as if the trip to St. Lucie County had sapped the last energies of the Hollywood PD. An internal supplemental report dated October 5, 1981, gave a terse, if somewhat inelegant, statement of the obvious: "As of this date this agency has not received any substantial leads that would implicate anyone to the crime."

Nine days later Detectives Hoffman and Hickman, acting on a tip, interviewed a man named Charles Elchwartzle, the owner of a blue Ford van, but, as it turned out, being in possession of such a vehicle in South Florida at the time was Elchwartzle's only misstep. On October 22, Hoffman and Hickman called in Jimmy Campbell to cover "areas possibly not covered in the previous interview . . . conducted by Mr. Joe Matthews," but that came to nothing as well. For all intents and purposes, and less than two months after the incident, the active investigation of the abduction and murder of Adam Walsh was at a standstill.

JACKSONVILLE, FLORIDA—JULY 28, 1981

When Ottis Toole returned to Jacksonville following his late July 1981 foray into South Florida, his life resumed without a hitch. He returned the Cadillac he had "borrowed" from the Reaves Roofing compound without anyone having noticed it missing. And though his brother Howard and his sister-in-law Georgia had tried to file charges against Ottis for the theft of their pickup truck that was abandoned in Delaware, the Florida state attorney's office found the case too shaky to prosecute.

With his mother's house a charred ruin, Toole needed a new place to live, so he rented a room in a blue-collar rooming house owned by a woman named Betty Goodyear. Toole then reconnected with his erstwhile wife, Rita, and convinced her to move in with him on July 31.

At about 4:00 p.m. the following day, Rita—twenty-four years Toole's senior—glanced out the window of their room to see a familiar-looking man striding up the sidewalk. "Hey, looks like your brother Howard's here," Rita said, turning. But Ottis was in full flight out the back door.

Howard was about to knock, but when he heard the back door bang, he realized it would be a waste of time. He vaulted off the porch and lit out after Ottis, who was running down Market Street for all he was worth. Ottis made it as far as the entrance to a Little Champ convenience store on the corner before his brother caught up with him.

"Someone's going to shoot me," Ottis cried to the clerk as he burst through the door.

"Go ahead and call the cops," Howard added as he ran in on Ottis's heels. He snatched Ottis by the collar and began slapping him. "This son of a bitch stole my truck."

The encounter might have given Howard Toole some minor satisfaction, but as the cops who arrived to quell the disturbance soon pointed out, there were no grounds upon which they could take Ottis into custody. For his part, Ottis had no interest in pressing assault charges against his brother, and the matter ended for the time being with Howard skulking off and Ottis figuring he'd taken his rightful lumps.

In the days that followed, Toole got by doing yard work for Goodyear at her various properties and helped out as best he could in her office, though the fact that he could not read well limited his usefulness there. He also found employment at the modest parish of the Church of God on Ramona Boulevard, where pastor Cecil Wiggins paid him $17.50 for lawn maintenance one day late in August and another $22.75 on the next.

In the meantime, Betty Goodyear's son James Redwine had returned home from some kicking around in Miami of his own, and he and Ottis were soon hanging out together, sometimes cruising the streets in an older-model Cadillac. One evening Toole showed Redwine a .22-caliber pistol that he pulled from under the seat of the Caddy. He told Redwine he was thinking of using the pistol to kill a couple of drifters who had been hanging around a local park. Redwine, who had also seen a large wooden-handled knife under the seat of the Caddy, didn't know if Ottis was serious about killing anyone, but he did see him fire a shot over the head of one of Goodyear's tenants shortly thereafter.

"What was that all about?" Redwine asked Toole as the tenant hightailed it in terror down the street.

"The guy just pissed me off," Ottis said.

Early in October, with the car theft charges dropped, Ottis Toole's former lover Henry Lee Lucas was finally released by Pikeville, Maryland, authorities. Lucas made his way back to Jacksonville, and before long found Ottis and was able to explain where he'd been all this time. Lucas had not abandoned Ottis for his niece Frieda. The separation was just bad luck, and once he'd been thrown in jail, there was no way for him to get in touch.

As to Frieda and nephew Frank, they were now in foster care somewhere in Polk County, down by Tampa. The children's mother had died of a drug overdose that might have been a suicide, and they'd spent a few weeks in the custody of their stepfather, A. J. Carr, until Frieda told Child Protective Services that Carr was physically abusing her. When a polygraph exam confirmed Frieda's story, Health Rehabilitation Services had stepped in to take custody of the children. All grim news by most standards, but in the world of Ottis Toole and Henry Lee Lucas, it was just the ordinary stuff of life.

Ottis was happy to know that Lucas had not forsaken him, of course. Things had not worked out so well between him and Rita, and before long he and Lucas had moved into another of Betty Goodyear's rooming houses. He and Lucas worked together for Reaves Roofing for one day right before Christmas, and then Ottis managed to get Goodyear to hire Lucas as a fellow maintenance worker. Indeed, five months after they'd split up and Toole had gone to South Florida on his little fling, things seemed to be working out for the two of them.

There was a troubling incident at one of Goodyear's properties right after the New Year, however. At about ten o'clock on the night of January 4, 1982, a fire broke out in one of the bedrooms of a house she owned at 117 East Second Street, near downtown Jacksonville. When firefighters responded, they found sixty-five-year-old George Sonnenberg unconscious in the room next to the vacant quarters where the fire had broken out, second- and third-degree burns covering most of his body. Another tenant had suffered burns to his hands while trying to escape through a blazing door, and a third had broken his leg jumping from an upstairs window. Sonnenberg lingered in the hospital for a week before dying on January 11. Fire marshals ruled it an accident.

About the same time, James Redwine, Betty Goodyear's son, overheard Ottis Toole and Henry Lee Lucas cooking up a plan that seemed sure to land them in serious trouble. They'd discovered the whereabouts of "Becky" Powell, now living with foster parents in Auburndale, a small town about halfway between Tampa and Orlando, two or three hours from where they sat. "Me and Henry Lee'll go on down to Auburndale," Ottis explained to Redwine, "and we'll bring Becky on back."

But what if the foster parents she was living with objected? Redwine wondered.

Toole smiled at Henry Lee before he answered. "What do you think, you dumbass? Anyone tries to stop us, we'll just kill 'em."

Redwine tried to talk the pair out of the plan, but they were resolute. As Toole explained to Redwine, he and Henry Lee had pulled off far more difficult things in the past. A few days later, as they were about to get in Ottis's car and head out for Auburndale, the front door of their rooming house on East Seventh Street flew open, and Redwine heard a female voice shouting, "Uncle Ottis! Henry Lee!"

It was fourteen-year-old Frieda "Becky" Powell with her arms outstretched, overjoyed to see Uncle Ottis and Henry Lee again.

To Redwine it seemed a miracle, but authorities in Auburndale were well aware of Frieda's history with Ottis Toole and Henry Lee Lucas, and it was not long before investigators were nosing around Betty Goodyear's office, wondering if anyone had seen a young woman matching Frieda's description.

If Toole wasn't sure what to do next, Frieda and Henry Lee had no difficulty making their decision. According to Redwine the pair had been gone from Jacksonville for two days before Toole realized that they had skipped out on him once again.

Toole, whose only real loves in life were his mother, his niece, and Henry Lee, took it hard. He paced his room for days, muttering to himself, and then, after buying a white-on-white two-door Cadillac from Spencer's Motors in Jacksonville, he disappeared.

Toole spent some time out west, made a few brief acquaintances in Louisiana, then finally turned up again in Jacksonville, where he was arrested on September 22, 1982, for driving without a valid driver's license. On November 1, he was arrested again by sheriff's deputies on the same charge, giving his address as 217 East Third Street and the name of his employer as Betty Goodyear.

Toole was through with wandering. He rekindled his relationship with Goodyear's son James Redwine and picked up his threadbare existence in Jacksonville where he'd left it a year before, though still without Lucas and "Becky" at his side. It is hard to say how long he might have carried on as it appeared he always had, just one more figure on the margins of life, managing somehow to stay afloat.

But the truth beneath the surface of Toole's dismal existence was far darker than anyone might have suspected. *Rotten teeth, unkempt hair, rank breath, and filthy clothes*—check! *Borderline intelligence, a bad attitude, poor coping skills*—on the mark. *Friends*—none. *Acquaintances*—few. *Skills*—nonexistent. *Prospects*—nil.

All dismal enough, perhaps, but what Toole had hiding in the wings made those attributes seem the stuff of a Disney hero in comparison. And if he hadn't finally had a little truly bad luck, the horror-show side of Ottis Toole might never have been known.

JACKSONVILLE, FLORIDA—MAY 31, 1983

Until the passage of the Uniform Holidays Bill in 1968, Memorial Day was always celebrated on May 30, a time set aside to honor U.S. men and women who died while engaged in military service. As John Logan, the commander in chief of the Grand Army of the Republic, wrote in his 1868 general order, the purpose of "Decoration Day," as it was originally known, was to fly the flag and strew graves with garlands in proud memory of all those heroes who had "made their breasts a barricade between our country and its foe."

Over time, Memorial Day has become a somewhat trivialized occasion, its luster dimmed by a series of unpopular wars over the past half century and its date now shifting year by year to coincide with the last Monday in May. Perhaps a weary workforce and school population now welcome a three-day weekend as an unofficial kickoff to the summer season, but surely the holiday achieves little to instill the sense of honor, duty, and sacrifice it was designed for.

Certainly there was no such apparent effect on James Redwine, Ottis Toole's sometime companion, and pal Charles Hammock, two juveniles picked up by police the afternoon following the holiday's observance in Jacksonville in 1983. That morning, Redwine and Hammock had expressed their own holiday passions by setting fire to an unoccupied house at 1203 Hubbard Street.

Tipped off by an informant, police tracked down the pair, who quickly admitted setting fire to both the Hubbard Street house and another unoccupied house in the same neighborhood of Springfield a week earlier. However, Redwine told officers, they had help in these arsons. A man named Ottis Toole, an erstwhile boarder in his mother's various rooming houses, had convinced them that burning down houses could be great fun, and they had gone along.

Accordingly, officers set out looking for Toole, who offered no resistance when they finally picked him up the following Monday, June 6. In fact, Toole not only confessed to the two arsons in question but told police that he had set dozens of fires in Jacksonville over the past twenty years, most of them in vacant buildings. He rode along with officers through a series of downtrodden neighborhoods, identifying thirty-six such sites where arson had been suspected, including his mother's house at 708 Day Street. He'd been setting fires since he was nine, he told police, doing it "to keep blacks out of the neighborhood" and also because it turned him on sexually.

During a court-ordered psychological examination, Toole told Dr. Ernest Miller that setting fires allowed him to "fantasize sex," and that he would characteristically watch the blazes from a distance and masturbate. He told the doctor that he was a homosexual, but claimed that while he enjoyed the company of children, he had never consummated a sexual relationship with a child. He also told the doctor that he'd been suffering seizures from the time in his childhood when he'd been struck in the head with a rock. He'd been taking Dilantin for years, he said, and was accustomed to drinking a little whiskey each night—"about half a pint"—plus several six-packs.

He told Miller that he had been suffering from depression for more than two years since the death of his mother and admitted that the overdose of pills that had landed him in the hospital in Newport News was in fact a suicide attempt. "At times he fancies he hears voices saying he should kill himself and 'go to rest,' " Miller wrote, adding that Toole was unclear as to whether the voices came from his own mind or from the devil.

While Toole told the doctor that he thought his memory was "poor" and that he "had trouble thinking," Miller adjudged that his basic cognitive functions were intact and that he exhibited only minor memory problems related to immediate recall. "Can tell time and is of average native intelligence," Miller said. "Is able to register, store, and retrieve data fairly well."

The doctor's clinical impression was that Toole exhibited borderline character disorder and that while he was a "severely disturbed man," he was nonetheless competent to stand trial. Meanwhile, Miller recommended that Toole receive treatment for "psychosexual conflicts, pyromania and alcoholism-drug dependency."

While Toole received no formal treatment for his problems, he was awarded a speedy trial where he was summarily convicted of the two May arsons he confessed to in his Springfield neighborhood. He received a fifteen-year sentence for one fire and a five-year sentence for the second, with the terms to run consecutively. On Thursday, August 11, 1983, he was received at the Union Correctional Institution at Raiford, Florida. At the age of thirty-six, and with a lifetime of bad news behind him, the tide of Ottis Toole's fortunes had finally begun to turn.

At the same time that Toole arrived at Raiford, his former partner Henry Lee Lucas was facing serious difficulties of his own in Texas, where he and Becky Powell had gone when they'd fled Jacksonville back in 1982. Lucas had been arrested in Stoneberg, a hamlet northwest of Fort Worth, near the Oklahoma border, on June 11, 1983, suspected in the murder of a woman named Catherine Powell. Powell had been discovered in her rural home outside Tyler, Texas, the previous summer, sexually abused and shot once in the head. In addition, Lucas had been questioned by Ouachita Parish, Louisiana, detective Jay Via about a series of unsolved murders in the county seat of Monroe and elsewhere in the area.

Finally, Lucas began to crack. He admitted that he had killed Catherine Powell the previous August, and he also said that he had killed Ottis Toole's niece Becky, then fifteen, in Denton, Texas, a few days later. Lucas would eventually claim responsibility for more than two hundred murders, though he also told police that he had been assisted in several of the crimes by a man from Jacksonville, Florida, named Ottis Toole. While authorities were uncertain as to just how much credit to give these claims, police with dead-end cases from around the South were soon on their way to Texas to speak with Lucas.

One such detective was Buddy Terry, from the Jacksonville Sheriff's Office homicide unit. On Thursday, August 11, during an interview with Terry, Henry Lee Lucas confessed to the murder of eight women in Jacksonville between 1979 and 1981.

Lucas also recounted another crime to Terry, one that involved Ottis Toole.

He'd been with Toole when he set fire to one of Betty Goodyear's rooming houses, Lucas told Terry. Toole was upset with several of the men who lived in that particular house because they would not respond to his sexual advances, Lucas said. While Lucas watched, Toole took a can of gasoline from the trunk of his car, made his way into a vacant back bedroom of the house, doused the room with the fuel, and lit it with a match.

Lucas told Terry that the two of them drove around the block several times, watching as the flames built, firemen responded, and residents leaped from windows. Lucas said that they also watched as EMS technicians dragged resident George Sonnenberg to the front porch and worked desperately to revive him. From Toole's point of view, Lucas assured Terry, things could simply not have turned out better.

JACKSONVILLE, FLORIDA—AUGUST 30, 1983

Following his interview with Henry Lee Lucas in Texas, Detective Terry returned to Jacksonville and made arrangements with Florida prison authorities to interview Ottis Toole at Raiford. Understandably, Terry was eager to learn whether Toole had in fact been complicit in the various crimes as Lucas claimed, or whether the convicted arsonist might simply be a convenient scapegoat for a guilty man to use in easing his own burden.

On August 30, 1983, Terry met with Toole at the prison's Reception and Medical Center. There, Toole confirmed that he had known Lucas since 1979 and that he had in fact been in love with him. He and Lucas had shared a homosexual relationship, Toole said, and the two of them had traveled together to several parts of the country.

As to the rooming house fire, Toole told Detective Terry that not everything that Lucas had said was true. For instance, Toole wanted Terry to know that he had not doused that vacant bedroom with gasoline before setting it ablaze . . . given his experience in starting fires, he explained, there was no need for such trouble. He had set the fire, sure, but to get it going he had simply torn the cover off a foam mattress and set that highly flammable substance ablaze with a match. And while he was aware that several men lived in the building, he had no idea that anyone, including the unfortunate George Sonnenberg, was home at the time. It was simply Sonnenberg's tough luck.

So if Toole hadn't set out with the intention of harming Sonnenberg, Terry wondered, then why had he set the fire in the first place? The question brought a guileless smile to Toole's face. Setting fires just made him feel good, he told Terry. He guessed he'd set a couple hundred of them around Jacksonville over the past few years.

Detective Terry nodded, finished up his notes, and gave Toole a smile of his own. "You're under arrest for arson—," he began, but Toole simply shrugged.

"I'm already here for that," he said, indicating their spartan surroundings.

"—and for the murder of George Sonnenberg," Terry concluded. The fool's luck that Ottis Toole had enjoyed all his life had finally run its course.

Nine days later, on Thursday, September 8, 1983, Toole was indicted in Jacksonville on charges of murder and arson, and on September 13 he was transferred from Raiford to the Duval County Jail to await trial. It is hard to know if Toole felt anything similar to the apprehension or fear that most individuals might experience at such heightening of circumstance, but judging from the conversations he had with some of his cellmates and other detectives drawn to interview him in his new quarters, it does not seem that he was guarded or fearful.

He seemed happy to discover that among his fellow prisoners in the Duval County lockup were two old friends from his days in the early 1980s at Reaves Roofing, Bobby Lee Jones and James Collins, a man who also used the alias of Julius Wilkes. Toole chatted freely with Jones and Collins/Wilkes about the circumstances that had finally led him to jail, and when a Brevard County detective named Steve Kendrick showed up to interview him about an unsolved homicide that had taken place in Cocoa Beach, some two and a half hours to the south, Toole was even more forthcoming.

During the interview, which took place on Monday, October 10, 1983, Toole readily confessed to Kendrick that he had probably committed or taken part in at least sixty-five murders, though he didn't have any recollection of the Cocoa Beach case that Kendrick had come to talk about. After a half hour or so, Kendrick sensed that he was getting nothing useful regarding his own case out of Toole and turned his tape recorder off. As the detective was packing up to leave the interview room, some switch seemed to flip inside the man who had just a few moments before admitted to killing scores of people.

According to Kendrick, Toole suddenly straightened in his chair and looked up at him intently. "You're from Fort Lauderdale, right?"

"No." Kendrick shook his head. It occurred to him that Toole had confused Brevard County with Broward County, two hours farther south along the coast. But being an able cop, Kendrick was not about to let it drop. "Were you expecting someone from Fort Lauderdale?" he asked Toole.

Toole nodded.

"You get into something in Fort Lauderdale?" the detective prompted.

"Yeah, I did," Toole said.

Given that the man in front of him had readily identified himself as a serial killer, Kendrick might not have thought too much of the exchange, were it not for the sudden shift in Toole's behavior. He was gripping the sides of his chair tightly now, shifting uneasily from side to side, his gaze dropping abruptly from Kendrick's to the floor and back again. As his case notes make clear, Kendrick sensed that he had stumbled onto something big: "Reporting agent felt that for a man to admit involvement in sixty five (65) murders, but get upset about Ft. Lauderdale, it had to be something appalling."

Kendrick sat back down across from Toole and folded his hands in front of him. "Why don't you tell me about it?" the detective said. And Toole began to do just that.

He had found a little boy at a Sears store, Toole said, and told the boy that he had some candy and wanted to talk to him and convinced him to get in his Cadillac out in the parking lot. Toole told Kendrick that he was intending to take the boy back to Jacksonville and raise him as his own son, but it all changed when this Adam started crying and saying he wanted to get out of the car. The boy's behavior made him mad, Toole explained, and so he hit him in the face to shut him up. And then he turned off the highway onto a dirt road that had a fork at the end of it. And that was where he murdered this Adam and cut off his head and threw it into a pond somewhere along the side of the road.

In hindsight, one might wonder why such a statement did not mark the end of the hunt for the killer of Adam Walsh then and there. True, Detective Kendrick was from another jurisdiction and was only vaguely familiar with the case, and there would understandably be a bit of time for sorting out just what Ottis Toole was talking about . . . but surely, one might think, a speedy resolution of the matter was at hand. As the old saw goes, however, that is the trouble with assumptions. In truth, the trouble was just getting under way.

When Kendrick left the room after his second interview with Toole, he was a man on a mission. He found Detective Buddy Terry in his office and quickly shared the news. "He's talking about killing a child down in Broward County," Kendrick told Terry. "He says he cut him up and left the body in two different places. This is all out of the clear blue sky."

Terry remembers the moment well, though at the time he was not familiar with any child-killing case in South Florida (if nothing else, Terry's obliviousness speaks volumes about how times have changed). Still, based on Kendrick's certainty that Toole was confessing to a gruesome crime that he had in fact committed, he began calling various agencies in Broward County.

"I finally got hold of the Hollywood Police Department," Terry recalls, "and they told me that it sounded like the Adam Walsh case." Terry had no idea what Hollywood was talking about, but once it had been explained to him, he hurried to Kendrick with the news.

The following morning, October 11, Kendrick reached someone in the homicide division at Hollywood PD and gave a brief account of what he'd come across. "I identified myself as an investigator for the Brevard County Sheriff's Office," he says, "and said that I had just interviewed an individual pertaining to a homicide I was investigating. During the interview with the individual, he said a number of things that led me to believe that he is in fact the one who killed Adam Walsh."

Whomever Kendrick spoke to took the information and said that someone would be back in touch immediately. But "immediately" seemed to have a relative meaning. "Probably a week after that," Kendrick says, "I got a call from someone and we spoke briefly about my conversation with Ottis Toole about Adam. I don't believe I had any additional contact with them [the Hollywood PD] after that. I think I only spoke to them once."

With notification having been made to the Hollywood PD, there was nothing more for Detectives Kendrick or Terry to do regarding the Adam Walsh case. Kendrick returned to his office in Brevard County, and Terry went off to Louisiana to confer with authorities there pertaining to Henry Lee Lucas and his own investigation of the murder of George Sonnenberg.

As a result of the information shared during Terry's trip to Monroe, three detectives from Ouachita Parish, Louisiana, traveled back to Jacksonville with him to interview Toole regarding the murder of sixteen-year-old Sherry Alford in Monroe. On Tuesday, October 18, 1983, Detective Jay Via, who'd been among the first to question Henry Lee Lucas following his arrest, began his pre-interview conversation with Ottis Toole while Toole was eating his lunch.

Via casually asked Toole when he was going to start talking about all the blacks that Henry Lee Lucas claimed the two of them had killed. Toole broke off from eating to smile his Alfred E. Neuman–like smile. Surely Via understood why he wasn't about to start talking about that subject, Toole told the detective. The population of the Duval County Jail was about 90 percent black. How long did Via think Toole would last if he started bragging about killing "brothers"?

Via nodded in appreciation of Toole's wisdom. But he'd also heard some rumors that Toole had killed a bunch of kids during his travels across the country, he said. Kid killers weren't very popular in prison either. Were those rumors true? Via wondered.

At that, Via recalls, Toole's manner suddenly changed. He stopped in mid-bite and put down his chicken leg. "You talking about the kid that got his head cut off around West Palm Beach, Florida?" Toole said, guardedly.

Via checked his watch, noting that it was 3:20 in the afternoon. Toole had become a different person, instantaneously. For the first time, he made direct eye contact with Via and inquired again in a somber voice whether or not he was talking about the "kid" he had killed in South Florida.

"What kid are you talking about?" Via asked.

Toole pulled his knees up to his chest and began to weep. It was the "kid" he got from the Sears store, he explained.

Via was genuinely puzzled. He'd just been baiting Toole, and he'd certainly heard nothing of any child murder case in Florida—in fact, his conversations with Detective Terry of Jacksonville had been confined to the Alford case connecting Toole and Henry Lee Lucas. "I don't know what you're talking about," Via told Toole.

By this time, Toole was racked with sobs. He thought Via wanted to know about the kid he'd grabbed from the Sears store, the one whose head he'd cut off, Toole said.

At that point, Via went to the door of the interview room and called to Buddy Terry, who was standing down the hallway talking with Lieutenant Joe Cummings of the Monroe Police Department, who had come over with Via to interview Toole. "You better come in here," Via told Terry and Cummings. "He's just confessed to killing a child in South Florida."

While Terry quickly realized what Toole must have been talking to Via about, there was no point in getting into a discussion with him at the moment. He simply followed Via and Cummings back into the interview room and listened as Via asked Toole to explain exactly what he was referring to.

Toole replied that he had traveled to South Florida in a black-over-white Cadillac to find a "kid" to keep for his own. After driving around for some time, he spotted a mall parking lot, pulled in, and saw a young white boy standing outside a Sears store. Toole told the officers that he forced the child into his Cadillac, pulled out of the lot, and ended up on a highway. When the child would not stop screaming and crying, Toole said, he backhanded him in the face with a closed fist and then struck him again in the stomach, at which point the child slumped down in the seat, unconscious.

Toole was relieved that the child had stopped making noise, but it was not long before he began to think that he had actually killed the child and that he would have to dispose of the body. He traveled some distance on the "freeway," Toole said, exiting a couple of times before he ended up in a remote swampy area.

He parked, took the child out of the car, and laid him facedown over a log. He took a long-bladed knife—maybe a machete—from the trunk of the Cadillac and went back to where he had left the boy . . . and cut off his head.

It took several blows to accomplish the decapitation, Toole said, and after that, he used the blade to dismember the rest of the body and scatter it about the swamp. As he described his actions to Via, Terry, and Cummings, Toole took care to illustrate how he'd used his knuckles to backhand the boy in the face and his closed fist to hit him in the stomach. He also pantomimed removing the child from the seat of the Cadillac and laying him gently against a log.

Crying now, he told the detectives how he decided to keep the child's head at first, tossing it onto the backseat floorboard of the Cadillac. After he had driven a bit, he began to think better of this notion, however, and he pulled over to toss the decapitated head into a drainage ditch or canal of some kind. And after that, Toole said, he drove back to Jacksonville.

At the conclusion of the statement, the three detectives stepped out into the hallway, and it was only then that Buddy Terry told Via and Cummings that it sounded to him like Toole had just repeated—albeit in far more grisly detail—a confession he'd made the previous week, the killing of a child named Adam Walsh, who had been abducted from a Sears store two summers previously. Adam's head had been found floating in a canal a couple of weeks after his disappearance, Terry explained, but his body had never been found, and the killer was still on the loose.

Via shook his head and glanced back through the window of the interview room, where a shaken Toole still sat. He'd never heard of the case, Via told Terry. But whatever terrible things had happened, it sure seemed as if they'd found the party responsible.

It seemed that way to Buddy Terry, too. But both he and Via were reasonable men. And what developed with Toole from that point on would have little to do with reason.

JACKSONVILLE, FLORIDA—OCTOBER 19, 1983

According to a Hollywood PD supplemental report, eight days went by before Lieutenant Hynds passed along word to lead case detective Jack Hoffman that Buddy Terry of the Jacksonville Sheriff's Office had called with information pertaining to the disappearance and murder of Adam Walsh. Hoffman notes that he returned Terry's call at 3:10 p.m. on Wednesday, October 19, and by 9:00 p.m., he and his partner Hickman were in Jacksonville to interview Ottis Toole.

When they arrived, Terry advised the two that Toole was just finishing up another interview with Detective Via, from Louisiana. Via was the investigator who had extracted the most specific information from Toole, he explained, and they would likely want to confer with him before talking with Toole themselves. Yes, they did want to talk to Via, Hoffman told Terry, and with that, the two Hollywood detectives sat tight-lipped until Via came out of the interview room and Terry made introductions around.

It didn't take Hoffman long to set the tone for their interchange. He fixed Via with his disdainful stare, then delivered a jaw-dropping accusation. "So you're the one who's been feeding Toole details of my investigation?"

Via stared at the pair across from him, incredulous. "I don't know what you're talking about," Via managed finally, glancing at Terry to make sure he hadn't misheard. "I was interviewing Ottis Toole about a murder in Ouachita Parish, Louisiana, when, out of nowhere, he started talking about killing some 'kid' in South Florida."

Via had the distinct impression that nothing he was saying mattered in the slightest to Hoffman, but still he continued. "I got Detective Terry in the room along with my colleague Joe Cummings from Monroe, and asked this Toole to take us through his story from the beginning. When he was finished, I still didn't know who he was talking about. We left Toole in the interview room and went out in the hall to talk, and that's when Detective Terry told me that it sounded like Toole was talking about killing Adam Walsh. That's the first time in my life I even heard the name."

Hoffman glanced at Terry then, as if he had just spotted someone else to blame for meddling in his investigation. "I'm going to need a written report on this," he said to Via, skepticism saturating his tone.

"You can read my notes any time you want to," Via said. "Furthermore, I don't appreciate your attitude, my friend. I'm trying to do you a favor, and you come in here insinuating I'm leaking information to some douchebag like Ottis Toole? Where the hell would I even get it?"

Apart from another sidelong glance at Terry, there was no response. "Can we have him now?" Hoffman said, waving toward the interview room.

"He's all yours," Terry said. "You won't mind if I sit in, though, will you?"

The look Hoffman gave Terry told him that Hoffman very much minded, but there was little the Hollywood detective could do to keep Terry out. "He's your prisoner," Hoffman told Terry tersely, and the three moved inside the interview room with Toole.

Hoffman introduced himself and his partner Hickman and told Toole that they were from the Hollywood, Florida, Police Department. He offered a standard rights form for Toole to sign, but Toole waved it away. He understood his rights, he told Hoffman, and he understood that he was waiving his right to have an attorney present during the questioning that was about to take place. He didn't read all that well, he told Hoffman, indicating the form on the table before him. He'd only gone through the seventh grade, but he understood the English language well enough and he understood exactly what they were saying about his rights.

With that established, Hoffman asked Toole to give him a statement about what he claimed he'd done down in South Florida, and Toole readily agreed. It was a couple of years ago, he began, when he and his partner Henry Lee Lucas drove down to Fort Lauderdale in a 1973 black-over-white Cadillac that Toole had purchased from a woman in Jacksonville named Faye McNett. Buddy Terry lifted an eyebrow as he heard the mention of Lucas in the matter for the first time, but he said nothing.

Toole explained to Hoffman and Hickman that he had been depressed over the death of his mother that May, and that he and Lucas had been traveling around the country, as far as Texas and California, with his niece and nephew Frieda and Frank Powell. He told Hoffman that he and Lucas had returned to Jacksonville some time in June, and that before they set out on the trip to South Florida, he'd taken a Pennsylvania license tag from a car on the street and switched the plate on the Caddy.

The two of them had snatched a kid from outside a Sears store in a shopping mall, he told Hoffman, who then asked how Toole could be sure it was a Sears. Toole looked at Hoffman as if he were the barely functioning individual in the room. " 'Cause I know a Sears when I see a Sears," he said, as if explaining it to an idiot. He didn't remember actually going inside the Sears, though he may have, he told Hoffman. He was just window shopping and remembered having passed a wig shop when he saw the boy.

As to the time of the abduction, however, Toole responded in a way that was typical of his tenuous grasp of matters that most take for granted. "It would have to have been . . . ah . . . the afternoon, afternoon, afternoon. I call afternoon around noontime and that."

There'd been trouble with the boy in the car, Toole continued, and he'd had to slap and punch him to get him to quiet
down. Eventually, he and Lucas had pulled off the turnpike, and
Lucas had killed the boy by decapitating him "with an 18-inch
bayonet" while Toole held Adam down on his stomach. He said
Lucas had to hit the kid three or four times to get his head cut
off. After that, they chopped the boy up and threw his body
parts out the window along the turnpike. They'd kept the head
for a while longer because Lucas wanted to have sex with it,
Toole said.

As to why he was making this confession, Toole told the
detectives that he wanted to get it out of his mind.

Hoffman next showed Toole the photo of Adam that the
family had reproduced on the missing person's flyer, but Toole
wasn't sure that it was the same boy that he and Lucas took.
When Hoffman showed Toole a second photo in which Adam's
hair was wet from swimming, Toole nodded. He believed that
the second photo did resemble the boy he killed, he said.

With that, Detectives Hoffman and Hickman concluded
their interview and left the room, leaving Detective Terry and
Ottis Toole alone.

"Why are you jerking them around?" Terry asked Toole, his
arms folded.

"What are you talking about?" Toole replied.

"You know as well as I do that Henry Lee Lucas was in jail in
Maryland when all this happened. What are you trying to pull?"

Toole looked away and stared at the wall for a few moments.
Finally he turned back to Terry. Yes, he'd lied about Lucas being
involved. "Tell them detectives I want to talk to them again," he
said to Terry, who shook his head and went to look for Hoffman
and Hickman.

It was well past midnight when the two detectives from Hollywood came back into the interview room and Toole announced
that he hadn't explained things exactly right the first time

around and would like to correct his statement. Hoffman gave Terry a skeptical glance, but nonetheless he and Hoffman sat down and began to take a second recorded statement from Toole.

The biggest thing he had to correct was that Henry Lee Lucas hadn't been involved in the crime, Toole told them. Then he set out to explain how things had really happened. Early in July of 1981, he and Lucas had borrowed Toole's brother's 1972 Ford pickup, supposedly to haul some scrap iron to the Jacksonville dump and sell it. In truth, Toole and Lucas lit out of Jacksonville immediately, accompanied by Toole's niece Frieda Powell, thirteen at the time, and his nephew Frank Powell, twelve. They'd abandoned the truck in Maryland about a week later, and on the fifteenth of July, Toole's sister-in-law Georgia reported the truck stolen to the Jacksonville sheriff. Toole had gotten separated from Lucas and his niece and nephew and, after a brief hospital stay, had returned to Florida by himself. Meantime, Lucas had been arrested by Delaware police on charges of vehicular theft and remained in jail there well into October.

Toole had traveled to South Florida alone, he told Hoffman and Hickman, and ran into Adam Walsh coming out of the Hollywood Sears store on the west side of the building. He enticed the boy into his Cadillac with the promise of candy and toys, then quickly rolled up the windows and locked the doors. Though the engine on the Cadillac had been giving him a little trouble ("It wasn't runnin' right. It would just roll off"), he got it started and pulled out of the parking lot, with Adam now asking about the toys and the candy. It took him about ten minutes to get from the store parking lot to Florida's Turnpike, Toole said, and by the time he went through the tollbooth to get a ticket, he had to start slapping and hitting the boy to get him to quiet down.

"The kid was getting on my nerves," Toole said. "I hit him quite a bit of times in the car. I think I did knock him out. I'm pretty sure that I knocked that kid out."

The rest of his account matched closely with what Toole had already told Detective Kendrick from Brevard County and Detective Via from Louisiana. He pulled off the turnpike onto a dirt road to kill the child. The child was unconscious when he carried him from the car and laid him facedown on the ground. And it took him four or five blows to sever the child's head.

"He was unconscious, so I didn't have a hard time chopping his head off," Toole said. "I laid him facedown and I did it."

Hoffman glanced up at Toole and asked whether he was right-handed or left-handed.

"Right-handed," Toole answered.

"And you said you kept the head for a while," Hoffman continued. "Just where in the car did you put it?"

Toole shrugged. "I say I switched it different times. I had it in the back one time on the floorboard and I ended up putting it in the front floorboard."

After the decapitation, Toole said that he dismembered and scattered the body parts, then got back onto the turnpike and drove another ten minutes or so northward before he began to think better of keeping the head. When he spotted a bridge railing up ahead, he told Hoffman, "I stopped the car and got out and I threw the head over in the canal."

How about the boy's clothes? Hoffman asked. "Oh his clothes were in the car," Tool said. While he was stopped, he used the clothes to wipe up some of the blood off the seat and then tossed the clothes out. Or maybe he had thrown the clothes away in a Dumpster in one of the roadside rest stops, Toole said, for that is what he remembered doing with his own blood-soaked clothes. "I threw them in the Dumpster."

And all this blood on his clothes had come from the child? Hoffman wanted to be sure.

Not only on his clothes but on his shoes as well, Toole assured the detective. "I threw my shoes away too and put on another pair."

He'd then driven on back to Jacksonville and junked the car at a yard on Holloway Avenue, Toole said, and that was pretty much the end of that story.

But why had he lied to them and implicated Henry Lee Lucas in his first statement? Hoffman wanted to know. "Because I figured I could tie him up in it and get even with his ass," Toole said.

"And you also said that Henry Lee got a blow job from the head," Hoffman continued, looking up from his notes. "Was that really *you* that got the blow job from the head?"

Toole shook his head at the question. "No," he said, dismissively, "I didn't even fuck it."

Hoffman then withdrew a third photograph of Adam and laid it beside the other two he'd already shown Toole. Was this the boy he was talking about? the detective asked. Toole studied the third photograph briefly, then glanced at Hoffman, "The other pictures, the other pictures look more like him than that one does," Toole said, but still there seemed no doubt in his mind. "Yes, I'd say. Yes, that's him."

It was almost two in the morning by the time Hoffman and Hickman wound up their second interview with Toole. "If we take you back down to South Florida with us, can you show us the places you've been talking about. This Sears store, the place where you decapitated the child, and where you threw his head in the canal?"

"I guess so," Toole said.

"We'll let you know," Hoffman said, and with that the interview was finished.

Once again, it might seem to any sentient observer that every element was in hand for a swift delivery of justice, or as swift as one is permitted in a system as full of checks and balances as our own. An individual with a history of violent behavior has made three unbidden confessions of murder to law officers from three different jurisdictions, providing details obviously known previously only to the medical examiners and the detectives in charge of the case. Surely justice was about to be dispensed. How could it possibly not be?

In the early hours following his second conversation with Toole, Detective Hoffman—whether or not he was miffed that his theory about Jimmy Campbell had been discredited, or simply that someone other than he and his partner Hickman had found Ottis Toole and extracted a confession from him—went quickly to work securing an order from a Duval County circuit judge allowing the two of them and Detective Terry to transport Toole to Hollywood for the purposes of identifying the purported crime scenes he had described. Meanwhile, Toole returned to his cell in the county lockup, where he began to pace and mutter, waking his cellmate James Collins.

What was the matter? Collins asked. He was trying to get some sleep.

Toole glanced around the cell nervously, then leaned close. What did Collins suppose other inmates would do to someone who had murdered children? Toole wondered, his voice low. Collins wasn't sure what might happen, but he did think that Toole was unusually agitated.

Toole went on to explain to Collins that the cops had found the head of this kid he'd killed, and that now they wanted him to go down to Fort Lauderdale and help them find the body. "I just hope it ain't there," Toole said, and then he went back to his pacing and muttering. Collins never told anyone whether he actually did get back to sleep that night. Ordinary people might have had great difficulty doing so. But if men believed everything they heard in prison, there'd be precious little sleep enjoyed there.

At nine on Friday morning, Toole was escorted by Detectives Hoffman and Terry from the Duval County Jail and flown by private plane to the North Perry Airport in Pembroke Pines, not far from Hollywood. They were met at about eleven thirty by two other detectives from Hollywood PD and driven by van to the nearby sprawling Broward Mall, which contained a Sears store.

This was definitely not the place, Toole said, as they pulled into the huge lot. The lot outside the store where he'd taken the boy was much smaller, and the mall had been a single-story structure, not a two-story like this one.

From the Broward Mall, they drove next to a Sears store that sat just off Federal Highway in Fort Lauderdale, but again, Toole shook his head. This was not the place.

Detective Larry Hoisington of the Hollywood PD, who been assigned to drive the team, was behind the wheel. Hoisington next drove to I-95 and piloted them the few miles south toward Hollywood. As they pulled off the exit ramp at Hollywood Boulevard, Toole gazed intently out the van windows. "This looks like the road I got off on," he told the detectives. As they passed the train station that abuts the boulevard there, Toole noted that the area looked familiar to him. "I think the store is up there," he said, pointing to the right.

Hoisington glanced in the rearview mirror to be sure which way Toole was directing them. Owing to his various deficiencies, Toole never used such words as *left* or *right*, *north* or *south*, *east* or *west*—just hand motions and phrases like "over there" and "down that way." Hoisington followed Toole's gesture and, a few blocks farther, pulled the van off Hollywood Boulevard and into the lot on the east side of the Sears store. He circled the store to the north, then turned along its west facade, where the garden shop was located. "This is it," Toole said, pointing. "This is where I picked up the kid."

Hoffman glanced around at his colleagues, then noted the time on his watch. He directed Hoisington to drive the few hundred yards to Hollywood PD for lunch before they started out for the turnpike.

After lunch, however, Toole asked if they could take one more look at the Sears lot, just so he could be sure. Hoisington took them back to the north entrance, where the catalog store was located, and parked the van. After a few moments, Toole nodded again. This was the place, he was more than sure of it. He pointed to a nearby bus bench located in the lot beneath an overhang. He'd been standing right there when he saw the boy come walking out of the doors by the garden department.

He repeated his story of luring Adam into the Cadillac with the promises of toys and candy and then showed the officers where he pulled out of the lot and made a right turn on Hollywood Boulevard, heading west toward Florida's Turnpike. It took about ten minutes, Toole told them, recalling there was a "sharp bend" in the road somewhere along the way. When Hoisington took them around a traffic circle on Hollywood Boulevard, Toole glanced out at a school located there and confirmed that this was the road he remembered driving on.

To test Toole, Hoisington decided that he purposely would not exit the roundabout where Hollywood Boulevard continued west toward the turnpike. Instead, he continued on toward the south exit of the roundabout. Toole laughed at that. "I did the same thing you just did," he told Hoisington. "You were supposed to turn back there." Hoisington glanced at Hoffman, but if he expected any recognition of his cleverness, none was forthcoming.

"Take the right fucking turn, will you?" Hoffman growled.

At the northbound turnpike entrance Hoisington brought down the van window to take a toll ticket; Toole said that he remembered doing the same thing the day he had Adam in his car. As they passed through the second toll plaza on the route north, Toole told the detectives it was where he'd pulled over to "quiet the kid down." Adam had been crying for his mother, Toole explained, and he had to beat him until he was unconscious to get him to stop.

By 3:30 p.m., as they clicked past mile marker 126 on the turnpike, well over an hour north of Hollywood, the van whisked beneath an overpass, and Toole pointed out the window toward the side of the road. "Hey, this is where I got off at," he called.

Hoisington pulled the van to the shoulder of the turnpike and, just as Toole had when he overshot the nearly hidden exit, backed cautiously to the service road leading to a desolate construction staging area. "You can pull off into there," Toole said, pointing. "This is where I stopped and killed the kid."

Hoffman told Toole to direct them to the place where he'd left Adam's body, and a shackled, handcuffed Toole gave it his best, even though he told them his memory was a little hazy—he'd been pretty intoxicated at the time, he said. He thought there was a fork in the road, to be quite honest, but there were no turnoffs to be found. Just a straight shot down the service road through the pine barrens to a spot where the road petered out at a guardrail blocking the road. "It was over in there someplace," Toole said, and a dubious Hoffman led his men, along with Detective Terry, out for an inspection of the area.

While Hoffman and the others tramped about the desolate woods, Hoisington and Toole sat alone inside the van. Hoisington had been ordered by Hoffman not to speak with Toole—"You're here for one reason, to drive the goddamned van, okay?"—and he was not about to start trouble. But Toole seemed agitated now, and the longer they sat together, the more restless he became.

"I killed a lot of people," he blurted to Hoisington suddenly. "But of all I did, I wisht I hadn't killed that little kid."

Toole indicated the area where the others were walking with a nod of his head. Hoisington followed Toole's gesture, but said nothing.

"It was right here," Toole said, tears welling in his eyes. "I took him out of the car and carried him yonder in the woods, and I cut off his head with a machete I always carried." He went on to explain how he'd dragged the body into the brush and covered it with leaves. He came back to the spot where he'd left Adam's head and took it back to the car and tossed it on the floor behind the driver's seat.

Hoisington knew that Toole was a suspect in the murder of Adam Walsh, of course, but he had no idea of the details of Toole's confessions. Everything that Toole was recounting to him sounded like the stuff of a nightmare.

"Why did you keep the head?" Hoisington heard himself asking.

Toole glanced at him as if he were explaining why you'd duck under cover when it started to rain. He'd already sodomized Adam's body, he told Hoisington. "I was going to have sex with the head later on."

As a cop, Hoisington had heard his fair share, but Toole's offhand declaration was enough to make his stomach heave. With great relief he saw an obviously irritated Hoffman leading his group back toward the van.

"We can't see anything over there," Hoffman grumbled as he climbed in, waving vaguely toward the tangle of vines and underbrush on the far side of the guardrail. He slapped at a mosquito on his neck, one of a cloud that followed him through the opened door. It had been more than two years, the hot and frustrated detectives reasoned, as they piled back into the van. A jungle could spring up around here in that amount of time. Heavy equipment would have to be brought in.

Meantime, Hoffman declared, Toole could show them where he'd disposed of the head. Sure, Toole assured them. It wasn't far, no more than ten minutes from where they were parked.

Hoisington piloted them back down the rocky trail, then waited for a break in the traffic to pull back on the highway. It wasn't like they'd pulled off into a paved rest area where there was some nicely banked reentry road. The very maneuver to regain the highway in a sluggish nine-passenger van was not without risk. Some hopped-up kid in a fast car comes up too quickly behind them, they'd all be toast. And all because of a scumbag like Toole? What a way to go.

Still, Hoisington managed it without incident, and had hardly got them back up to cruising speed when Toole called out again, this time near mile marker 130. The group exited the van at roadside this time, and Toole directed them a few yards eastward to the bank of a nearby canal, where a wooden dock jutted out over the water. He'd walked out onto the dock there and thrown the head into the water, Toole said.

Detective Hoffman, who was well aware that they were standing near the spot where Adam's head had been discovered by fishermen more than two years previously, said nothing to his colleagues. It was after 6:00 p.m. by this time, and Toole said he was hungry and wondered if there was anything to eat. Detective Hoisington handed Toole one of the sandwiches they'd brought along, but another detective swatted it out of Toole's hand.

"You don't need to do this guy any favors," Hoffman told Hoisington. "He's just jerking us around."

Toole glanced at the sandwich that had landed in the dirt. "Fuck you," he said to Hoffman.

"No," Hoffman replied. "Fuck *you*."

At that point, they all got into the van and drove home.

Back at Hollywood PD, Hoffman took another recorded statement from Ottis Toole in which he yet again formally confessed to the murder of Adam Walsh, and provided a detailed account of the circumstances under which he had committed the act. Toole broke into tears several times during this statement, claiming that he liked the little boy and had only wanted to take him home to raise him to be his own child. He had to kill Adam, though, because he realized the boy was very smart and could probably identify him as his kidnapper. When asked why this, of all the killings he had confessed to, bothered him so much, Toole said, "Because that was the youngest person I ever killed."

While that interview was taking place, Detective Hoisington ran into deputy chief Leroy Hessler in a hallway. "So how'd it go?" Hessler asked.

Hoisington hesitated but decided he should give the chief an honest answer. This was a pretty important matter, and he wasn't so sure things were running as they should. He explained to Hessler that he was surprised that Toole was cooperating at all, given Hoffman's treatment of the man, and also shared with Hessler some of the details that Toole had told him about the crime when Hoffman was out of earshot. Hessler listened patiently, then asked Hoisington if there was some point to all this.

Hoisington hesitated. He wasn't assigned as an investigator to this case, as Hessler well knew, but he was a detective, after all. "I just thought maybe I should write a supplemental report, or at least give Detective Hoffman a formal statement for his files," Hoisington said, still taken by Toole's offhand ghoulishness. "If what Toole told me independently corroborates or contradicts something he's said elsewhere, that might be useful."

Hessler stared at Hoisington for a moment. "You understand that this is Detective Hoffman's case, right?"

"Yes sir," Hoisington responded.

"Then you go talk to Hoffman about all this," Hessler said and walked away.

Hoisington made an effort to do what Hessler ordered, but by the time Hoffman and his partner Hickman had finished with Toole, it was past ten thirty at night. When Hoisington caught Hoffman coming out of the interview room, the lead detective warned him to make it quick. Chief Martin had already called a press conference for eleven, and was waiting on Hoffman in his office.

Hoisington had hardly begun his explanation when Hoffman cut him off. "I thought I told you not to talk to that asshole," he said, pointing inside the interview room where Toole still sat.

"He was talking to *me*," Hoisington protested, "and some of those things he said—"

Hoffman held up a hand impatiently. "I heard you. I'll include it in my report," he said; then he hurried down the hall to confer with Martin.

At 11:00 p.m. during a hastily arranged press conference, Hollywood chief of police Sam Martin made the momentous announcement. They had found the man who killed Adam Walsh, and on Monday, Ottis Toole would be officially charged with the crime.

Toole was a confessed serial killer, Martin told reporters, though of the thirty-five to fifty murders he had committed, Adam's was the only one over which he had expressed any regret. "Listening to him talk about the things he's done makes Charles Manson sound like Tom Sawyer or Huck Finn," Martin said. And Assistant Chief Hessler added his own opinion that Toole's stories were "grisly and heinous beyond belief." But as to the murder of Adam Walsh, Hessler said, there could be no doubt. "There are certain details only he could know. He did it."

Hessler assured reporters that his detectives had been grilling Toole ten to twenty hours a day for two days solid, and that he had finally broken down earlier Friday evening. As to the confessions that Toole had made to Detective Kendrick on October 10 and to Detectives Via and Terry on October 18, Hessler was curiously—or not so curiously—silent. As far as the outside world was concerned, then, Jack Hoffman and the Hollywood PD had cracked this case without assistance.

Indeed, Martin assured those gathered, they had finally found their man. Ottis Toole, already convicted of another crime in Jacksonville, would be returned to that city this night or the following morning, but soon he would face justice for the murder of Adam Walsh.

Any reasonable individual would have been inclined to take Martin's assertions as fact. An unhinged psychopath, finally snagged by a system through whose cracks he had tumbled for most of his miscreant's life, had confessed details of a heinous crime only he could have known. It might have been a shame for the murdered boy's family that so much time had passed, and it might be galling if it was learned that his apprehension was almost accidental, and perhaps it was annoying that a public defender would have to be engaged at the taxpayers' expense, along with a costly trial to be followed—were a death penalty handed down—by any number of appeals based on what would be surely specious ground . . .

But despite all that, a grievous wrong could now be righted, and some shred of society's order might be restored.

HOLLYWOOD, FLORIDA—OCTOBER 22, 1983

The news of the break in the case was trumpeted across the region on Saturday, and any viewer, listener, or reader who caught it might have assumed that though it had been two long and agonizing years for John and Revé Walsh, the grieving parents were about to see justice done. John Walsh's stirring response upon being given the news was replayed again and again on network and local outlets: "Just give me three minutes alone in a room with this guy." Finally, it seemed, the long-suffering parents would find some measure of relief.

However, it was not necessarily the call of Chief Martin or Leroy Hessler as to whether or not Ottis Toole would in fact be charged. It is true that a police officer can arrest and charge a suspect at a crime scene or in the course of an investigation during which a suspect makes a confession. Following such an arrest there is an arraignment, normally held within twenty-four hours, at which the suspect pleads guilty or not guilty, where bail is set or denied, and at which a public defender is appointed if necessary. In most jurisdictions, the state attorney then has a set period of time—twenty-one days in Florida—in which to file formal charges or drop the case. In fact, it is not unusual for a case initiated as an arrest to be dropped or negotiated, owing to something overlooked or unknown during the relatively hasty process of arrest.

In this instance, however, Toole was already in custody for other crimes, and there was no risk of him fleeing—and thus no reason for immediate arrest. Accordingly, the department took the alternative route toward charging a suspect: that of seeking a warrant for the suspect's arrest on new charges from the state attorney for Broward County.

In most cases, a state attorney asks that as much evidence as possible be presented before issuing an arrest warrant, for obvious reasons. No reputable prosecutor wants to be involved in harassing innocent citizens, for one thing; but also, the more ironclad the evidence presented, the easier it is for a successful prosecution to be brought. It was common knowledge among police agencies in Dade County during Janet Reno's tenure as head of the state attorney's office that unless an arresting agency presented its case in fail-safe terms, no warrant would be forthcoming. As a result, Reno compiled a sterling record as a prosecutor, one that eventually vaulted her into the office of U.S. attorney general.

In the case of Ottis Toole, a prosecutor in Broward state attorney Michael Satz's office advised Hollywood PD that the case would be bolstered considerably if physical evidence were obtained that placed Toole at the scene of the crime, or at least confirmed his presence in South Florida during the time that the crime took place.

If Hoffman and Hickman had done a more meticulous job of documenting the information revealed by Toole in his confessions to Detectives Kendrick and Via, and if they had presented the results of their own investigation in a way that made it seem they were independently corroborating what only the killer could have known about the crime, perhaps Satz would not have asked for more. But because Hoffman had not even mentioned the fact of the previous confessions, claiming that he had "broken" Toole after hours of relentless grilling, the state attorney's request for corroborating physical evidence was not out of the ordinary.

For most who heard Chief Martin or Leroy Hessler trumpet the news of an impending charge on radio and television, however, all the fine points of arrests versus warrants were the stuff of "inside baseball." What most ordinary citizens believed was that a suspect had confessed to the killing of Adam Walsh, and he would soon be tried and convicted and fried in the electric chair—good riddance to bad rubbish, on to better news ahead.

One of those watching as the news concerning Ottis Toole was broadcast across South Florida was Bill Mistler, the man who had been on his way into Sears to pick up some supplies for a camping trip on that fateful day when he had seen a neatly dressed young boy go off into the parking lot with a disreputable-looking man who seemed all wrong for him. When Mistler heard the news anchor's eager pronouncement that at long last a break had come in the Adam Walsh case, he glanced up at the television with an interest that soon grew into astonishment. As Chief Martin named the suspect in the case and a picture of Ottis Toole filled the screen, Mistler jumped straight from his bed.

At that moment, certainty filled his mind. The face he was staring at was that of the down-and-outer who'd led the young boy away from the Sears store that day. He had in fact witnessed the kidnapping of Adam Walsh, Mistler thought, a kind of awe filling him.

As other images connected with the story swirled across the screen, Mistler could do nothing but gape, his mind whirling. He thought about calling Hollywood police on the spot, to recount to them what he'd seen that day, but then he hesitated. As a teenager Mistler had spent a year in prison for his ill-advised participation in a robbery. He had put that all behind him, and he was now a respected businessman, the owner of a successful pest control company.

If he came forward and his name and face ended up in the newspapers or on television, who was to say some malcontent wouldn't call in to dredge up his past mistakes? Besides, the cops made it sound like they had Toole dead to rights. There must have been other witnesses who'd seen what happened at Sears that day and had identified the kidnapper. Why else would there be all the hullabaloo? Finally, and though it pained him a bit to do so, Mistler convinced himself to let it go. His help wasn't needed. Justice had prevailed.

Mistler switched off his television and lay back down to stare quietly up at his ceiling. And finally, he fell asleep.

The following Sunday morning, lead detective Hoffman was quoted by the Associated Press as saying that his men had not yet verified that Toole was in the area the day that Adam Walsh had been abducted, but that nonetheless the suspect knew details of the murder that only the killer could have known. Hoffman was not at liberty to discuss the evidence that the department had shared with the state attorney's office, but he was confident that they had plenty to base a case on.

And, moreover, if Bill Mistler did not come forward to place Ottis Toole in South Florida at the time of the kidnapping, there was at least one other person who did. Arlene Mayer, the woman who had taken her daughter Heidi to Kmart for some house-hold supplies less than forty-eight hours before Adam Walsh went missing, was having coffee at her kitchen table on Sunday morning after Chief Martin's announcement, the newspaper trumpeting the news laid out beside her. She was about to take a sip when Heidi walked into the room and stopped dead.

"Mom—" She pointed at the picture on the front page. "That's *him*."

Arlene stared up at her daughter, who was already beginning to cry. "That's the man who tried to get me that night in the Kmart."

Arlene looked down at the photograph of Ottis Toole emblazoned there, then shook her head, fighting the chill that began to envelop her. "Now, Heidi, are you sure . . . ?"

"I wouldn't say it if I wasn't sure," Heidi said, her voice rising to a near shriek. "That's the man who tried to get me!"

Arlene Mayer rose to comfort her daughter, and when she finally had Heidi calmed down, she picked up the phone and dialed the Hollywood police.

Shortly after 5:00 p.m. on Monday, Detectives Hoffman and Hickman conducted a formal interview with Heidi, who recounted her memory of the visit to Kmart the night she was accosted. Following the completion of her statement, the detectives presented her with a photo lineup to see if she recognized anyone.

"That's him," Heidi said, pointing without hesitation at a photograph of Toole. "There's that big gap between his two front teeth."

Following their interview with Heidi, Hoffman and Hickman then interviewed Arlene, who independently selected Toole's photo out of the array they presented her. She told the detectives that following the confrontation between Toole and her daughter, she'd found a Kmart security guard to walk them to her car, and that the big white car that both she and her daughter had seen the man get out of was still sitting in the lot at the time. Furthermore, she told Hoffman, she had driven straight home and called Hollywood PD to report the incident, though the detective couldn't locate any record of that call.

Meanwhile, an intensive search for the rest of Adam's remains was under way at the spot near mile marker 126 on Florida's Turnpike, where Toole told detectives he'd left the body. Detectives from Hollywood PD had discovered from the lessee of the property, Sergeant James Carter of the St. Lucie County Sheriff's Office, that the guardrail fence that had stopped their progress on the service road the day they'd first visited the area with Toole had been in place for only ten months.

Carter took them down the faint trail on the other side of the fence to show them that there was indeed a fork in the road, one branch that ran about a mile east to a grazing pasture, the other heading south to a shallow valley where Carter maintained a trailer park. At least that much seemed promising. The day he'd been out here with Toole, the man seemed incapable of any reliable memory.

Meantime, Hollywood PD had called in the Florida Department of Law Enforcement, an agency far more experienced and better equipped to conduct the kind of search at hand. FDLE technicians used steel probes to examine the ground on the north side of the fork in the road, where Toole had claimed he'd left the body. In turn, the FDLE was assisted by specialists from the Florida Department of Agriculture, who surveyed the entire area with a special ground-penetrating radar unit. By late Wednesday, the team had identified seven locations just beyond the fence and north of the road as having unidentified objects buried beneath the ground. Because it was nearly dark, they decided to wait until morning to begin the actual digging.

Detective Hoffman had flown back to Jacksonville, in search of evidence that would prove Toole had been in South Florida at the time of Adam's abduction. In discussing his movements in late July of 1981, Toole had told Hoffman that following his release from the hospital in Newport News, he received a check for $78 from the local Salvation Army to pay for a bus ticket back to Jacksonville. Hollywood detectives followed up, speaking to a Mrs. Hall in that Newport News agency. After a bit of rummaging about, Hall confirmed that in fact a check in the amount of $71.93, payable to the Greyhound Bus Corporation, had been given to someone named Ottis Toole by her agency on Friday, July 24, 1981. That was the amount the bus company had quoted for a one-way fare from Newport News to Jacksonville, she said.

When he arrived in Jacksonville, Hoffman met his counterpart Buddy Terry, who took him directly to the Duval County Jail, where Toole was being held. Terry was buoyed by the fact that a local judge had just declared Toole competent to stand trial in the boarding house arson that killed George Sonnenberg, but Hoffman couldn't have cared less. He couldn't wait to get to the county lockup, where he took Toole through another recounting of his movements in late July of 1981.

Toole told Hoffman that he'd taken the check from the Newport News Salvation Army and walked directly to the nearby bus station, where he'd had to wait for a couple of hours. He said it was "nighttime" when he finally boarded a bus bound for Jacksonville, and that he was not sure when he arrived back in the North Florida city, though bus schedules suggest it would have had to have been sometime early Saturday morning.

Nor was Toole exactly sure what he'd done the moment he stepped down from the air-conditioned bus into the cloying summer heat. Maybe he'd walked to Reaves Roofing to see if they might need him to work that day, or maybe he went instead to the residence of a Nancy Jackson over on Iona Street, where his wife Rita was staying at the time.

Probably he had gone to work and stayed in Jacksonville "a pretty good while," he told Hoffman that evening, because he was broke, and his wife was getting tired of staying with this Jackson woman and wanted him to get them a place of their own. Everything was a little hazy in his mind, Toole said, but he did remember that he rented himself and Rita a place in one of Betty Goodyear's rooming houses on East Second Street, and that is where his brother Howard came to beat him up for stealing his truck.

Hoffman left the matter of the chronology of Toole's movements aside for a moment and returned to the details of the kidnapping and murder. When Hoffman asked what Toole had done with the machete and the shovel he'd used to bury the body, Toole told Hoffman that he had been wondering about that himself. With his mother's house all burned up, he couldn't have hidden those items there, now could he?

So what *had* he done with them? Hoffman wanted to know. And that is when Toole delivered a thunderbolt. "That's why I'm trying to give you all these statements," he told Hoffman. "I'm not really sure that I really *did* kill Adam Walsh."

Hoffman took a deep breath. So Toole was now saying that he had stayed in Jacksonville to work after he got back on Saturday, July 25? He was broke and had to make some money before he took his trip to South Florida. Did Toole realize that Adam had been taken from that Sears store in Hollywood on Monday, scarcely two days later?

Toole blinked, apparently trying to rack his thoughts into something resembling logical order. "So the only thing, if I really didn't kill Adam Walsh, I would have to have been working the Monday, on the twenty-seventh?" he said to Hoffman.

Hoffman leaned back in his chair. "That's the long and short of it," he said. "We'll check the company's records. If you were working on July twenty-seventh, then everything you've told us about the murder is a load of BS."

At this point, Buddy Terry could hold himself back no longer. Without asking Hoffman, he leaned across the table toward Toole.

"Ottis," Terry interjected, "are you lying today? Are you sure you didn't kill Adam Walsh? Now, come on now, let's don't do it this way. Look at me. Look at me, Ottis."

But Toole wouldn't look at Terry. "My mind ain't gonna take much more of this shit," he mumbled; then he began to cry.

"Just tell me the truth," Terry said quietly, "that's all I want to know."

Through his sobs, Toole shook his head. "No, I didn't kill Adam Walsh."

Terry ventured a glance at Hoffman, who wore his characteristic scowl of disgust, then turned back to Toole. "Are you sure, or are you not sure?"

Toole was still staring down at the interview table. "I'm sure I didn't," he said.

"How are you sure?" Terry persisted. "What makes you sure you didn't kill Adam Walsh?"

Toole finally looked up at Terry, his voice plaintive. "Because if I was really sure, I could come up with his body," he said.

Hoffman broke in then, demanding to know where Toole had come up with all the details he'd been giving them about the crime.

"*I made it all up,*" Toole said in an anguished voice, and then he began to cry again.

It was enough for Hoffman. He glanced at his watch and saw that it was 10:30 in the evening. They'd been listening to Toole ramble on for forty-five minutes, and they were just going in circles. He snapped his notebook shut and stood to leave the interview room. Terry, however, stayed behind with Toole.

For the next ten minutes, while Toole wailed in misery, Terry sat patiently, making the occasional reassuring sound, gradually calming the prisoner down. Finally, Toole stopped sobbing and appeared to pull himself together.

"You okay now?" Terry asked. He glanced at his watch. It had been exactly twelve minutes since Hoffman left the room.

Toole nodded. "I need to talk to that guy again," Toole said. Terry glanced toward the door through which Hoffman had departed.

"Detective Hoffman?"

Toole nodded again.

"And why do you need to talk to him?" Terry inquired, carefully.

"Because I wasn't telling the truth just now," Toole said. "About not killing Adam Walsh."

Terry nodded. "I'll just go get him, then."

In his *fifth* interview regarding the abduction and murder of Adam Walsh, recorded shortly after Terry brought Hoffman back to the interview room that night, Toole spoke calmly and in an assured tone of voice, adding details to his account that he had not included in any of his previous statements. He told of walking directly from the Jacksonville Greyhound station to the yard of the roofing company where he knew the Cadillac he'd given back to Faye McNett was stored. He used the keys he'd kept to get inside the fence and took the car, driving to the burned-out site of his mother's home. From under what was left of the front porch, he dug up the can he'd used as a bank and pocketed the $300 or so that was there, then went down to the gas station on the corner, filled the tank, and got on I-95, headed south toward Miami.

"I had everything right in the car," he told Hoffman. "I had all kinds of tools, a shovel, a machete underneath the seat."

As to his encounter with the child outside the store, Toole was even more forthcoming. "He told me his name was Adam, that his mom was in the store shopping. He told me he liked baseball, that he was playing on some kind of Little League team," Toole recalled. He liked talking to the boy, and it was then that he decided that he was going to take him and raise him for himself.

As to the moments when his plans began to fall apart, Toole was appallingly graphic. "He was crying more and getting a little bit louder. And so that's when I really did slap the daylights out of him. I slapped him pretty . . . pretty darn hard. I slapped him dead in the face. Dead across the eyes."

But it seemed not to be enough. "He kept getting a little bit wilder and I hit him real hard in his stomach and that would take the wind out of him. And I did punch him in the eyes a couple times . . . more . . . more than a couple of times."

Finally, Toole said, "I really hit him hard in the stomach. I grabbed onto his throat and started choking him, with both hands. He was unconscious. He never . . . never gained consciousness."

Toole took the detectives back through his account of finding a place to pull off the turnpike, of stopping the Cadillac at the fork he'd mentioned in the service road, and of carrying Adam's body out. "I pulled the bayonet out from underneath the seat," he said, repeating the use of that term for the weapon before he began once again to refer to it as a "machete." And then Toole said, "Well, I done chopped him down. I chopped his head off. I had to come down real hard."

After it was done, Toole said, "I pulled his shirt off, wrapped his head up in it and put it in the car." When he finally decided that he should get rid of Adam's head, he had been driving no more than five or ten minutes. That is when he spotted the canal and the wooden bridge and pulled over and threw the head into the water. He stood and watched to be sure it would sink, and then he turned and got back into the Cadillac. He drove to the next rest plaza, and pulled in beside the entrance to a gas station restroom, where he went in "to clean up and all . . . got all this blood off me."

He filled his tank then and drove back to Jacksonville to the site of his mother's burned-out house, where he parked and slept in the car through the night. In the morning, he woke and cleaned up the car and his tools, and that was pretty much that.

Detective Hoffman noted that it was 11:41 p.m. when he asked Toole his final question of the evening. Just why was it that Toole had lied to him earlier about not having killed Adam Walsh? Hoffman wanted to know.

Toole shrugged. "I couldn't get my head together," he told the detective, as if that ought to explain everything.

While it was surely a blow to Hoffman that Toole had briefly recanted his confession, a more experienced homicide investigator might have reassured the Hollywood detective that this was not out of the ordinary. According to Toole's own words, the killing of "that little boy" was the worst thing that he had ever done. And while it is not out of the ordinary for a guilty person to confess in order to find some peace, neither is it unusual for that same person to later recant. The reasons are many: fear of reprisal, a wave of psychological denial that one has actually done the worst thing possible, and on and on. Furthermore, if one were looking for the model of rational behavior, you wouldn't be searching among convicted killers in the first place. The fact remained that Ottis Toole had confessed to this killing on multiple occasions, citing details that only someone who'd been present could have known.

But Hoffman had not joined the Hollywood Police Department until late in 1975, and he served as a uniform patrolman for nearly three years before he was transferred to the Criminal Investigations Division as a detective. When he took over the investigation of the Adam Walsh case, he had less than three years of time in grade as an investigator, and no experience at all with a case of such magnitude and difficulty. If his reputation as a know-it-all was merited, such an individual would be especially prone to second-guessing himself in his heart of hearts.

Furthermore, one might wonder why on earth the detective did not take this opportunity to question Toole as to whether or not he'd had an encounter with a young girl in a Kmart during his foray to Hollywood back in 1981. After all, only two days before, Hoffman had listened to Arlene Mayer and her daugh-

ter Heidi describe their frightening evening in minute detail
and witnessed them independently identify Toole's photograph
as the man they had seen. Had Toole verified the encounter—
which had not been reported anywhere—it would have placed
Toole in Hollywood at the time of Adam's murder and in all
likelihood put the matter to rest.

VERO BEACH, FLORIDA—OCTOBER 27, 1983

The following Thursday morning, Judge Trowbridge of the
Nineteenth Judicial Circuit of Florida, which includes Indian
River County, where the crime was presumed to have occurred,
ordered the appointment of a temporary public defender for
Toole. Before a local defender could be appointed, however,
Elton H. Schwartz, an attorney practicing in Miami, drawn by
the publicity inherent in the case, offered his services to Toole
free of charge. Subsequently, the court—now absolved of any
expense in the matter—approved the arrangement.

While that was going on, Detective Hoffman set out on his
rounds about Jacksonville, trying to substantiate the details of
Toole's story. First, Hoffman tracked down Faye McNett, who in
fact recalled selling a 1971 Cadillac to Toole. It was a white car,
with a black vinyl top, a four-door, McNett said, and while Toole
wanted it badly, he didn't have enough money to pay for it. He
gave her a few dollars down, she recalls, and agreed to have her
take $20 or $25 a week out of his paycheck until the balance was
satisfied. Ultimately, he told her he couldn't keep up the payments and would have to return the car, which she then kept in
the roofing company's compound.

If he had an extra set of keys to the car and was prone to
"borrowing" it, she hadn't known about it, but sure, she supposed it was possible. Lots of people had keys to the yard fence,
McNett said. That was just how it was.

After he spoke with McNett, Hoffman interviewed John

Reaves Jr., owner of Southeast Color Coat and the son of John Reaves Sr., owner of Reaves Roofing, where Toole had also worked occasionally. The last day Toole had received any pay for either company was June 4, 1981, Reaves said after a check of his records. Furthermore, Reaves did remember getting a phone call from the Salvation Army in Newport News, Virginia. They'd wanted to confirm that Toole did have a job to return to in Jacksonville, and Reaves had vouched for him. Toole had never actually come back to work at either his company or his father's, though, Reaves Jr. said. As to whether or not Toole had a set of keys to the company compound where McNett's Cadillac was kept, Reaves thought it was possible—one of Toole's responsibilities was to let employees and their trucks in and out of the gate.

Meantime, just off Florida's Turnpike at mile marker 126 in Indian River County, FDLE technicians were using a front-end loader to excavate the area where their scans had indicated buried objects were to be found. The machine scraped off four inches of earth at a time in all seven spots, down to a depth of two feet, but no clothing or remains were found.

Also that afternoon, Hoffman received a call from a Detective Steve Upkirk of the Oklahoma City Police Department. Based on statements made by Henry Lee Lucas and Ottis Toole, his department had concluded that Toole was likely responsible for somewhere between four and six unsolved homicides in his jurisdiction, Upkirk said. In addition, there were other unsolved cases in other Oklahoma jurisdictions that Toole was probably responsible for as well. It wasn't necessarily information that would help Hoffman in his own investigation, but it did seem to confirm that Ottis Toole was a very bad person indeed. With him in prison, the world was surely a better place.

On the following morning, Friday, October 28, Hoffman's boss, Hollywood chief of police Sam Martin, found a letter from an attorney's office in Miami waiting for him when he came to work. It was a notice from Elton Schwartz, Toole's newly appointed public defender, advising Martin that forthwith his men were to cease interviewing his client, unless Schwartz was present.

At the same time, Hoffman was at the offices of Southeast Color Coat in Jacksonville, where clerk Ilene Knight dug out records to show that Ottis Toole had been employed by the company from 1976 through June 4, 1981. She did find that Toole had returned for work at the company after that, but it was only for a single day, in December of 1981. Toole had not worked for the company since, Knight was certain.

Next, Hoffman tracked down Georgia Toole, Ottis's sister-in-law, who confirmed that she had in fact tried to have him arrested for stealing her pickup truck, just as the sheriff's records showed. She also told Hoffman where he could find Norvella "Rita" Toole, Ottis's wife. Rita told Hoffman that she had married Toole on January 14, 1977, and that in fact they were still married to that day. "But," she told Hoffman, "he was always running me off, and I couldn't figure it out, and one day I got thinking, I said, well, what would a man tell his wife to leave all the time for, unless there's something wrong?"

Rita told Hoffman that she was away from Ottis so much that there wasn't really a lot she could tell him. "The only thing, Ottis was good to me, and that's all I know, he never mistreated me. He never beat me, he always called me baby, and I was kinda shocked when I heard all this."

Following his interview with Rita, Hoffman met briefly with Vernon Toole, Ottis's brother, and then with Mack Caulder, a foreman for the roofing company, but obtained little of use from either. A bit after 3:00 p.m. that Friday, Hoffman interviewed John Reaves Sr., the owner of Reaves Roofing. He confirmed that Toole had worked for him at times and was responsible for cleaning the compound and had access to the company gas pump and keys. He also told Hoffman that owing to a number of thefts on company property, he had all the locks changed back in 1982, some time after Toole had left his employment. Reaves remembered that Faye McNett had sold her Cadillac to Toole, and he assured Hoffman that indeed his company kept a number of tools on the property, including crowbars, shovels, and the like.

When Hoffman asked if they had any machetes, Reaves thought about it. "I believe we got one or two of them too," he said. "It had a wood handle, I'd say about 10 or 12 inches, but I don't remember seeing it lately." At the conclusion of their interview, Reaves Sr. took Hoffman out to the company tool shed to look around for the machete, but they had no luck.

For all his work in Jacksonville, Hoffman had developed little of value. On the one hand, he had ruled out any possibility that Toole had been working for his old employers on Monday, July 27, 1981, the day that Adam was abducted, but on the other, he had found no one who could place Ottis Toole in any specific location—particularly Hollywood—between July 26 and July 30. This makes the failure to corroborate Toole's encounter with Heidi Mayer all the more confounding.

In any case, while Hoffman had been busy with his interviews, Buddy Terry had set to work on actually finding the Cadillac that Toole claimed he had used during the abduction and murder, and which Faye McNett had long since sold. Terry finally tracked the then-twelve-year-old vehicle to an outfit called Wells Brothers Used Cars, at 4334 Brentwood Avenue in Jacksonville, and found that indeed it was a black-over-white four-door model with a black leatherlike interior, a black dashboard, black carpeting, and power window and door locks that could be controlled by a master panel in the driver's armrest.

On Monday, October 31, technicians from the Florida Department of Law Enforcement were dispatched to pick up the Cadillac from the Wells Brothers lot and take it to the FDLE crime lab on Platen Road in Jacksonville, where it was to be examined for fingerprints, blood, and fibers. That same day, public defender Schwartz met with his client for the first time, and on Tuesday the attorney announced to reporters in Tallahassee that Ottis Toole now claimed that he did not murder Adam Walsh or anyone else. "Ottis Toole has denied every one of the crimes he's confessed to," Schwartz somewhat predictably said. Asked to comment, Hollywood chief of police Martin told the Associated Press that he felt his department still had a prime suspect in the case.

On that same Tuesday, Detectives Hoffman and Hickman were still in Jacksonville, interviewing Howard Toole, Ottis's brother, at a halfway house. Yes, Howard told the detectives, when he found out that Ottis was back in Jacksonville on August 1, 1981, he had gone to Betty Goodyear's rooming house to confront his brother about the theft of the pickup, and in fact he had chased him down to the nearby mini-mart, where he caught Ottis and slapped him around.

But as far as Ottis having keys to the Reaves Roofing compound or driving a 1971 black-over-white Cadillac, Howard claimed to have no knowledge. Nor did he know that Ottis had been hospitalized in Newport News. It was not unusual for Ottis to take off for weeks at a time without notifying him or anyone else in the family, Howard told Hoffman.

On Wednesday, November 2, 1983, FDLE technicians began their processing of the 1971 Cadillac that Ottis said he'd been driving when he kidnapped and killed Adam Walsh. Five rolls of film were used in photographing the interior and exterior of the vehicle, and the carpets were removed to be treated with luminol, a substance that glows when it comes in contact with blood.

In addition, the car was vacuumed and hair samples retained. Following all that, the vehicle was turned over to technicians in the latent prints section for processing. The various samples were sent off to the department's microanalysis section in Tallahassee and its serology lab in Jacksonville, while the photographs were retained by FDLE's Jacksonville office.

On the same day, Detective Hoffman spoke with Spencer Bennett, of Spencer Motors, at 1401 North Main Street in Jacksonville. Bennett claimed to have known Toole since he was seventeen and also said that he had sold him a two-door white Cadillac in 1982. That car had ended up with Ottis's brother Howard, Bennett said, because—once again—Ottis couldn't keep up the payments. Bennett described Toole as a quiet, meek individual. And if he was in fact a homosexual, Bennett said, it was news to him.

Hoffman then asked Bennett if he knew if Ottis ever carried a knife or machete around with him. Bennett told Hoffman that in fact he had found a machete in one of his vehicles a while back, though he didn't remember exactly when or which car he'd found it in. He rummaged around in a closet and finally produced a machete with a wooden handle wrapped in black electrician's tape, and housed in a green canvas sheath. The blade was rusty and had what looked like tar smeared on it. Hoffman was welcome to it, Bennett said.

Hoffman took the machete and traveled to the offices of Reaves Roofing, where he showed it to John Reaves Sr. Reaves glanced at the machete, but said it didn't look familiar. For whatever reason, Hoffman didn't bother to show the blade either to John Reaves Jr. at Southeast Color Coat or to company foreman Mack Caulder, both of whom worked more closely with Toole. While he was at the offices, however, Hoffman did take a statement from Helen Reaves, who told him that she had heard from a neighbor, Catherine Butler, that back in 1982 quite often a white car would turn up at the company gates after everyone had gone home. Whoever was in that white car would enter and leave the compound at will, Butler told Mrs. Reaves.

From Reaves Roofing, Hoffman drove back to Wells Brothers Used Cars to check on the provenance of the 1971 black-over-white Cadillac that FDLE was now processing. The records were spotty, but it appeared that they'd had the car since some time in the summer of 1982. They'd sold the car to a person named Ronald Williams on December 31 of that year, for $1569.75, but Williams had defaulted on the payments, and they'd had to repossess it. The Wells Brothers had had the car to themselves again until Detective Terry showed up and the FDLE came to take it away.

If all this seemed less than consequential, Hoffman had something of a more interesting conversation that evening at the Duval County Jail, where he interviewed Bobby Lee Jones, who not only had worked with Toole at Reaves Roofing and Southeast Color Coat, but had recently shared a cell with Toole for about a month.

In the days that the two of them had worked together, Jones told Hoffman, he knew that Toole had what he described as an "18-inch butcher knife" with a wooden handle under the driver's seat of his car. Toole's car was a white '72 Cadillac with a dent in the right side of the rear bumper, Jones said. He remembered the dent clearly because he had put it there. "I ran into the back of him," Jones said. "I never said anything about it, but I remember that dent."

Jones said that Toole always carried a big ring of keys when he was working for the company and would often disappear from work for several days. He'd show up and explain that he'd been partying, Jones said, though Toole also claimed that he burned down houses for money.

As to their recent time together in the Duval County Jail, Jones told Hoffman that Toole had told him all about the kidnapping and murder of Adam Walsh. He said that Toole talked about driving up and talking to the boy and making friends with him, and then for some reason starting to beat him up and cutting him apart with a big knife. "I told him to shut up and lay down," Jones said.

Following his conversation with Jones, Hoffman then interviewed James Collins, aka Julius Riley Wilkes, the other cellmate who had also worked with Toole at Southeast Color Coat.

According to Collins, it was common knowledge that Toole was gay. Collins related an on-the-job incident at Southeast Color Coat where another worker was making deprecating remarks to Toole about his lover Henry Lee Lucas. According to Collins, Toole didn't say much, but simply walked off the job abruptly. A few minutes later, Toole returned to work in his Cadillac with a shotgun under his arm. He approached the man who had been making fun of Lucas and pointed the barrel of the shotgun in the man's face. "Just keep on talking and I'll blow your brains out," Collins reported Toole as saying.

When Hoffman asked Collins to describe the car that Toole was driving that day, he replied that it was either white or black, one of the two. In any case, Collins thought it looked like the Cadillac that was on the news just the other day. It was toward the end of this interview that Collins divulged the recent conversations he'd had with Toole in their cell about the fact that he was leaving jail to help the cops in Fort Lauderdale look for the body of a child he'd killed down there, and his fears as to what other inmates might do to a fellow convict known to have murdered children.

On the following morning, Thursday, November 3, Hoffman drove the forty miles to Raiford, where he interviewed a man named James Michael Poole, who'd shared a cell with Ottis Toole in the Butler Transient Unit back in July. Poole told Hoffman that Toole had made various strange statements about being in the "child repossession business." Another time, he told Poole that he had "taken" his own son from Broward County and that somewhere on their way back to Jacksonville he had just dropped the boy off along the highway. Poole thought that odd because the boy was supposedly only seven or eight years old, but then again, people did strange things—especially the kind of people you meet in jail.

While at Raiford, Detective Hoffman also spoke with Boyd Earl Gilbert, another cellmate of Toole's in the Butler Transient

Unit. Gilbert told Hoffman that the two of them had met on August 31, some two months previously, and that at that time, Toole claimed that up until the time of his imprisonment, he had been earning a living burning down buildings for people who wanted to collect the insurance. Unfortunately, there'd been an old man sleeping in the last place he burned down, and the guy died.

During that same conversation, Gilbert said, Toole also told him that he had murdered a little kid down around West Palm Beach, the son of a policeman. Though it might seem a puzzling claim, it is quite possible that Toole had confused the adult-sized boat captain's hat Adam was wearing when he was taken with the similarly styled patrolman's dress cap worn by most South Florida cops at the time. In any case, if Gilbert was being truthful, it meant that Toole was talking openly about his involvement in the killing of Adam Walsh for more than a month before he'd made his first formal confession to Detective Kendrick of Brevard County on October 10.

As Hoffman was conducting these interviews at Raiford, Buddy Terry took the machete that Hoffman had picked up at Bennett Motors to the FDLE offices in Jacksonville to have it tested for blood. Technicians had already identified eight different areas of carpet and padding from the floorboards of Toole's Cadillac to test for blood as well.

Terry was hopeful that something would come of the tests, of course, but his mind kept wandering to what awaited him at his next stop. A call had come into his office the previous evening from Ottis Toole, something Terry was hardly expecting, given the public pronouncements of his newly appointed attorney.

Toole had said that he needed to speak with Terry right away. He was upset with this lawyer from Miami who'd come up to talk with him. According to Toole's message, the guy was actually trying to get him to say he wasn't guilty of the murder of Adam Walsh.

JACKSONVILLE, FLORIDA—NOVEMBER 3, 1983

Ottis Toole's seventh recorded statement to police regarding the murder of Adam Walsh began shortly after noon on November 3 with a preamble from Detective Terry. "I came to the county jail to talk to you because you contacted Detective Ron Carool and told him that you wanted me to come over and talk to you," Terry said. "Is that correct?"

It was indeed correct, Toole assured him. "The lawyer I had from Miami and the lawyer I got in Jacksonville told me that I don't have to talk with you at all," Toole said, "but I still want to talk to you. And the detective is trying to get me to say I ain't guilty on the Adam Walsh case."

Terry looked at Toole closely. "The detective, or the attorney?" he asked.

"I mean the attorney," Toole answered. "I really know myself that I really did kill Adam Walsh but the lawyer I got from Miami, he's trying to tell me I didn't kill Adam Walsh."

Though it was frustrating, Detective Terry told Toole that he was sorry, but they could go no further. They couldn't talk about Adam Walsh anymore, not without Toole's attorney present. Whether he liked it or not, Toole had a lawyer now. They could talk about other things, Terry said, but their private conversations about Adam Walsh were at an end.

That same afternoon, Detective Hoffman drove from Raiford another three and a half hours south to a State of Florida foster care facility in Lakeland, Florida, where he interviewed Frank Powell, Ottis Toole's nephew and brother of Frieda "Becky" Powell. Young Frank told Hoffman that he had not seen Ottis Toole since they all were separated one night on their way up to Maryland back in July 1981.

He told Hoffman that he often rode around Jacksonville with his uncle and that he had been with him on several visits to Reaves Roofing and Southeast Color Coat, when Ottis used keys on his ring to unlock the gates so that he could fire up the tar kettles and such. And Frank also remembered that Ottis kept a leather-sheathed hunting knife under the front seat of his black-over-white Cadillac. He'd had the car in 1980 and '81, Frank said, and had used it even after he'd had to give it back to Mrs. McNett.

All the information seemed to confirm that Toole in fact had access to a car that he could have used to drive to Miami, one with a resemblance to a car seen in the vicinity of the abduction of Adam Walsh. Also, it seemed that Toole probably had kept a sizable bladed weapon of some sort under the seat of that car. But aside from the reported sighting of Toole by a woman and her daughter in a Hollywood Kmart a day or two before Adam's disappearance and Toole's apparently wobbly confessions to the crime, Hoffman had still not come up with the solid evidence he was after. He thanked young Powell for his help and began the long drive back to Jacksonville.

Early on Friday morning, as Toole was being escorted by Detective Terry toward an interview room in the Duval County Jail, where yet another team of out-of-state homicide detectives were waiting to interview him regarding a set of unsolved cases, Toole glanced down the hallway to see Detectives Hoffman and Hickman conversing with each other, and he called out to them. He'd remembered this church where he used to work back in 1981. It was out off Lane Avenue, near I-10, Toole told them, near a Days Inn. Maybe they could track it down and find out exactly what days he was working, Toole told the detectives.

Detective Terry suspected that Toole's attorney wouldn't be happy with his client's offer of such information, but since Toole had initiated the conversation, it did not violate counsel's dictates that no interview be scheduled independently. Certainly, Terry made no move to intervene. Hoffman and Hickman made a note of Toole's information and told him they'd look into it.

First, though, the two Hollywood detectives followed up with Betty Goodyear, to see if they could confirm the date when

Toole had moved into one of her houses with his erstwhile wife Rita. As was the case with employment records, any piece of evidence that would place Toole in Jacksonville on July 27, 1981, would render all of his statements regarding Adam Walsh null and void.

But Goodyear insisted that if she did nothing else, she kept accurate records. She produced a pair of receipt books for the period in question, the first of which showed that she had rented a room to Ottis Toole on July 31, 1981. She also showed them another book with a copy of a receipt made out to V. Toole on August 7. Toole did have a brother named Vernon, but as to why his name was in her book, Goodyear did not know.

From there, Hoffman and Hickman traveled to University Hospital, where Ottis's wife Rita was a patient. When they asked her about Betty Goodyear's records, Rita cleared the mystery up quickly. She'd moved out of living with Ottis shortly after they'd reunited there at the end of July, and moved in with his brother Vernon for a week. Since he paid the rent, that's why his name was on the receipt. As for her time together with Ottis during that period, it began the day she moved into the Goodyear Apartments on July 31. She'd been staying with a woman named Nancy Jackson for seven or eight months before that, and she hadn't seen Ottis at all during that time.

The two detectives left University Hospital to follow up on Toole's recollection that he had done some work for a church around the time of Adam Walsh's murder. After some digging, they finally found a Church of God next to a Days Inn just south of I-10, about fifteen minutes west of downtown. The church's pastor, Reverend Cecil Wiggins, didn't recall anyone named Toole ever working for him, but, prodded by the detectives, he agreed to consult his records. Somewhat to his surprise, the good reverend discovered that the church had in fact paid Toole for lawn maintenance work on two separate occasions in 1981: $17.50 on August 27, and $22.75 on August 28.

Hoffman and Hickman could only stare at each other. After all their digging, they had been able to place Ottis Toole in Jacksonville on July 25, when he'd arrived from Virginia on a Greyhound bus. And they knew that he was back again on July 31, when he'd rented a room for himself and his wife from Betty Goodyear. But as to where he was during the time in between, and especially on the afternoon and evening of July 27, when Adam Walsh was kidnapped and murdered, they had only the sighting reported by Heidi and Arlene Mayer and the word of Toole to go on.

Given the amount of time that Hoffman had spent in Jacksonville talking to Toole's family and associates, it might seem in hindsight that he was more intent on proving that Toole was in that city on July 27 and thus could not possibly have committed the murder of Adam Walsh than he was with trying to find evidence placing Toole in South Florida at the time. Perhaps Hoffman was simply following the line of least resistance in interviewing individuals who knew Toole and might exonerate him; but it is puzzling, at the very least, why Hoffman or his team did not expend a greater effort on trying to place Toole at the scene of the crime: broadcasting appeals to witnesses in local media, for instance, or canvasing the ranks of Sears shoppers.

Possibly it seemed easier to Hoffman to track down and talk to people who knew Toole than to search for needles in the haystacks of South Florida; possibly, given his relative inexperience with crimes of such magnitude, he was simply out of his depth as an investigator; or possibly he simply believed Toole was lying when he said that he had kidnapped and murdered Adam Walsh. Were this his reasoning, though, he had committed the cardinal sin of an investigator—allowing his subjective feelings to interfere with his work. And whatever his reasoning, it seems odd that Hoffman was spending most of his time and effort trying to prove that the person who had confessed to the crime did not do it instead of the other way around.

In any case, and out of leads in Jacksonville for the time being, Hoffman and Hickman returned to Hollywood to await the results of the various tests being performed by the FDLE labs. On the following Wednesday, November 9, Hollywood police chief Sam Martin called Hoffman in to share the report that the FDLE had finally sent him. The eight sections of carpet and padding from the front and rear floorboards of the Cadillac had been treated with luminol to indicate the presence of blood, the report noted, and areas of strongly persistent luminescence were observed on the portion of carpet taken from the driver's-side floor, the carpet from the left rear floorboard, and on the padding beneath the carpet on the left rear floorboard. While it would have taken a considerable quantity of blood to soak through the carpet and into the padding itself, the report stated that—given the amount of time that had passed (and the limitations of DNA technology at the time)—there was an "insufficient" amount of blood present for further testing.

As to the machete that Hoffman had confiscated at Bennett Motors, chemical tests on the blade edge also demonstrated that traces of blood were present, but once again, the quantity found was insufficient to allow for further testing. While such results may seem maddeningly inconclusive to a present-day audience conditioned by the mind-boggling feats achieved by *CSI* investigators on contemporary television, those were the unequivocal findings of the most sophisticated crime technicians working in Florida law enforcement at the time.

Tests for blood on the canvas sheath of the machete were also inconclusive, the report added. And as for other debris found on the blade and sheath, that would be examined by FDLE's microanalysis section in Tallahassee. Five rolls of film had been taken to document the various forensic procedures performed on the Cadillac, the report noted, though the disposition of that film was not made clear.

The thought of setting science aside for the moment and simply showing the machete to the several people who had reported seeing Ottis Toole in possession of such a weapon might have occurred to almost anyone at that point. After all, Hoffman had gone to the trouble of taking it to *one* of Toole's employers for the purposes of identification. But if Chief Martin or Detective Hoffman or anyone else at HPD thought of such a low-tech undertaking, there is no indication of it.

WILLIAMSON COUNTY, TEXAS—NOVEMBER 12, 1983

In November 1983, two days before what would have been the celebration of Adam Walsh's ninth birthday, Henry Lee Lucas wrote from his jail cell in Texas to his former lover and partner in crime, Ottis Toole. He wasn't sure if word had reached Toole yet, but Lucas wanted him to know that he had confessed to the murder of Toole's niece, Becky Powell. Lucas hadn't written sooner regarding the matter, he explained, because he didn't want to "hurt" Toole.

Despite the fact that he had killed her, Lucas assured Toole that Becky had been his life: "I loved her more than anything else," he said, and then, having dispensed with that matter, went on to ask Toole for help in piecing together the details of the many crimes they had committed together, "so we can get the [w]hole thing out in the open." Lucas had not yet implicated Toole in anything, he said, but he had found considerable peace in coming clean, and he was writing now to find out if Toole as well might be willing to talk about their various misdeeds.

On Monday, November 14, Lucas followed up with a phone call, one that was being tape-recorded by the Texas Rangers, a fact that Lucas passed along to Toole at the beginning of their conversation. Certainly the warning did not deter Toole from being forthright.

"Remember that one time I said I wanted me some ribs?" Toole asked Lucas. "Did that make me a cannibal?"

"You wasn't a cannibal," Lucas assured him. "It's the force of the devil, something forced on us that we can't change. There's no denying what we become," he added. "We know what we are."

Toole seemed quick to pick up on Lucas's theme. "Remember how I liked to pour some blood out of them?"

Once again, Lucas—whose first murder victim was his own mother, in 1960—seemed compassionate and reasoned. "Ottis, you and I have something people look on as an animal. There's no way of changing what we done, but we can stop it and not allow other people to become what we have. And the only way to do that is by honesty."

Apparently Lucas had achieved some sense of salvation by baring his soul to investigators about his many misdeeds (quite a few of them fanciful, as it turned out), and it seemed as if his words had some effect on Toole. The following day, Tuesday, November 15, Toole was interviewed by Calcasieu Parish chief of detectives Donny Fittz about the murder of twenty-year-old Catherine Martin back in 1982, near Lake Charles, Louisiana. She'd been stabbed sixteen times with a screwdriver. Yeah, he had done it, Toole said. And his account of the crime reflected that he saw nothing unusual in his choice of weapons. If you had a hammer, you'd use a hammer. If there was a knife, use a knife. What was so different between a knife and a screwdriver anyway?

As he was winding up his interview with Toole, Fittz casually tossed out something he'd heard in the hallway.

"We understand you say you really didn't kill Adam Walsh," Fittz said to Toole, who seemed surprised by the statement.

"Oh no, I killed him too, there's no doubt about that," Toole replied. "It was like the kid, he wouldn't shut up. I was driving him in the car. I slapped him. I hit him several times."

Fittz gave an interview to reporters concerning his own investigation of the murder of Catherine Martin, but thought enough of what he'd heard from Toole about the Walsh case to pass that information along as well. Thus, in a story published on November 23 in the *Fort Lauderdale Sun-Sentinel*, the public was assured once again by Toole that he was the man responsible.

Meanwhile, Detective Hoffman had returned to Jacksonville yet again, looking for something that would pin down Toole's whereabouts between July 25 and July 31, 1981. On Thursday morning, November 17, Hoffman went to the Jacksonville Sheriff's Office homicide unit to meet with Buddy Terry. Toole was in the unit as well on this day, being interviewed by detectives from agencies near Houston and others from Colorado.

The door to the interview room was open, and when Toole glanced up to see Hoffman walking by, he called out after the detective. "Hey, Jack," he said, "I need to speak with you."

Hoffman grudgingly stopped to acknowledge Toole. "So where's Detective Hickman?" Toole wanted to know.

Hoffman glanced at his two colleagues. "He's back in Hollywood," Hoffman said to Toole. "This is Lieutenant Smith and Sergeant Standley," he added. "And neither one of them believe a thing you've said about Adam Walsh."

Toole had already complained to detectives Kendrick from Brevard County and Via from Louisiana that he didn't like the way that Hoffman treated him. Hoffman had called him a "retard" and an "asshole" on several occasions the day they were out there by Florida's Turnpike looking for the body, Toole said, and that "really pissed him off."

"I know I'm an asshole," Toole told Kendrick earlier. "And I am a retard." But if the Hollywood cops thought they were so smart, then let them go find Adam's body themselves, that's what he'd decided.

Thus, it is not difficult to imagine what Toole thought of the three Hollywood cops glowering at him from the hallway. Hoffman would later note in his log that Toole seemed quite upset, in fact.

"You want me to go on national TV and state that I killed Adam Walsh?" Toole called angrily to Hoffman. But despite the fact that he had no other leads in the case of a lifetime, Hoffman apparently felt he'd already been sufficiently played the fool by Ottis Toole. He simply shrugged and led the other officers away down the hall.

That day, Hoffman looked at medical records supplied by jailors that indicated that since his arrival, Toole had been receiving 50 milligrams of Benadryl at bedtime, presumably to help him fall asleep, along with regular dosages of Meladril, an herbal supplement sometimes used in the treatment of herpes. Though medical records showed that he had been diagnosed as having suffered convulsions from grand mal epilepsy some fifteen years previously, Toole was taking no epilepsy medication at Duval County. Little of import there, it seemed.

On the following day, Hoffman interviewed Toole's stepfather, Robert Harley, who told the detective that he had married Toole's mother Sarah in 1957, when Toole was ten. He told Hoffman of the thefts that occurred from his home after Toole's mother died and of his suspicions that Toole and Henry Lee Lucas were responsible for those, as well as for the fire that destroyed the house on June 23, 1981.

At the same time, other detectives from Hollywood were at the Lake Butler facility, interviewing James Redwine, Betty Goodyear's troubled son, who had fallen in with Toole after his return to Jacksonville from a treatment center in Miami. Redwine, serving time for arsons he committed along with Toole, said that while Toole often acted meek and timid, he could fly into rages, especially if he had a weapon available.

Redwine described a few such incidents for the detectives and also confirmed that he had seen Toole in possession of a large knife with a brown wooden handle. However, Redwine said, he was not going to submit to a sworn statement about any of this. He did not want to get involved in the investigation, period.

On Saturday, Hoffman and his cohorts, Smith and Standley, were back in the homicide unit at the Jacksonville Sheriff's Office. Once again, Toole spotted him passing the open interview room and called out after him. Hoffman ignored Toole, but Buddy Terry caught up with him and explained that Toole was being insistent. "Just go see what he wants," Terry urged.

Hoffman may not have cared what Ottis Toole wanted, but he was on Terry's turf and needed some element of cooperation if he was going to accomplish anything in Jacksonville. Thus, he walked into the interview room and informed Toole brusquely that he, Toole, was being represented by public defender Elton Schwartz and that Schwartz did not want Toole talking to any investigators without his attorney present.

To Toole, none of it mattered. "I do not want to be represented by anyone," he told Hoffman. "I want to speak to you about Adam Walsh, and I do not want to be represented by any attorney."

Hoffman glanced about the room, where any number of fellow law officers stood watching, waiting for his call. Certainly, Toole seemed well aware of his rights, and this was anything but a coercive situation, as cops from several different jurisdictions could testify. He was stymied in his own investigation; what was the harm of hearing Toole out? Suppressing something of a sigh, Hoffman sat down and began to take the *eighth* statement offered by Ottis Toole concerning the murder of Adam Walsh.

Toole began by telling Hoffman that essentially everything he had confessed to concerning the murder was correct, from the time of his arrival in South Florida and the abduction of Adam Walsh from the Sears Mall in Hollywood until his arrival at mile marker 126 on Florida's Turnpike and the subsequent decapitation. But the part about burying Adam's body in that same location was not exactly right, Toole said.

"Everything I told you about the killing, about the chopping, all that's true," Toole told Hoffman. As to Adam's torso, though, "I wrapped him in some blankets and put him in the trunk."

Following his brief stop to dispose of the head in the canal, Toole said, he drove on to Jacksonville, arriving in the evening hours at 708 Day Avenue, where the remains of his mother's gutted house still stood. At that time, Toole said, he took Adam's body out of the trunk and carried it around to the backyard and placed it in a gutted-out refrigerator that he had used as a kind of incinerator in the past. He'd start a fire and toss in coils of coated wire to burn the insulation off and expose the copper, he explained, which he could then sell at junkyards around town.

In this instance, however, his aim was quite different. After he'd gotten Adam's torso inside the refrigerator, Toole heaped on some pieces of wood and doused it all with gasoline. He lit the fire then, hoping to cremate the body, but to his disappointment, the fire went out fairly rapidly. Some of the skin on the body had turned black and crumbly, but it was not in any way completely burned. So he did what he had to do: he heaped on more wood, poured on more gasoline, and set the blaze going again.

After he was finally satisfied with the results, Ottis tried to push the gutted refrigerator on its side, so he could dump the remains onto a blanket he had spread out. But the refrigerator was heavy to begin with, and with all the debris and ash that now filled the insides, Toole couldn't budge it. So he went back to the Cadillac, found a shovel, and used that to scoop out the remains onto the blanket.

He gathered up the blanket and its contents, wrestled the bundle to the Cadillac, and managed to heave it up and into the trunk. He was about to slam the lid down when something occurred to him: What if there were hot ashes still lurking in that mess somewhere? They could smolder for hours and eventually start a blaze in his trunk. Toole might not be smart, but he knew about fire.

He also knew that no one had bothered to turn off the water at the ruined house and so he went to fetch the hose that still dangled from a spigot outside. He opened the faucet and doused the trunk and its contents until he was sure that no embers could have survived.

By then it was late, and Toole, who'd had himself a full day, was tired. He slammed the lid of the trunk, climbed into the Cadillac, and slept there through the night. In the morning he rose to clean off his machete and his shovel, and then hid the tools under a still-standing portion of the ruined house.

After that, he drove the Cadillac to the city of Jacksonville's northernmost dump, where he backed up to a muddy area and tossed the water-soaked bundle out. Satisfied that the wadded blanket looked no different from any other bundle of discarded goods in the vast wasteland, he was about to get back into the car when it struck him that the sodden carpeting of the trunk might now contain traces of blood, so he pulled that up from the floorboards of the trunk and tossed it out into the dump as well. That night, long after he knew all the employees would be gone, Toole returned the Cadillac to the yard of Reaves Roofing.

And whatever happened to that machete he had used? Hoffman wanted to know. Toole wasn't sure what he had done with the blade, finally, he told Hoffman. It could have ended up over at Spencer's Motors in Jacksonville, though. He'd left a lot of his stuff in paper bags over there at one time or another.

Hoffman's notes do not indicate whether or not his heart quickened at this chance comment of Toole's, but if it did not, one would surely wonder why. Finally, after all the fruitless searching, Ottis Toole had unknowingly suggested that Hoffman was in possession of a piece of evidence that would directly link the killer to the crime.

Asked to describe this machete further, Toole told Hoffman that it was in a green canvas holster that kept the blade covered, and that he had wrapped tape on the wooden handle, "to keep from getting blisters from chopping." It seemed a perfect match to the machete that Hoffman had confiscated at Bennett Motors: the handle had been taped, the grips were wooden, the blade was housed in a green canvas sheath, and one of the substances on the blade looked very much like tar, indicating its use by someone involved in the roofing trade.

Hoffman next asked Toole where he had stayed between the time he took the Cadillac back to the roofing company on the evening of July 28 and the afternoon of July 31, when he moved into one of Betty Goodyear's houses with Rita. Toole wasn't too sure. He might have slept in a portion of his mother's house that still had its roof, or he might have slept in one or another of the parks in the area.

Hoffman concluded the interview at 11:08 that morning, asking Toole to explain why he had lied before about burying Adam's body down near mile marker 126 on Florida's Turnpike. Toole didn't say anything about the sandwich that Hoffman had slapped out of his hands the day he'd led detectives to the site where he'd decapitated Adam. Nor did he mention that it pissed him off mightily that Hoffman had called him an asshole and a retard on numerous occasions.

Yes, he had told Hoffman that he cut off Adam's head and buried his body nearby on that day, he admitted, but there was a very simple explanation: "I was just fucking around with the police department," he said.

SATURDAY, NOVEMBER 19, 1983

Following that interview with Toole and a break for lunch, Hoffman and his fellow officers from Hollywood tracked down David Gillyard, who'd worked as sales manager for Wells Brothers Used Cars, starting in November 1982. He remembered taking in the 1971 black-over-white Cadillac, Gillyard told the detectives, and recalled very clearly that there was no carpeting in its trunk. Rather than go to the expense of paying for new carpet for such an old vehicle, he had ordered one of his lot men to simply "paint splatter" the trunk to give it some appearance of finish for sale.

After they'd spoken to Gillyard, the detectives went back to Faye McNett, just wondering, they said, if the Cadillac she'd sold to Ottis Toole had carpeting in its trunk. Indeed it did, McNett told them. What kind of a question was that, anyway?

On Sunday, Hoffman, accompanied by Lieutenant Smith and Sergeant Stanley, took a drive to the North Jacksonville dump, where they took photographs of the area—with more than two years of trash heaped on the site since Toole said he had disposed of the body there, it seemed little else could be done.

Early Monday morning, seeking further corroboration of what Toole had told them, the detectives spoke with the Jacksonville Fire Department arson specialist who had investigated the burning of Toole's mother's house at 708 Day Avenue in June of 1981. The lot had been leveled back on December 10, 1982, by an outfit called Realco Wrecking. But as to what had and had not remained standing after the fire, there were numerous photographs in the files, Captain Hinkley said. The Hollywood detectives were welcome to them.

At about nine thirty that morning, Hoffman interviewed Robert L. Hammond, who owned Hammond's Grocery at 700 Day Avenue, next door to Toole's mother's house. Yes, he knew both Toole and Henry Lee Lucas, Hammond told the officers, and he well remembered the day that Toole's mother's house burned down.

He had also observed that Toole stayed at the house on several occasions after the fire, and he had often seen Toole digging up and burying various articles of trash in the backyard. Toole eked out a living by collecting junk, Hammond said, and often stored various items he'd found in his mother's yard. He brought back discarded refrigerators, then hacked them apart for the aluminum he could sell at salvage yards. And he also used the gutted refrigerators as incinerators where he burned the insulation off wiring to expose the salable copper underneath. Hammond's mother Sarah was present at the interview, and she too told Hoffman that she had seen Ottis Toole back at his mother's house after the June 23 fire.

Hoffman next spoke with a man named Charles Lee Hardaman, who claimed to have known Toole for about three years. The two of them would ride around picking up junk like refrigerators, stoves, and furniture, and then bring it back to 708 Day Avenue, where they'd break it apart for whatever salvageable materials might be obtained—and yes, he had also seen Toole use the carcasses of refrigerators as incinerators.

When Hoffman asked if he ever knew Toole to carry weapons, Hardaman confirmed that there was a shotgun around sometimes. And how about any large knives? Hoffman wanted to know.

"I never seen him with knives," Hardaman said first, but then corrected himself. "Well, he had one like they used in the old days."

Just how large a knife was this? Hoffman asked.

"I don't know," Hardaman said. "I saw it," he added, holding his hands a foot or more apart. Then he raised his thumb and forefinger, with perhaps a two-inch gap between them. "A blade about this wide."

"What kind of case?" Hoffman asked.

"A steel case."

"What color?"

Hardaman shrugged. "Rust," he said, going on to explain to Hoffman that it was the kind of knife that you could fix onto a gun barrel.

"A bayonet?" Hoffman asked.

"Yeah," Hardaman said.

In his first confession to Hoffman, Toole had begun his description of the decapitation by saying he'd used a bayonet. But Hoffman had responded by saying, "Like a machete?" and Toole had subsequently followed the detective's lead in referring to the weapon he'd used as a machete. It could have been a simple misstatement, given the limitations of Toole's intelligence, but then again, the matter was certainly worth pursuing.

"When did you see that knife?" Hoffman asked.

Hardaman gave him a look. "Well, it was mine," he finally admitted. "I left it there at the house and told him to sharpen it."

"And he kept it? Never returned it to you?"

"Right," Hardaman said.

"When did you give it to him?" Hoffman next asked.

Hardaman thought. "It was when his momma was living, that much I know."

"So that would have been before May 1981?"

"Yeah," Hardaman said.

Following the conversation with Hardaman, Hoffman drove with Smith and Standley to Daytona Beach, about two hours south, where they met briefly with William O. Toole, another of Ottis's brothers. William refused to speak with them in any detail about Ottis, however, and the trio drove home to Hollywood that evening.

It was on Wednesday of that week that the *Fort Lauderdale Sun-Sentinel* ran the story in which Louisiana detective Donny Fittz told reporters that Ottis Toole had confessed to the killing of Adam Walsh during an unrelated interview. When reporters called Hollywood PD for a comment on Fittz's allegations, public information officer Tony Alderson dismissed it as nothing new. "We believed Toole the first time," Alderson said.

Meantime, the FDLE lab in Jacksonville had concluded its examination of Toole's Cadillac for Adam's fingerprints. Alas, no latent prints of any value had been found.

Almost a week went by without any significant develop-

ments, though the treatment center in Hialeah where Betty
Goodyear's son John Redwine had stayed prior to meeting Toole
did confirm to Hollywood PD that Redwine had gone on vacation from the facility on July 24, 1981, and had boarded a bus
bound for Jacksonville at nine that morning. Conceivably, Redwine could have been helpful in placing Toole's whereabouts if
Hoffman could find him.

On Wednesday, November 30, 1983, Detective Hoffman
reached a clerk named Filiore in the Jacksonville Water Department, who confirmed that water service to the home of Toole's
mother at 708 Day Avenue had in fact been disconnected for
nonpayment, but not until September 9, 1981. "This information was needed in order to verify a part of Ottis Toole's confession in which he indicated that he used the hose in the rear of
his mother's residence to wash out the 1971 Cadillac trunk area
in which there was trace evidence of blood," Hoffman wrote in
his notes, adding that the information did corroborate Toole's
claim that there was water available to him on the date in question.

Later that day, Hoffman phoned Dennis Bedwell, supervisor
of the City of Jacksonville Sanitation Department. Since Toole
had claimed that he disposed of the body of Adam Walsh in the
North Jacksonville dump on the morning of July 28, 1981, Hoffman needed Bedwell to provide the names of the employees who
were on duty between the time of that facility's opening and,
say, 3:00 p.m. Bedwell checked his records and came up with a
couple of names and phone numbers for Hoffman, but there is
no indication that the detective ever spoke to either employee or
searched sanitation department records (or those of other land-
fill operations) for any information that might have confirmed a
visit by Toole at the time he claimed to have been there.

The following day, Thursday, December 1, Hoffman took the
machete he'd found at Bennett Motors to the Metro Dade Police
Department crime lab with a request that technicians per-

form tool marking tests on the weapon. Though the blood tests were inconclusive, Hoffman hoped that the striations found on the spinal column at the base of Adam Walsh's skull could be matched to the blade.

The Broward County medical examiner's office had also found a couple of embedded "paint chips" during their further cleanup of Adam's skull, and Hoffman brought the fragments along for Metro Dade's analysis as well. If the chips could be identified as paint or other materials traceable to the 1971 Cadillac, that too might serve as evidence linking Toole to the crime.

The following Tuesday, December 6, Hoffman and Lieutenant Smith traveled to the Williamson County Jail near Austin, Texas, where Henry Lee Lucas was being held, hoping that Lucas might be able to implicate Toole in the killing of Adam Walsh. Lucas told Hoffman and Smith that it was quite possible that Toole could have been responsible for such a crime, for he and Toole had traveled various parts of the United States together at one time or another and had committed any number of murders both independently and as a team. However, as to this particular crime, Lucas said he had no knowledge of it whatsoever.

On that Friday, Hoffman received more disheartening news, this from the Miami Dade crime lab, advising that their "best efforts to date" had not been able to produce a positive identification of the tool markings on Adam's vertebrae as having been made by the machete he'd submitted. Analyst Bob Hart had "worked the evidence with great vigor," Metro Dade crime lab commander Edward Whittaker assured Hoffman, but all the physical factors combined appeared to be leading to no positive identification.

As to the "white fragments," or paint chips, that Hoffman had submitted, those were still being analyzed. Though the chips did not appear to be composed of automotive paint, the report said, they had obviously come from *something*, and the fracture patterns observed at the edges of these chips were deemed very likely sufficient to permit an absolutely positive ID if whatever material they had broken from could be recovered. Thus, "the questioned vehicle should be searched with extreme care for such material and if found, for any defect or break in any surface."

A few days later, however, on December 14, lab commander Whittaker called to inform Hoffman that in fact the examination of the machete against the markings on the vertebrae had come up negative. They were still trying to identify what the white fragments he'd submitted might have come from, Whittaker said, and they would let him know the moment any information was available. There exists no record in the case file that Hoffman ever contacted the FDLE crime lab regarding a search within the Cadillac for any object from which the chips might have derived.

On Thursday, December 22, FDLE got in touch with Hoffman to report that no fibers from the vacuum sweepings from the front or rear seat carpets of the Cadillac had matched fibers from the machete's canvas sheath. On the following Tuesday, December 27, FDLE technician Glen Abate traveled to the then-vacant lot at 708 Day Street and began to dig in what had been the rear yard, searching for evidence that the body of Adam Walsh might have been placed there. At one spot, about a foot below the surface, Abate uncovered a pair of light green shorts and advised Buddy Terry of the Jacksonville Sheriff's Office of his findings.

Since Revé Walsh had told detectives of dressing her son in a pair of light green shorts on the morning of July 27, 1981, Terry thought it a significant discovery. He called Detective Hoffman in Hollywood to let him know, and had the shorts placed in an evidence locker until he could pick them up.

New Year's Day of 1984 dawned with Hoffman back in Jacksonville, still trying to trace Toole's movements at the time of the crime. On January 4, he met with Timothy Harold Jones, the clerk who was behind the counter of the Little Champ store the day that Ottis Toole burst in, screaming that someone was going to shoot him. The clerk also recalled that, moments later, Howard Toole followed Ottis in and proceeded to slap him around. That all had taken place on August 1, 1981, Jones said, though he also stated that he remembered selling Ottis a pack of cigarettes and a can of beer "one or two days" prior to the fight—which would have meant July 30 or 31, if Jones's memory was accurate.

Meantime, Lieutenant Smith checked the various distances between the Jacksonville Greyhound bus station and the places Toole might have walked to upon his arrival on July 25. It was 3.6 miles from the station to his mother's home at 708 Day, and 7.8 miles to the Reaves Roofing lot from which he claimed to have taken the Cadillac—a hour's walk to one, two hours to the other.

At 8:00 a.m. on Thursday, January 5, Hoffman arrived at the former site of the home at 708 Day Street, along with Lieutenant Smith and two other detectives from Hollywood PD. Also present were Detective Terry, three technicians from the FDLE crime investigation unit, and a representative of the Jacksonville Public Works Department. They were convened to excavate the property in a systematic search for evidence.

Using a front-end loader with an eight-foot-wide bucket, the team employed the standard method for excavating crime scenes, dragging the property two inches at a pass, until they had reached depths anywhere from four to six feet. About two hours into the search, as they dug in the northwest section of the lot, the machine unearthed bone fragments that resembled a section of a human pelvis. Three hours later, in a different section of the lot, two other unidentifiable bones were uncovered. And at about 3:30 p.m., in a third quadrant of the lot, a left-footed yellow rubber "zori," or flip-flop, in a small child's size, was found. All of the items were duly cataloged by FDLE crime scene technician Abate and turned over to Detective Terry.

While Hoffman stayed behind to watch over the rest of the search, Terry and Lieutenant Smith hurried to the Duval County medical examiner's office with the bone fragments. Whatever hopes they had, however, were soon dashed. These were the remains of some type of animal, the ME said. No chance they had come from a human.

On Friday, Hoffman spoke with Yvonne Grant, the manager of the Little Champ where Howard Toole committed his battery on his brother Ottis. That day was August 1, 1981, Grant confirmed, and like her employee Timothy Jones, she remembered that Ottis Toole had in fact been in her store previously, only a day—or at most, two days—prior to the incident.

The entire period from October 1983, when Toole made his first confession to the murder of Adam Walsh, to the following January 1984, during which Toole made at least seven more confessions to the crime, must have seemed very much a time of "one step forward, two steps back" for Detective Hoffman and the Hollywood PD. After two years with essentially nothing, a man already convicted of another senseless murder and implicated in dozens of others around the country had come forward to claim responsibility for the abduction and murder of Adam Walsh.

Yet despite the repeated confessions and the offering up of detail of the crime that it seemed only the killer could have carried with him, Hoffman could find no evidence linking Toole directly to the crime. It must have been a period of intense frustration for Hoffman, and one senses from a pattern of dogged, repetitive inquiries down the same oft-tracked trails a desperation in his actions.

But whatever degree of frustration Hoffman may have felt or whatever adjective one might employ to describe the tenor of his investigation, it seemed that he was weary of whatever Ottis Toole had brought to the table. As evidence, consider what happened next.

JACKSONVILLE, FLORIDA—JANUARY 6, 1984

Though there is no indication as to who called for the meeting between Detective Jack Hoffman and Ottis Toole on the first Friday of the new year of 1984, there is certainly no reason for Hoffman to have requested it. He already had seven sworn statements from Toole confessing to the killing of Adam Walsh, and, if Hollywood PIO Tony Alderson is to be believed, most everyone at Hollywood PD "believed Toole from the beginning."

In any case, at 9:56 on Friday morning, January 6, Hoffman, accompanied by fellow Hollywood PD detectives Smith, Naylon, and Banks, entered the interview room at the Jacksonville Sheriff's Office, and once again sat down with Ottis Toole.

"What is the reason that you are giving us this statement regarding Adam Walsh?" Hoffman began.

Toole fumbled a bit, but he seemed clear enough, ultimately. "Ah, I didn't, ah, I didn't kill Adam Walsh."

Hoffman glanced at his fellow officers, then back at Toole. "You didn't kill Adam Walsh?"

Toole shook his head. "No."

Hoffman's next question had an odd ring to it. Instead of asking Toole who or what had motivated him to call them in to say such a thing, Hoffman took more of a petulant tack. "Then why have you stuck with your confession all these months, from the first time I met you?" Hoffman asked. "Can you tell me why you stuck to your story all this time?"

Though there may seem a certain relevance to the question, it also seems that Hoffman had been prepared for what he was going to hear during the interview. In any case, Toole managed an answer for the detective, lame as it may have sounded:

"Ah, I was trying to hang Henry Lucas at first, but I found out he was in jail."

Another interviewer might have pointed out to Toole that he had known for months that Lucas was in jail, and then gone to work on Toole, trying to determine just who had drawn up the scenario for the present morning's meeting. But Hoffman did none of those things, and by 10:06, ten minutes after it had begun, the lead detective on the case signaled to his associates that the interview was over.

Hoffman then asked Buddy Terry to hand over the green shorts and yellow rubber zori that had been recovered during the excavation of the property where Toole's mother's house had stood, and Terry complied. Hoffman took the shorts and flip-flop back to Hollywood with him that evening, and placed them in the PD evidence room, where—rather than being shown to John and Revé Walsh for purposes of identification—the items inexplicably remained unexamined for more than thirteen years.

For all intents and purposes, Jack Hoffman's investigation of Ottis Toole as a suspect in the murder of Adam Walsh was over. For whatever reason—his innate distrust of Toole, his inability to let go of Jimmy Campbell as a suspect, or simply a natural inclination to step away from a frustating task—Jack Hoffman had finished with Ottis Toole.

Shortly thereafter, the last vestiges of Detective Hoffman's investigation of Toole were wrapped up without fanfare: in late January, the Tallahassee lab reported that hairs found in Toole's Cadillac—vacuumed from the seats, headrest, and carpet— did not belong to Adam Walsh. Subsequently, according to an FDLE memo, all the evidentiary items examined by both the Tallahassee and Jacksonville labs were returned either to the Hollywood PD by registered mail or directly to Detective Terry of the Jacksonville Sheriff's Office.

Ottis Toole's difficulties with the law were scarcely over, to be sure. Just two weeks later, at the end of a three-day conference in Monroe, Louisiana, hosted by the Ouachita Parish Homicide Task Force, law enforcement officers from nineteen states issued a joint announcement that Henry Lee Lucas and Ottis Toole had been positively linked to 81 murders out of the 150 or more that they claimed to have committed.

During his various interviews with those agents, Toole explained that quite often, after Henry Lee had sex with some of the female victims, he would turn them over to Toole to be killed. Toole, inflamed with anger and jealousy, was only too happy to comply. A number of the victims had suffered extensively, with multiple stab wounds and deep—though not fatal—cuts along the arms, thighs, and lower legs. Several had been disemboweled, and a number had been doused with diesel fuel—stolen by Lucas and Toole during erstwhile stints on roofing crews—then set afire.

In Jacksonville, Buddy Terry had enjoyed far more success with his own investigation of the arson case in which Toole had caused the death of Betty Goodyear's tenant George Sonnenberg. Toole went to trial on those charges in late April and somewhat predictably testified that he did not in fact set the fire that he had on numerous occasions previously confessed to. The defense introduced Dr. Eduardo Sanchez, a psychiatrist, who testified that Toole was a pyromaniac, his intelligence on the borderline of retardation. He was childlike and impulsive, Dr. Sanchez said, subject to bouts of "overwhelming tension" that had to be relieved. "Setting fires is one of the ways he does it," Sanchez said, and in such terms it might sound almost rational.

Whatever the jury thought of Dr. Sanchez's explanations, they seemed far more compelled by the evidence presented. On Friday, May 11, that body took thirty-five minutes to reach its verdict: Ottis Toole was guilty of the arson murder of George Sonnenberg, and the recommended penalty was death.

As he was being led from the courtroom, a furious Toole whirled on Detective Terry, who had supplied much of the evidence during the trial. "Friends don't testify against friends," Toole shouted at Terry. "I'm going to fuck you."

Toole, who had been formally charged with nine other murders in Texas, Colorado, and Louisiana by that time, was sentenced to death for the murder of Sonnenberg and was finally transferred back into the State of Florida prison system at Lake Butler on May 18, 1984. Shortly after his arrival at Lake Butler, Toole granted an interview to *Jacksonville Times-Union* reporter Mickie Valente, during which he repeated his confession to the murder of Adam Walsh.

He took Valente through the details of the abduction, explaining once again that he had done it to "keep him for myself," and the decapitation—"I put both hands on it [the machete] and I chopped his head off." And he included the information that he had given Hoffman about what he had actually done with Adam's body, though he had a grisly coda to add.

He had taken the body back to Jacksonville and stuffed him into a discarded "icebox" on his mother's property, Toole told Valente. And then he said, "I took that machete and I cut out some of his side and I ate some of it." And following that, he burned the corpse and tossed the remains into a Jacksonville city dump on the following day. As to the specter of execution for his current conviction, Toole told the reporter that he was not really concerned. "It might not really happen," he said. "You can always appeal, for years and years."

Only three days after that sensational story appeared, on May 24, 1984, the FDLE returned the principal piece of evidence in the case—Toole's Cadillac—to the Jacksonville Sheriff's Office. There had been no word from Hoffman or the Hollywood PD in the wake of Toole's sordid public confession, and with no hold placed on the car as evidence, it was subsequently sold by the sheriff's office to a used car dealer. A St. Augustine resident named Sirree Safwat bought the vehicle, despite his complaint that it lacked carpeting on the floorboards and trunk. Less than a year later, after the car began to exhibit serious engine problems, Safwat said, he sold it to a junk dealer as scrap for $50.

On October 18, 1984, Detective Hoffman granted an interview with the *Florida Today* newspaper in Cocoa. In it, he told the reporter unequivocally that Ottis Toole was no longer considered a suspect in the murder of Adam Walsh. "He was a suspect until we were able to put holes in his story," Hoffman told a reporter, though he did not say what those "holes" were. "His confession only vaguely matched" the actual details of the killing, Hoffman claimed. An aide to Broward County state attorney Michael Satz said that his office concurred, though he also made it clear that the call was entirely Hoffman's: "Hollywood police apparently saw fit to say that Toole is no longer suspected and we're just agreeing," press aide Dave Casey offered.

When Buddy Terry heard the news, he was not surprised. As far as he could tell, Hoffman had never really taken Toole seriously. He believed that Hoffman had missed an opportunity to nail Toole for the Walsh murder, but at least Toole was in prison, Terry thought, and facing execution. Clearly, he would have to put the rest out of his mind.

Which he might have done, were it not for the astounding news that Terry soon was to receive from his superiors. Hoffman, it seemed, was not quite finished with Ottis Toole and the Adam Walsh case, after all. He had filed a complaint with Duval County authorities that Terry had supplied Toole with case file information that Toole used to concoct his confession. Terry had done this, Hoffman alleged, because the Jacksonville detective and Toole had formed a secret agreement to write a book based on Toole's sensational confession.

Terry, who hadn't even heard of Adam Walsh the first time he overheard Toole confessing the crime to Brevard County detective Steve Kendrick, was dumbfounded by Hoffman's allegations. Still, while the matter was investigated, he was to be transferred out of the robbery and homicide unit where he had served as a detective for more than twelve years, back to the uniform patrol division, assigned to the graveyard for wayward detectives, otherwise known as the Communications Center.

Sears video game display and west exit doors where Adam was escorted out of the store on July 27, 1981.
Hollywood Police Department evidence file

Adam Walsh in the captain's hat he was wearing the day he was abducted. *Courtesy John and Revé Walsh*

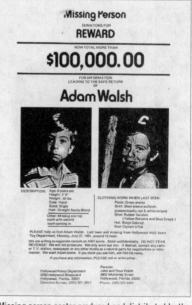

Missing person poster produced and distributed by the Walshes. *Courtesy Broward County Medical Examiner. Photograph by Gerlinde Photography/Michael Hopkins*

Hollywood Police Department detective Jack Hoffman,
original lead investigator on the Adam Walsh case.
Courtesy Hollywood Historical Society

Detective Ron Hickman, Hoffman's partner. *Courtesy
Hollywood Historical Society*

Sam D. Martin, Hollywood chief of police at the time of
Adam's abduction. Martin served as chief from 1974 to
1986. *Courtesy Hollywood Historical Society*

John and Revé Walsh, on their way to *Good Morning America,* on August 10, two weeks after Adam's disappearance. *Courtesy Hollywood Historical Society*

The grieving Walshes at Adam's memorial service, August 15, 1981. *Courtesy Hollywood Historical Society*

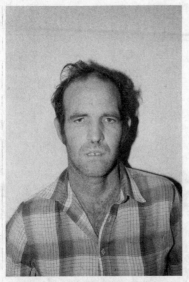

Ottis Toole, gap-toothed and with a wandering eye, shortly after he gave his first confession to police.
Hollywood Police Department evidence file

Clown drawing signed by Ottis Toole and given to niece Sarah Patterson during a prison visit in December 1995.
Courtesy Joe Matthews

Detail of extortion letter sent to John Walsh by Ottis Toole, October 4, 1988 (see text on page 152).
Hollywood Police Department evidence file

Canal beside the Florida Turnpike near Vero Beach where Adam's severed head was found.
Hollywood Police Department evidence file

Ottis Toole's Cadillac (with dented rear bumper) used in the abduction of Adam Walsh.
Florida Department of Law Enforcement evidence file

Aerial view of the turnpike service road west of Vero Beach where Ottis Toole admitted dismembering Adam Walsh.
Hollywood Police Department evidence file

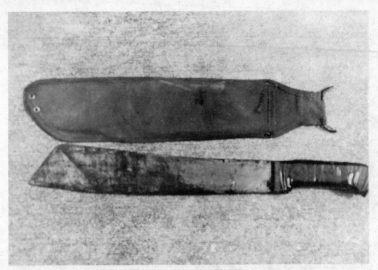

Machete believed to have been used in the dismemberment of Adam Walsh's body.
Hollywood Police Department evidence file

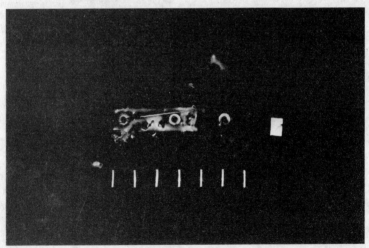

Luminol enhanced photograph of machete handle indicating presence of blood.
Florida Department of Law Enforcement evidence file

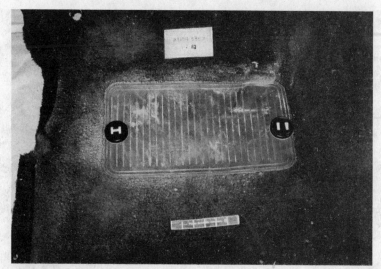

Driver's-side floorboards of Ottis Toole's Cadillac.
Florida Department of Law Enforcement evidence file

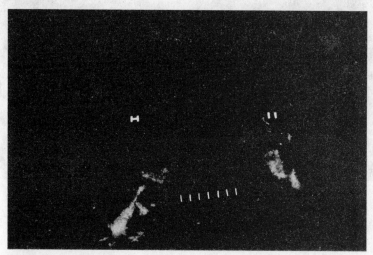

Luminol enhanced photograph of driver's floorboards indicating bloody footprints.
Florida Department of Law Enforcement evidence file

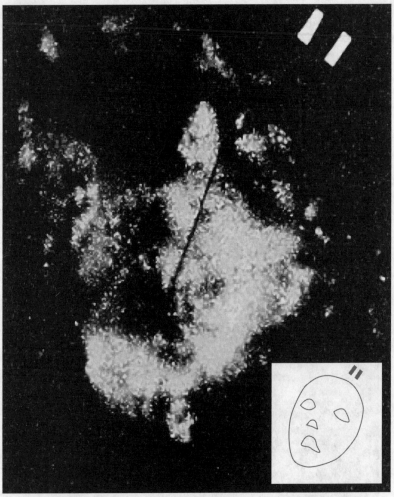

Luminol enhanced photograph of Cadillac's rear floorboard carpeting with imprint of bloodied face. *Florida Department of Law Enforcement evidence file*

Inset showing outline of face in luminol.

CHAPTER FIVE

As Evil Does

Q: Tell me about some of the weapons you've used to
   kill your victims.

A: I've used jack handles, two by fours, shovels, axes.
   Run them over with a car. Strangled them with
   stockings, skip ropes, phone cords. You name it.

Q: And shot them?

A: Oh yeah, shot 'em. Sure. In the head. In the chest. In
   the back. In the stomach.

Q: And sometimes in the top of the head . . .

A: . . . sometimes, if somebody's been going down on
   you. You have to be careful there, though.

Q: And this is with a handgun?

A: Usually. A .22, a .25, a .357 magnum. But sometimes
   a shotgun. And I've used a rifle, too.

Q: Is there any weapon you never used?

A: I never used an ice pick. That would have been
   good, though. I wish I would have used an ice pick,
   just once.

—OTTIS TOOLE TO TEXAS RANGERS,
MARCH 24, 1984

HOLLYWOOD, FLORIDA—NOVEMBER 14, 1984

Given the train wreck that the investigation of Ottis Toole had become, the November Wednesday that would have marked the celebration of Adam Walsh's tenth birthday instead seemed to serve as a milestone of frustration. A year or so before, it appeared that his killer had been found, and while it would not bring their son back, John and Revé Walsh might have found a certain kind of relief had Toole been charged and tried. At the very least, some sense of justice might have prevailed, some semblance of the possibility of order restored to their world.

The Walshes were certainly not the first parents to be visited by such predation and calamity. As they soon found out in the aftermath of their loss, thousands of families around the country had suffered similar tragedies and had been similarly frustrated in their ability to find help from local law enforcement agencies and the justice system. Children went off to corner stores, or out in backyards to play, and they simply never came back. Or sometimes were brought back in body bags.

In most cases, stricken parents could do little but grieve, but more than a few took the time to share their sadness and their frustration in letters to the Walshes. None of the aggrieved parents who had suffered the disappearance or murder of a child had any idea exactly what to do, but many sent checks to the Walshes urging them to use the money any way they saw fit.

And then, in September 1981, less than two months following Adam's murder, the Walshes received a call from the office of Florida senator Paula Hawkins, who had tried unsuccessfully to get the FBI involved in the search for Adam at the outset. Senator Hawkins had joined the push on Capitol Hill to pass legislation that would require the federal government to maintain a centralized database on missing children and those who had been found dead but unidentified.

It seemed ludicrous to supporters of the bill, the Missing Children Act, that you could report your stolen car—or horse—

to the FBI and have that agency spring immediately into action, while a child could disappear without so much as an eye blink from federal crime fighters. Outrage over the 1932 Lindbergh baby kidnapping had resulted in the passage of the Federal Kidnapping Act (the so-called Lindbergh Law), making it a federal offense to transport a victim across a state line or use the mail to send a ransom note. Ostensibly, the act gave the FBI the authority to pursue kidnapping cases, but the agency had maintained a long-standing reluctance to interfere with local police in such matters. It often made for bad politics, for one thing; for another, most kidnapping cases turned out to be the result of messy, interfamilial wrangling; and for yet another, they were reluctant to create more work for themselves. The official FBI line was that "local agencies have more mobile manpower," necessary to efficiently pursue kidnappings.

Indeed, though Walsh had pleaded with the FBI to get involved in the initial search for Adam, and the agency pledged its support, records show that no such action was ever taken. The message that was passed down was this: If it got to the point where Hollywood PD was searching for a suspect somewhere out of state, then the feds would be happy to lend a hand. Otherwise, the local cops were on their own.

Though the prospects for passage of the proposed legislation were dim, a staffer for Senator Hawkins wanted the Walshes to go to Washington to lobby on behalf of the bill, and though it was a mission they would have to carry out at their own expense, they were more than happy to do so. At the very least, it was a way to vent some of the frustration they had felt from the outset of Adam's disappearance.

It did not take the Walshes long to sense the enormous weight of indifference they were confronting, however. As even newly elected presidents have learned, trying to correct the conduct of business as usual in the federal bureaucracy is like trying to nudge an ocean liner off its path by standing on a rubber raft and pressing on the liner's hull with your bare hands as it speeds by. But, fueled by their outrage and sense of injustice and buoyed by the support of so many strangers around the country, they had already formed their own nonprofit agency, the Adam Walsh Outreach Center for Missing Children, and they now threw themselves wholeheartedly into lobbying Congress on the Missing Children Act.

In October 1982 the effort, which had been joined by a number of prominent politicians, including Henry Hyde, Paul Simon, Arlen Specter, and even staunch FBI supporter Strom Thurmond, paid off with the act's passage—and though it simply provided for the establishment of separate categories for missing children and the unidentified dead in the FBI's national database, the legislation marked the first time in history that missing children, runaways, child prostitution, family abductions, and a host of associated ills were formally recognized as matters that impacted an entire nation.

For nearly two years following, John Walsh balanced his work for Paradise Grand Hotels and his efforts on behalf of the Walsh Outreach Center and various legislative efforts around the country. *Adam*, a made-for-television movie based on the case, had aired on October 10, 1983, just as Ottis Toole was making his first confession to Brevard County detective Steve Kendrick. Though one of Toole's cellmates later told investigators that they had turned the movie off that night and watched a football game instead, in other parts of the republic the film was well received, critically and popularly. Forty million viewers watched as a roll call of photographs of fifty-five missing children played at the end of the film, and thousands of calls flooded the 1-800 number provided. As a result, thirteen of those fifty-five missing children were reunited with their families.

The Walshes, realizing the limitations of the Missing Children Act, next turned their attention to the establishment of a national version of their own nonprofit, a center where parents of missing and abducted children could go for practical help. Limited in effect as it was, the passage of the Missing Children Act had nonetheless broken the political logjam that impeded progress on such issues, and even President Ronald Reagan threw his support behind the establishment of a National Center for Missing and Exploited Children. Finally, on June 13, 1984, the center was opened, in the form of a private organization, funded at the outset by a $3.3 million grant from the U.S. Department of Justice. The only hitch was that John Walsh had to agree to serve on the center's board of directors, which in turn meant that he would have to leave his job with Paradise Grand.

In some ways it was a difficult decision. Revé had given birth to a daughter, Meghan, in July 1982, and in 1984 she was pregnant again. John's pay would be a fraction of what he was making in the hotel business, but there was no fighting the tide. The Walshes had in fact helped accomplish the impossible—and once you had pushed against the hull of a massive ocean liner and felt it wobble from its intended course, you couldn't simply stop.

There was great satisfaction for both John and Revé Walsh in what they had accomplished, but even though their work in Florida and Washington had helped other parents regain their children and see that persons who had committed such crimes received their just deserts, it did not ease the ache that filled them every time they thought of Adam. It did not matter that other children had come along. It did not matter that time had passed, and that life had brought them many blessings. Their firstborn was gone forever, and his killer remained unidentified. And despite their suspicions that Ottis Toole was responsible, the police certainly didn't seem to think so. For all the Walshes knew, then, the person responsible was still out there somewhere, and was killing still.

Adam's eleventh birthday, November 14, 1985, came and went with no word from the police, and as the years piled up and no progress was reported, the prospects that a break in the case would ever come dimmed. In January 1986, Hollywood police chief Sam Martin retired, and though insiders presumed that Leroy Hessler—prominently involved in the Adam Walsh investigation—would be his replacement, city commissioners were troubled by reports of rampant favoritism in matters of promotion, transfer, and assignment within the department. Instead of going along with Hessler, they appointed Richard Witt, a twenty-seven-year veteran of the City of Miami Police Department, to take Martin's place.

If the Walshes thought it would mean anything in terms of progress on the case, however, they would be sadly disappointed. Witt had plenty to attend to without diverting his department's resources down what was to him a dead-end road, and thus Adam's twelfth birthday passed with no word, as did his thirteenth in 1987.

Then there arrived some news from a quarter the Walshes could scarcely have envisioned. A letter dated October 4, 1988, began:

Dear Walsh,
My name is Ottis Toole. I'm the person who snatched, raped, murdered, and cut up the little prick teaser, Adam Walsh and dumped his smelly ass into the canal. You know the story but you don't know where his bones are. I do.

Now you are a rich fucker, money you made from the dead body of that little kid. OK, he was a sweet little piece of ass! I want to make a deal with you. Here's my deal. You pay me money and I'll tell you where the bones are so you can get him buried all decent and Christian.

Elsewhere in this despicable letter to John Walsh, Toole explained that he wanted $5,000 right away as "good faith money" and Walsh's signed promise of $45,000 more once Toole had shown him Adam's bones. Toole closed by telling Walsh that Adam had been crying for his mother as he sodomized him.

"If you send the police after me before we make a deal then you don't get no bones and what's left of Adam's hot pussy can rot," Toole warned. "Tell the cops and you don't get shit."

"Tell the cops," of course, is exactly what John Walsh did. He immediately gave the letter, signed by Ottis E. Toole—in script that precisely matched Toole's signature on various prison forms—to Detective Hoffman at Hollywood PD. Walsh had become aware that Hoffman was unwilling to believe that Toole was Adam's murderer—it had gotten back to Walsh that Hoffman thought Toole was simply trying to draw attention to himself by claiming responsibility. And while Walsh was willing to accede to Hoffman's claims that there was no physical evidence linking Toole to the crime, he was sure that this blood-boiling message would reignite the detective's interest.

Walsh was wrong—Hoffman simply filed the letter away. As it turns out, it was not the only letter that Toole sent out at the time. On the same day, he had also written an extortion note to Sears, explaining that he had cut a deal with a magazine to tell the story of how he had kidnapped, raped, and murdered Adam Walsh, and now, he said, he was threatening to tell the world how easy it was to abduct and assault children at their stores. "I do my shopping for juicy little kiddies at Sears," he said in his missive to the company. But for a "fast check," Toole said, he was willing to omit any direct mention of the chain in his magazine account. "See you soon," he closed. "Bring money."

On the following day, Toole sent off another letter to the *Orlando Sentinel*: "Someone told my ear that a big paper" like theirs might pay a "nice amount" for his personal account of the murder of Adam Walsh. And maybe once he told the story, people would leave him alone about it, Toole explained. But there were conditions: "No cops, no lawyers. Just me and a reporter. Please make me your cash offer promptly."

For its part, the *Sentinel* summarily forwarded the letter from Toole to Detective Hoffman. "Probably not anything new to you, but here it is for what it's worth," reporter Sean Holton said, before adding, "Let me know if anything comes of it."

Toole sent a similar letter to the *National Enquirer*, which prompted reporter Charlie Montgomery to place a call directly to Jack Hoffman. His paper wasn't about to offer Toole any money, Montgomery said, but it was his intention to write Toole back and ask what new details he might be willing to supply. If he got anything interesting in response, he would let Hoffman know. Meantime, he reminded Hoffman, he would very much appreciate hearing should anything new turn up in the case. More than seven years had passed since Adam's death, and five since Ottis Toole had first confessed, and still, it seemed, the case exerted its great power over the collective psyche of the country.

By October 12, having received no offers from any of the major outlets he'd written, Toole was drafting "To whom it may concern" appeals, trying to find anyone who might be willing to pay him for his story. "Dear Editor," began one such. "My name is Ottis E. Toole. I am the one who kidnapped, raped, murdered and hacked to pieces the boy Adam Walsh in 1981. I also murdered 3 women and a man up around Holmes County, Florida." Toole went on to explain that he had already written to the sheriffs of both Broward County and Holmes County, a rural enclave in a part of the Florida Panhandle often referred to as L.A. or "Lower Alabama," claiming that he was ready to confess to the aforementioned five murders. Furthermore, Toole said, he had decided to invite one member of the media to sit in on the confessions to ensure that police did not abuse him in the process. "If your paper is interested then let me know," Toole said in closing.

Copies of this letter and the one that had been sent to Sears were forwarded to Hoffman without apparent effect, but another letter sent to Broward County sheriff Nick Navarro finally prompted some action. In this missive Gerald Schaffer, a fellow inmate of Ottis Toole's at Florida State Prison, explained that he was actually writing on behalf of Toole, owing to Toole's difficulties in reading and writing. However, Sheriff Navarro should have no doubt: Toole was responsible for the murder of Adam Walsh and for other unidentified murders in Broward County, and he was willing to admit formally to his involvement.

There were conditions, said Schaffer, a former Martin County sheriff's deputy serving two life terms for the murder of two teenage girls. He was to be present during all interviews with Toole; the interviews were to be of short duration; and both Schaffer and Toole wished to be relocated to the Broward County Jail. It may have seemed a presumptuous offer, but if most of the other letters that Schaffer wrote on Toole's behalf were dismissed, this one received significantly more attention.

MONDAY, OCTOBER 17, 1988

Shortly after Navarro's office heard from Toole, on October 17, 1988, Captain Walter Laun, the commander of the Broward County Sheriff's Office criminal investigations unit, summoned Detective Sergeant Richard Scheff, supervisor of the homicide unit, to a meeting where he handed over a copy of the letter they had received.

Laun instructed Scheff to take one of his men up to the Florida State Prison to meet with Schaffer and Toole and try to assess whether there was any validity to the claims. Because Laun was aware of Toole's history of recanting his confessions, he wanted Scheff to try to extract some detail or form of evidence that would lend credence to Toole's assertions.

Two days later, on October 19, Scheff and Detective Sergeant Fantigrassi made the five-and-a-half-hour drive north to Florida State Prison, the state's maximum security facility. "Starke," as it is sometimes referred to, for its proximity to that aptly named town, houses the inmates considered to be the most dangerous in the system. It is also the location of the death-row cell blocks, and while lethal injection would become the standard method of execution in 2000, at the time of Scheff and Fantigrassi's visit, it was still "Old Sparky," the electric chair, that held the preeminent place of prominence at Starke.

Scheff and Fantigrassi first met with Gerald Schaffer, who told the detectives that he had become acquainted with Toole while both were incarcerated there, and that at present he was functioning as Ottis Toole's legal representative. Furthermore, Schaffer told them, he was interested in claiming the various reward monies still outstanding for the clearing of the Adam Walsh case.

Toole had admitted to abducting and killing Adam Walsh, Schaffer said, and to dismembering the body, partially devouring it, and discarding what was left in a canal. Toole was willing to formally confess to the killing and appear before a grand jury in the matter. Toole also had told Schaffer about numerous other slayings he had committed in Broward County, in the vicinity of U.S. 27 and south of State Road 84, but at present Schaffer was unable to provide specific detail about those cases.

That was all well and good, Scheff told Schaffer, but neither he nor Toole would be taken out of Starke on any pretext until such time as they provided verifiable, independent evidence that could be used to support Toole's claims. Schaffer seemed to have anticipated this demand. Without hesitation he pointed to a matter that no investigator had seized on in the seven years that had passed since the murder. Toole had told him that he'd used *two* weapons to cut Adam up, Schaffer said: a machete *and* a bayonet.

In his first confession to Hoffman, Toole had made passing reference to using a bayonet, but Hoffman began referring to the weapon as a "machete," and Toole apparently began to follow the detective's lead in subsequent references. In any case, the possibility of Toole's use of two weapons had never been pursued. Even the claim of erstwhile companion Charles Lee Hardaman that he had given Toole a bayonet prior to the time of Adam's murder apparently elicited little interest. But Schaffer's claim would seem to have changed all that. Whatever had led to the confusion, Toole would be able to provide a more detailed description of both items, Schaffer assured the Broward County detectives.

Accordingly, on the following day, October 20, 1988, Detectives Scheff and Fantigrassi met with Schaffer and Ottis Toole. Scheff recited the Miranda warning to Toole, who assured the detectives that he was well aware of his rights and was happy to waive them. Then Toole got quickly to the point, repeating his confession to the killing of Adam Walsh and stating that he was willing to testify to the matter in court. He had used a "straight knife" with a black plastic handle as well as a bayonet to kill and dismember the boy, he said, adding that the knife (presumably the machete) had been in the possession of Jacksonville authorities since shortly after his arrest, when it was taken from his car. The bayonet, Toole said, belonged to his sister Vinetta Syphurs, and was part of a display mounted on the living room wall of her home in Bostwick, Florida, about forty miles southeast of the interview room where they were sitting.

The detectives then pressed Toole to tell them where he had disposed of the body, and Toole told them that he had tossed various parts into the same canal where he had disposed of the head. The canal paralleled the turnpike for a ten-mile stretch or so, Toole said, and every so often he would pull to the side of the road and rid himself of another piece of the corpse. He couldn't recall anything memorable about any of the places he had stopped, save that little wooden bridge where he had thrown the head into the water.

At times, Toole seemed to need help from Schaffer in formulating certain of his answers, the detectives noted, leaving them uncertain as to whether or not Schaffer had been coaching Toole in this undertaking from the outset. In the end, the only new information that Toole had provided was that pertaining to the bayonet. But on the other hand, all they needed was one piece of physical evidence to tie Toole to the crime, so off the two went to find Vinetta Syphurs.

It took about an hour to drive to Bostwick, a remote, unincorporated community just west of the broad St. John's River several miles south of Jacksonville. It is the sort of place one works hard to get to, a sparsely populated expanse of piney forest and scrub that has changed little since that part of the continent was formed, perhaps the perfect place to be if you wanted to keep your distance from a relative like Ottis Toole.

When they got to Bostwick, the detectives made their way to the local post office, where a clerk checked the records. Vinetta Syphurs had indeed once resided at 2942 Cedar Creek Road, he told them, but she had moved a while back and had left no forwarding address. Scheff and Fantigrassi drove to the address the clerk had given them and knocked on the door of the modest house they found. A woman named Violet Fleck answered. She had never heard of anyone named Syphurs, she told them.

Scheff and Fantigrassi weren't particularly daunted by the response. Most cop work consists of exactly what they were doing. You knock on doors, you ask questions. One day someone behind the screen will have the right answer, or so you hope.

Across the street, at 2941 Cedar Creek Road, Charles B. Council answered their knock and told them that there had in fact been a Rodney and Vinetta Syphurs living opposite him, but they'd moved out about a year earlier. He had no idea where they might have gone. Scheff and Fantigrassi thanked Council for his help and moved along.

It wasn't all that unusual—in the dimension of American life through which they were moving, and often moved as cops—to trail after individuals whose existences seemed as transitory as those of tribal huntsmen or migrating birds. Yes, there was the America where people left forwarding addresses, and kept in touch with old friends and neighbors, and were as easy to find as a schoolhouse or a bank branch. But when you were looking for criminals, or the associates of criminals, or the families from which they'd sprung, you often found yourself traveling through such a netherworld as this in Bostwick, where identity and even existence often seemed as tangible as smoke.

From the Council residence, Scheff and Fantigrassi traveled southward ten miles or so to Palatka, population 10,000 and the seat of Putnam County. At the offices of the tax assessor, they learned that the property at 2942 Cedar Creek Road in Bostwick had been purchased by Violet Fleck, with whom they'd talked earlier in the day. She and her husband David had bought it from a Ralph Nelson Green of Jacksonville.

Armed with this information, the two detectives then visited the Putnam County clerk's office, where they discovered a record of Green's eviction of Rodney and Vinetta Syphurs from his property on Cedar Creek Road in 1987. And as it turned out, Mr. Green had employed the services of a Jacksonville attorney in the matter, one Wesley Wallace, Esq.

Detective Scheff got Wallace on the phone and explained who they were looking for. Finally, it appeared, he had knocked on the right door. Wallace happened to know that the Syphurs were now living with Vinetta's daughter, who was married to a man named Greg Bishop. And if Wallace was not mistaken, the Bishops had a place in Orange Park, in Clay County, just south of sprawling Jacksonville.

Scheff accordingly called the Clay County sheriff, who in turn located Greg Bishop, who dutifully called Detective Scheff as requested. He listened to Scheff and promised to have his mother-in-law call right back. Thus, following such a trail of crumbs, did Scheff and Fantigrassi finally find the woman with whom they wished to speak.

Perhaps it is not the glamorous stuff of series television, but this is the way detectives work, the real ones, the dedicated ones. There are those who weary of such deadening chores, of course. They let things slide. They get tired of traipsing through the rat warrens and the pine barrens after the smoke people. They never find the right door.

At approximately nine on the evening of October 20, Scheff and Fantigrassi, accompanied by Lieutenant Redmond of the Clay County Sheriff's Office, finally sat down with Vinetta and Rodney Syphurs. Mrs. Syphurs told the detectives that she had purchased an antique bayonet in 1979 and had mounted it as a decoration on the wall above her mantel. If her brother Ottis, or anyone else, had removed it for any period of time, she would have certainly noticed its absence. When the detectives asked if they could take a look at the bayonet, Mrs. Syphurs paused.

All this fuss over Ottis had resulted in an unbelievable amount of hounding of her and Rodney by the press, she told the detectives. That is why the two of them had moved in with her daughter, to get away from it all. It had all happened rather suddenly, she explained—omitting any mention of eviction proceedings—and quite a bit of their personal property was still stored in boxes. But she would find the bayonet, Mrs. Syphurs assured them, and as soon as she did, she would bring it to Lieutenant Redmond's office.

The following day, Scheff and Fantigrassi went to the Jacksonville Sheriff's Office to check on the machete. There they discovered that Detective Terry had in fact turned over such a weapon to the FDLE for testing, but that the department's labs had not been able to tie it definitively to Toole or the crime. Also that day, and somewhat to Detective Scheff's surprise, Vinetta Syphurs actually showed up at the Clay County Sheriff's Office with the bayonet in hand. Scheff arranged to have it sent to the Broward County Sheriff's Office crime lab, where it would be tested for blood and the blade compared to markings on the base of Adam Walsh's severed head.

Though the recovery of the bayonet from Mrs. Syphurs constituted the sum of the efforts of Broward County detectives in their pursuit of physical evidence and their interview with

Toole, Sergeant Scheff concluded his report on the matter with the observation, "No review of this matter would be complete without a thorough understanding of the background of Ottis Toole's original confession in the Adam Walsh case." Scheff went on to reiterate that many of the confessions to other killings made by Henry Lee Lucas and Ottis Toole had not been substantiated (there was no mention of the eighty-plus murders that *had* been attributed to the pair).

And while Scheff went on to point out that Toole was presently imprisoned "in reference to a Duval County murder," he did not mention that Detective Terry had carried out the investigation upon which that conviction was obtained. However, Scheff did take the time to reiterate the details of the complaint that Jack Hoffman had lodged against Terry.

"Apparently believing that he could enrich himself," said Scheff, "Terry entered into an arrangement with Ottis Toole in regards to book and movie rights to Ottis Toole's life story. Detective Terry then provided Ottis Toole with confidential information he had obtained from the Hollywood Police Department."

According to Scheff's report, Terry then contacted Hollywood PD to let them know that Toole had confessed to the killing of Adam Walsh. "Detectives from the Hollywood Police Department . . . invested one year in the investigation before uncovering Detective Terry's actions," Scheff continued, and finished by noting, "Ottis Toole's statements were dismissed, and Detective Terry was removed from the Homicide Unit."

It was proof, said Scheff, "of the ease with which Toole, a brain-damaged and troubled man, can be manipulated by others. Ottis Toole now appears to be under the influence of Gerald Schaffer who may be using Toole for his own purposes." As to the exact nature of the purposes of Schaffer—a convict with an IQ of 130, suspected in the deaths of thirty-four women in three states—Scheff was not clear.

Scheff's conclusions might carry weight, save for the fact

that at the time he compiled his report, only three days had passed since his interview with Toole. The analysis of possible new evidence in the case—i.e., the bayonet he had obtained from Vinetta Syphurs—had not even begun, and the complaint against Detective Terry, the man whose work had put Toole on death row in the first place, remained an unsubstantiated claim made by one of Scheff's fellow investigators working just down the road from the Broward County Sheriff's Office. There is no evidence that Hoffman himself pressured Scheff to include his uncalled-for coda, but at the very least, its presence in the report carries something of the scent of home cooking.

About a month passed before D. P. Hughes, chief investigator for the Broward County medical examiner's office, passed along to the Metro Dade crime lab the weapon that Scheff had taken from Vinetta Syphurs. The knife was described as a Japanese army bayonet, with wood grips and a fifteen-and-a-half-inch blade, held in a sheath, and Hughes asked that since the Dade crime lab had already performed a comparative analysis against the machete that Hoffman and Terry had provided, they be the ones to compare the bayonet against the markings made at the base of Adam's skull.

It took Robert Hart, the same forensics specialist who had performed the earlier analysis on the machete, nearly three months to get back to Hughes, and when he did, on February 14, 1989, the news was once again inconclusive. "Although the class characteristics are consistent [with the marks on the skull]," Hart said, "insufficient similarities are present to determine if this bayonet was the weapon used to inflict the injuries."

While it might have been disheartening news, it does not explain why Hoffman did not, at the very least, carry the bayonet to Jacksonville and simply ask Charles Hardaman if it was the same bayonet he had once given Ottis Toole to sharpen. Had Hardaman been able to identify the weapon, it would have corroborated yet another aspect of Toole's story.

HOLLYWOOD, FLORIDA—NOVEMBER 14, 1988

While Broward County detectives pursued their leads, Adam Walsh's fourteenth birthday came and went, marking the passage of more than seven years without significant progress in the case. On December 6, 1988, something of a milestone was reached when FBI deputy director Alan Burgess made it known that the case of Adam Walsh had finally been entered into the new nationwide database known as VICAP, the Violent Crime Apprehension Program.

The program had come into existence in 1985, and had developed in large part due to the work of former LAPD captain Pierce Brooks, who was involved in the investigation of the notorious "Onion Field" killing of a Los Angeles police officer in 1963, an incident later popularized in a Joseph Wambaugh best seller. Brooks was among the first to apply formal statistical analysis to determine patterns in violent crime and to theorize that psychologists might be able to provide useful profiles of the type of individual responsible for a violent crime or a series of such crimes. At the very least, if details of unsolved crimes were shared in a national computerized database available to police departments everywhere, the likelihood of apprehending "pattern" or "repeat" killers would surely be increased.

In 1983, John Walsh had been asked to testify before an Arlen Specter–chaired Senate Judiciary subcommittee looking into the efficacy of such an undertaking, and as he recalls, it was the sort of thing that people assumed was already in place. The truth was, however, that in the early 1980s the very concept of "national computer database" was something of an exercise in wishful thinking. At the time such notions as e-mail and the Internet were for most Americans only fantasy. A certain amount of information on unsolved crimes was shared between jurisdictions via teletype and snail-mail-carried bulletins, but the notion that anyone, anywhere, was paying much attention to what clattered off those machines or piled up in the mailroom, or was investing the time to catalog, file, and analyze the data on hundreds and thousands of violent crimes all across the country, was simply laughable.

But by this point, Walsh was well versed in the psychology of the Ted Bundys and the John Wayne Gacys of the world, and he had become increasingly convinced that it was such an individual who was responsible for Adam's death. He was more than happy to appear on behalf of the initiative. There was also a great deal of support for such a database within the FBI itself, where behavioral sciences unit special agent Robert Ressler had advanced the practice of profiling repeat rapists and killers through the 1970s. Ressler, generally credited with coining the term *serial killer*, played a key role in the eventual formation of VICAP, advocating it as an invaluable tool to a local agency when and if a nomadic predator came calling.

In 1985, the program was approved by the Department of Justice, and FBI-VICAP become the national repository for violent crimes, collating data on homicides, sexual assaults, missing persons, and unidentified human remains. Comprehensive case information concerning crimes anywhere in the country would thenceforward be submitted to FBI-VICAP, maintained in a comprehensive database and automatically compared to all other cases to identify similarities. The program also provided for a staff of agents trained specifically to analyze data and provide profiles where evidence suggested repeat and nomadic offenders might be at work, especially those involving abduction; those apparently random, motiveless, or sexually oriented; or those known or thought to be part of a series.

If such a program had been in place in 1981, would the actions of Henry Lee Lucas and Ottis Toole have landed them a place on VICAP's most-wanted list or prevented Adam's abduction and murder? John and Revé Walsh had no idea, but at least the fact that such a program was now in place and that the details of their son's case were thus operative gave them some sense of a shred of order restored, some vague assurance that Adam had not died in vain.

So far as progress on the case went, however, there was none forthcoming, and Adam's fifteenth birthday, in November 1989, passed uneventfully.

There was something of an ironic footnote deriving from the brief partnership of jailhouse lawyer Gerard Schaffer and Ottis Toole in 1990, however, when news came that a federal appeals court had dismissed Schaffer's complaint that his public defender had deliberately botched his court case to make sure he would stay in jail. In his complaint, Schaffer pointed to the fact that immediately after his conviction on murder charges, his attorney had married Schaffer's ex-wife, Theresa. Schaffer's attorney happened to be a public defender by the name of Elton Schwartz, the same man who had represented Ottis Toole back in 1984. Schwartz, apparently passionate on behalf of the rights of accused serial killers, had taken on Schaffer's case in the wake of his involvement with Toole.

And then, in early November 1990, twelve days before Adam's sixteenth birthday, an event took place that would almost by accident draw Joe Matthews back into the orbit of this story and eventually change the course of the investigation. At first, the event might have seemed without any bearing on what had befallen the Walshes, but that is the thing about cause and effect in all effective narrative. What might seem an unimportant or "butterfly" moment at the outset is one thing; but once a profound conclusion is reached, it is a simple matter to trace backward through all the possible turning points where a different decision might have been made. In this way, the investigator comes to a simple realization: in the story at hand, things couldn't have turned out any other way.

On November 2, 1990, Detective Sergeant Joe Matthews was called in from vacation by his superiors at Miami Beach PD to investigate a particularly heinous crime. The body of an unidentified three-year-old boy had been found discarded beneath a hedge that surrounded a home in one of the Beach's most exclusive residential neighborhoods. The emaciated child, weighing 18 pounds, with weeks-old Pampers duct-taped to his body, had died from multiple fractures to the skull, leading the Dade County medical examiner to call it the worst case of child neglect, abuse, and torture that he had ever witnessed.

It was not by accident that Matthews had been summoned. In the more than nine years that had passed since he'd rejoined his colleagues at Beach PD, he had continued to rack up accolades for his work as a polygraph examiner, interrogations expert, and homicide investigator. In 1987, during a period of civil unrest and racial rioting in Miami, German national Dieter Reichmann stopped a Miami Beach policeman and pointed to the body of his girlfriend in the seat beside him. While driving the streets of downtown Miami, Reichmann claimed, an unidentified black male had approached his car, then shot and killed his German girlfriend as part of a botched robbery attempt.

Matthews was placed in charge of the charged investigation, while an outraged community demanded justice, if not ultimately a lynching. From the outset, however, Matthews spotted various minor inconsistencies in Reichmann's story, and following forty to fifty hours of interviews and his usual persistent digging, Matthews discovered that Reichmann had taken out $2 million in German insurance policies on his girlfriend's life. It was fuel for a reconsideration of everything, and eventually Matthews had assembled a substantial amount of circumstantial evidence implicating Reichmann as the killer.

However, Janet Reno, Dade County state attorney at the time, advised Matthews that she deemed his evidence insufficient for the issuance of a warrant. Though Reichmann was arrested and tried on a federal weapons charge, he was found not guilty. He was ordered to be released from custody and allowed to return to his native country. As Matthews was escorting Reichmann to the property room to reclaim his personal effects, including a number of items that Matthews considered potential evidence in his murder investigation, the grinning German turned to tap him on the cheek with his palm. "Ah, my friend Matthews," Reichmann said in condescension, "you'll have to try harder next time, eh?"

At which point Matthews responded by pulling a pair of handcuffs from his belt and snapping them onto Reichmann's wrists. "Ah my friend Reichmann," Matthews said. "You are under arrest for first-degree murder."

Matthews's actions astounded Reichmann, of course, and they infuriated Janet Reno as well, for she wanted no part of a case that she considered dicey. Fortunately for Matthews and for the legal system, however, several on Reno's staff were convinced that Reichmann was guilty, and the case was prosecuted vigorously.

Ultimately, Reichmann was convicted of the murder and sentenced to death—even though the perpetrator had never confessed, the firearm used was never recovered, no witnesses ever appeared, and the exact location of the murder was never determined. The Florida Supreme Court reviewed Reichmann's case twice, but upheld the conviction. No wonder, then, that with no apparent leads, his superiors wanted Matthews on the case of the three-year-old discarded under a hedge off North Bay Road like so much garbage.

But even Matthews was having difficulties with this new case. No one had seen anything, and without an identification of the victim, it was difficult even to know where to begin an investigation. During a canvasing of the neighborhood where the child was discovered, he found himself talking to a little girl who knew very little about the crime save that it had terrified her and that the little boy had been found wearing only a T-shirt with lollipops printed on it.

"Poor baby Lollipops," the little girl told Matthews. "I hope you catch who did it."

He hoped he'd catch who killed "Baby Lollipops" too, Matthews told the little girl, and even if he had little by way of leads, he now had a name that seemed to galvanize the interest of the public in the case. On Monday, November 26, 1990, almost two weeks after Adam's sixteenth birthday, Joe Matthews called the producers of the television show *America's Most Wanted*, asking how he might get details of the "Baby Lollipops" case aired, in order to help identify the child.

Matthews was well aware that John Walsh was the host of the program, the brainchild of media mogul Rupert Murdoch's Fox Television Network. The show had begun its run in February 1988, the second piece of original programming produced by the network after *21 Jump Street*, which starred a then-unknown actor named Johnny Depp. *America's Most Wanted* was devoted to the dramatization of various violent crimes around the country and the apprehension of the persons responsible.

It was the first in what would become a landslide of "reality" shows, and it was a smash hit from the beginning, despite the fact that Walsh was initially anything but a polished performer. But as a result of his obvious sincerity, his status as a victim of violent crime, and his well-known work as a champion of the victimized everywhere, he had grown into the role of citizen crime fighter. By the time that Joe Matthews made his phone call, Walsh had hit his stride. The show had resulted in thousands of tips and the capture of more than a hundred criminals who had evaded justice previously.

Still, as a staffer explained to Matthews, their show was focused on the capture of wanted fugitives, not on the identification of a victim. Rather than argue that the one generally was the first step leading to the other, Matthews talked the staffer into connecting him with John Walsh's administrative assistant. He briefly explained the purpose of his call and made a simple request: just tell Mr. Walsh what he was asking, and that it was the same Detective Matthews who had conducted the polygraph examination for the Hollywood police when his son Adam was abducted.

The assistant did as Matthews asked, and the results were

exactly what the detective hoped for. Three days later, Thursday, November 29, 1990, John Walsh and his film crew were on their way to Miami Beach, where they filmed an *AMW* segment devoted to the crime and seeking the public's help in making the true identity of "Baby Lollipops" known.

After the filming, Matthews and Walsh spent some time together along Government Cut at the south end of Miami Beach, where the *AMW* motor home, Walsh's traveling office, had been parked. The two sat in a pair of lawn chairs, watching the sun descend and the glittering ocean liners dock and sail, discussing the handling of Adam's case over the past nine years.

It wasn't that the rank-and-file detectives didn't care or were totally incompetent, Matthews assured Walsh, it was just that from the beginning the department seemed overwhelmed by the task before it. Furthermore, there seemed to be no supervision emanating from Jack Hoffman, the lead detective on the case. As Matthews recalled the helter-skelter comings and goings of well-meaning detectives and the flutterings of their unfiled scraps of paper, Walsh nodded glumly. He'd been in the detective's bullpen one day, too. He'd seen one guy writing down information on a matchbook cover.

There was that, Matthews said, and there was also the fact of Jack Hoffman's personality. Hoffman, he thought, always seemed on "send," never on "receive." To Matthews, the effective way to get help, and information, was to present yourself with some humility—"Hey, I need a hand here, can you help out?" To Matthews it was a far more effective approach than the one that went, "Don't bother telling me anything. I know it all already."

Until that evening, Walsh had not realized that Matthews had been on loan to the Hollywood PD from Miami Beach at the time, and he was more than interested in Matthews's critique of the shoddy procedures he had witnessed there. Nor had he ever heard another piece of news that Matthews passed along. Years ago, Hollywood PD had officially cleared Jimmy Campbell of any involvement in the case, Matthews told him. It was a welcome surprise to Walsh, even though he had never really suspected Jimmy. But he also wondered why the Hollywood PD had never passed along word that they had exonerated his old friend. In fact, Walsh told Matthews, he had never heard any news unbidden from Hollywood PD.

To Matthews it was quite a surprise to hear that Hollywood police had not informed the Walshes that Campbell had been cleared. For John Walsh, it might be important enough— validation that a person he considered a friend was innocent. But imagine what a burden would be lifted from Revé. She had lived with enough guilt for simply having left Adam alone for a few moments. To have it confirmed that Campbell was in no way responsible would have been more than a courtesy. It simply seemed insensitive in the extreme that Hoffman had not bothered to share such information with the Walshes.

Matthews could only shake his head. The fact was, he was not surprised by anything that smacked of Hoffman's unwillingness to part with Jimmy Campbell as his prime suspect. He didn't say anything more to Walsh about the matter, but simply commiserated with him over the frustrations he'd experienced over the years, and asked that his sympathies be extended to Revé as well.

He did tell Walsh that he wished he had been allowed to stay on the case originally, for it was his professional opinion that the Hollywood PD was simply too ill equipped, and the lead detective assigned to the case too inexperienced, for a proper investigation. Furthermore, so far as the viability of a case against Ottis Toole, Matthews had been involved in other successful murder prosecutions where far less evidence was at hand. In his estimation, the Hollywood PD seemed unnecessarily obsessed with the need for physical evidence linking Toole to the crime scene. Given the circumstantial evidence that had come to light, they already had more than what they needed to present the case to a prosecutor.

Walsh heard Matthews out, but at that point, he was still reluctant to divorce himself entirely from the system, though he did share his own feelings that Hoffman and Hickman were less than stellar investigators. Shortly after Adam had gone missing, Walsh told Matthews, Detective Hickman had taken him aside for some private counsel. Hickman handed over a religious pamphlet that invited Walsh to become "born again." Hickman took Walsh's arm and explained. "I know how you feel," he said. "But if you'd take Jesus as your savior, your son will return."

He didn't know what to say to the detective at the time, Walsh told Matthews, but on a number of occasions since he had wondered if it was Jesus or the Hollywood PD he should have been counting on. He had lost sleep on many a night owing to his frustrations with the lack of progress in the case, but to repudiate the police department that he and Revé had placed their trust in for ten years was a difficult leap. He thanked Matthews for all his good work and expressed his hope that the segment they had just filmed would lead to a break in the Baby Lollipops case, and the two parted amicably.

Walsh needn't have worried. On Saturday, December 1, the Baby Lollipops segment aired, and a tip came in, identifying the murdered child as Lazaro Figueroa, his mother a thirty-year-old Cuban immigrant named Ana Cardona, and her lover as a woman named Olivia Gonzalez. Eventually, Cardona confessed to Matthews that she had left her seriously injured son to die in the bushes that night.

While an autopsy determined that young Lazaro's skull had been crushed by repeated blows from a baseball bat, Cardona claimed that the abuse of young Lazaro was begun by her lover, Gonzalez, with whom she had begun an affair following the murder of the victim's father. Owing to depression stemming from an abusive upbringing in Cuba and a dependency on cocaine that she had developed in the United States, she had lacked the courage to defend her child, Cardona claimed, and eventually joined her companion in starving, abusing, and beating Lazaro.

Though Cardona would ultimately plead not guilty to the crime, her lover turned state's evidence and testified against her. In the end, Olivia Gonzalez received a forty-year sentence. Anna Cardona was sentenced to death.

As a result of his work on the case, Joe Matthews was named Police Officer of the Year by the Dade County Association of Chiefs of Police in 1991.

MIAMI, FLORIDA—JUNE 26, 1991

Both Matthews and Walsh were gratified by what had come of their collaboration in the Baby Lollipops case, but neither could be happy with the continued lack of progress in the investigation of Adam's murder. And then, some six months after the break in the Baby Lollipops case, there came—seemingly by accident—an interesting development.

On June 26, 1991, the *Miami Herald* ran an article on the retirement of Major J. B. Smith of the Hollywood Police Department. Smith had been a cop at the agency for twenty-one years, the story noted, and was a sergeant in the robbery and homicide unit, assisting in the investigation of the disappearance and murder of Adam Walsh in 1981.

Smith spoke to the writer at some length about the still-unsolved case, adding, "Ottis Toole was probably the most complete investigation we've ever done to prove somebody didn't do it."

If the department had in fact unearthed any evidence to prove that Ottis Toole had not committed the crime, he did not share it, and the reporter—who apparently was content to believe that Toole had been "proven" innocent—did not inquire further. One person was dumbfounded by J. B. Smith's comments, however.

In Hollywood, Bill Mistler read, then carefully reread the

story, just to be sure he understood correctly. Back in 1983, when Ottis Toole was identified as the prime suspect in the abduction and murder of Adam Walsh, Mistler had wavered about coming forward to tell police what he had seen outside the Hollywood Sears store that day. But from the tenor of the stories he read at the time of the announcement, Mistler assumed that his testimony was unnecessary. Furthermore, until he read Detective Smith's comments that day in 1991, he thought that Ottis Toole had been charged and that the matter had been concluded.

Mistler, who'd been carrying a burden of guilt for almost ten years, got up from his chair and went into the kitchen where his wife was fixing dinner. Did she know that Ottis Toole had never been charged with the murder of Adam Walsh? he asked, brandishing the newspaper. She didn't, she told him, then listened as he recapped the details of what he'd read.

"What do you think I ought to do?" Mistler asked his wife when he'd finished.

She couldn't tell him what to do, she answered. But did he remember how scared they'd been the day their own son had wandered off for half an hour during a camping excursion?

Mistler remembered very well how he felt, and the recollections were enough to send him finally to the telephone, where he did what he'd been meaning to do for a long, long time. When he finally got through to Hollywood PD, an operator transferred him to Jack Hoffman, still the lead detective on the case. Mistler told Hoffman who he was, and then gave a brief account of what he had seen in the parking lot outside the Sears store that day. "I'm telling you, I saw Ottis Toole kidnap Adam Walsh," he said.

Hoffman waited for Mistler to finish, then thanked him for the call. It had been ten years since the incident, and here was some guy out of nowhere claiming he'd seen it all? Hoffman explained that he was a little busy right now, getting ready to go on vacation. If Mistler didn't mind, why not get back to him in a couple of weeks, and they'd take it up again?

Mistler, who'd just battled past any number of fears and uncertainties to make the call, stared at the phone in disbelief as Hoffman hung up. The detective hadn't even asked for his phone number or his address. He wasn't even sure the guy had caught his name.

Still, Mistler had made up his mind. He'd felt better about himself from the moment he'd picked up the phone and began to dial the police. And so, at about noon on Monday, July 22, Mistler called again. "I'm the guy who saw Ottis Toole take Adam Walsh from the curb outside the Sears store that day and put him inside a car," Mistler reminded Hoffman. He'd had no reason to believe he was witnessing a kidnapping at the time, for the child showed no signs of resistance or alarm. He simply assumed it was a family member taking the child home.

Mistler also explained to Hoffman that in 1983, when Hollywood PD announced that Toole was the chief suspect, he believed that Toole had in fact been charged with the crime and that the matter had been dispensed with. It was not until he stumbled upon the article concerning Major Smith's retirement, Mistler said, that he'd realized the case was still unsolved. Hoffman listened to it all, and when Mistler was finished, the detective scheduled a meeting at department offices for the following Monday.

On Sunday, July 28, the *Miami Herald* ran a ten-year anniversary piece on Adam's murder and included an interview with Jack Hoffman during which he told a reporter that he still hadn't "totally eliminated" Ottis Toole as a suspect. Whether or not it was Mistler's phone call that had reawakened his interest in Toole is difficult to say. Nothing of note had been added to his case file since the day in late October 1984 when Hoffman assured reporters that Toole had been unequivocally eliminated as a suspect.

In any case, on Monday, July 29, 1991, Bill Mistler appeared as scheduled at the offices of Hollywood PD, where he met with Detective Hoffman to make a voluntary sworn statement. Mistler broke into tears on two different occasions during the interview, explaining that he felt tremendous guilt for not having reacted differently to what he witnessed that day outside Sears. If he had approached Toole, or if he had summoned security or called police, he might have prevented Adam's death. Make no mistake about it, Mistler said. It was Ottis Toole he had seen leading Adam Walsh away from the Sears store that day, and he had lived and relived every moment in his mind ever since.

He arrived at the Sears lot via the northwest corner entrance near the garden shop, he told Hoffman. He was waiting for an older woman to park her car when he first saw Toole, driving past him in his Cadillac, headed the opposite direction. He recollected that the car was in good condition, other than what looked like rust stains from well water and a sizable dent in the right rear bumper. It was bearing a Florida license plate, and there were what appeared to be a number of gardening tools in the backseat.

Mistler said that he saw Toole stop his car in the opposite driving lane, get out of the driver's door, and walk around the car toward the curb. He remembered that Toole appeared to be checking out his surroundings, glancing left and right, and that the two actually locked eyes for a few seconds. Toole was an odd-looking type, he said, around six feet tall, with a wandering eye and reddish brown hair. He was dressed shabbily, his T-shirt filthy—hardly the picture of the typical suburban Sears shopper.

Mistler said that he watched as Toole approached the curb outside the entrance to Sears, where a small boy—maybe five years old—was standing. Because he was so caught up in Toole's idiosyncratic appearance, Mistler said, he didn't pay as much attention as he might have to exactly how the child was dressed, though he thought he remembered that the boy was wearing a hat.

Mistler said that Toole knelt down in front of the boy and began to talk to him. On the sidewalk nearby, he recalled, was a woman with a boy of fourteen or so, apparently searching for something in her purse. To Mistler, there was something wrong with what he was seeing. Toole and the boy with whom he was talking simply did not seem to belong together, if for no other reason than the comparative condition of their clothing, a guy off the streets talking to a kid who obviously came from a suburban home.

"I made the wrong call," Mistler said. "I kept looking for Adam to give me some sort of a signal . . ." But it never came.

Mistler watched in his rearview mirror as Toole took Adam by the arm, but he saw no signs of resistance there. The two walked past the front of the Cadillac, with Toole talking to Adam all the while. Toole opened the driver's door to the Cadillac, and Adam crawled in and across the front seat. By this point, Mistler noted that the parking space he was waiting for had finally been vacated.

He parked his truck, got out, and walked toward the curb. He glanced at the spot where the Cadillac had been stopped, but by then it was gone.

Mistler picked up a few items for the family's camping trip, but inevitably he hadn't managed to get everything everyone wanted. At 3:00 p.m. or so, he was back at the Sears store, accompanied by his wife and his nine-year-old son. Shortly after they entered, they noted a woman and a man involved in a heated discussion with "a fat security guard." Mistler's son nudged him and said that he knew the man and the woman. They were the parents of Adam Walsh, a kid his son knew from the playground at school. Mistler didn't think much of it at the time.

Later, as they were shopping for the things Mistler had forgotten, they heard an announcement on the store's PA system, paging Adam Walsh. But again, Mistler did not connect the announcement with what he had witnessed in the parking lot more than two hours earlier. They simply picked up the things they needed, Mistler explained, and then they took their trip.

When they got back the following Sunday, one of his son's friends came by the house and told them all about Adam's abduction, Mistler said. At the time, he reminded his wife that they had seen Mrs. Walsh in the Sears store the previous Monday—that is why she had appeared so upset. Still, Mistler said, it did not occur to him to connect what he had witnessed in the parking lot earlier that day to Adam's disappearance.

In fact, Mistler told Hoffman, it was not until a month to six weeks later, when he returned to Sears on yet another shopping trip, that a news story came on the radio and it suddenly hit him. He might in fact have witnessed Adam's abduction. He actually turned his truck toward the nearby headquarters of the Hollywood PD right then and there, Mistler said, but that was the point at which the news was all about the search for the "blue van" that someone had seen Adam being pulled into. The story he'd been listening to closed on news of the search for that van at that very moment, Mistler said, and he decided that perhaps what he had to offer wasn't that useful after all.

As to why he hadn't come forward in 1983, when Ottis Toole's picture was splashed across television and newspapers as the prime suspect in the case, Mistler told Hoffman that he thought other witnesses had come forward, or they wouldn't have named Toole as the man responsible. Hoffman listened to Mistler's account, then asked him if he would agree to take a polygraph exam and undergo hypnosis to see if those procedures would corroborate the truth of what he was claiming all these years later.

Mistler agreed without hesitation and returned to police headquarters the following day for the polygraph. While no record of the exam itself remains in the case file, a supplemental report filed by Detective Hoffman notes that the results of Mistler's polygraph were "inconclusive."

Three days later, on Friday, August 2, 1991, Mistler again reported to Hollywood PD, this time to be placed under hypnosis by a doctor attached to the Broward County Sheriff's Office psychological services unit. However, during the prehypnosis interview, Mistler again became so upset regarding his recollections of the day that the physician adjudged him unfit to be hypnotized at the time. Instead, detectives drove him back to the west parking lot of the Sears Mall in hopes that revisiting the scene might jog Mistler's memory as to what Adam had been wearing on the day of the kidnapping. But Mistler could simply not recall those details.

Finally, on Monday, September 2, Mistler returned again to police headquarters, where this time he successfully underwent hypnosis. During the session, he was able to recall that Toole had rotten, greenish teeth, a two-week beard, strange eyes, and was wearing dark pants and brown shoes. As far as Adam's clothing went, Mistler said that the child was wearing a baseball hat.

Mistler, of course, was interested in what effects his decision to come forward would have on the long-stymied case. If the cops had not received proof that Toole had committed the crime, they now had an eyewitness who could give them exactly what they needed. Furthermore, during his initial interview with Hoffman, when he'd first begun to detail the sighting of Toole in the Cadillac that day at the Sears store, Hoffman suddenly snapped alert. He'd been listening idly to Mistler's account of the day, cleaning his nails with a pocketknife. But at the mention of the Cadillac, Hoffman sat upright, making eye contact with Mistler for the first time.

"Nobody knows about that Cadillac," Hoffman told Mistler, then left the room to get photographs of the car for Mistler to identify.

When Hoffman originally asked Mistler to submit to a polygraph and to undergo hypnosis, he assumed that it meant that the cops were excited and interested in what he had to tell them.

But Mistler began to worry the day of his second hypnosis session, when he ventured to ask Hoffman what was going to happen with Toole now. Hoffman glanced away, Mistler says.

"I don't know," the detective said. "I don't think this is going anywhere."

Stunned, Mistler asked him what he meant.

Hoffman shrugged. "Well, the mother doesn't want to go into court and listen to all the gory details about what happened to her child. And Ottis is already convicted of another murder . . ." The detective trailed off.

At that point, Mistler had the chilling sensation that his decision to come forward meant absolutely nothing to the lead investigator in the case, but he went ahead with his session nonetheless. How could he not?

A few days later, he called Hoffman to check on how he'd done. If the polygraph exam and the hypnosis supported his account of what he had seen, then surely the cops would go after Toole for the killing, he reasoned.

"So how's it going with the case?" Mistler asked when Hoffman came on the line.

There was a pause, and the sounds of paper being shuffled in the background. "Ah, well," Hoffman said, "I went up and talked to Ottis, and Ottis assured me he didn't do it. He told me, 'Why would I lie to ya, Jack, I'd tell ya if I killed this kid.' "

Mistler had to take a deep breath. "Let me get this straight," he said to Hoffman. "You give me a polygraph exam, you hypnotize me twice, you interview me four times, and you go up and have a little chat with this psycho and you believe him and not me?"

When Hoffman didn't respond, something occurred to Mistler. "Look, tell me the truth, tell me what's going on. If the Walshes don't want to go through with this, that's one thing, but at least you have to tell me you told them about what I saw."

"Oh, yeah," Hoffman said. "I told the parents."

The offhand tone in which he said it so angered Mistler that he hung up the phone and turned to his wife to explain what it was all about. "He's lying," Mistler told her. "He never said anything to the Walshes. I'm gonna go over there to the PD and make him look me in the eye and tell me the same lie."

But Mistler's wife had the last word on that score. "I don't think that's such a good idea," she said.

Upon reflection, Mistler decided she was right. Instead of confronting Hoffman, he placed a call to the FBI, asking to speak with the agent assigned to work with the Hollywood police on the Adam Walsh case. After some delay, he was transferred to a Mrs. Grey or a Mrs. White—"some kind of color," Mistler recalls—who asked him again why he was calling. Mistler explained that he had witnessed the abduction of Adam Walsh by Ottis Toole and that though he had come forward to Hollywood police, he was worried that Detective Hoffman was not taking him seriously.

The person to whom Mistler spoke took down the information and said that someone would get back to him, but no call ever came. To Mistler it meant that perhaps what Hoffman said about the Walshes wanting to bury the case was true. They must have been told that he had come forward, Mistler reasoned, or the FBI would have called him back. "So it's okay," he told himself. He'd done everything he could. "It's over. It's done."

TALLAHASSEE, FLORIDA—AUGUST 14, 1991

At the same time the drama between Bill Mistler, Jack Hoffman, and the FBI was playing out, Joe Matthews was in Tallahassee conducting a three-day seminar on investigative interviewing and interrogation techniques for the University of North Florida's Institute for Police Technology and Management. Matthews's coinstructor was a retired FBI agent named Bill Haggerty who had been involved in the investigation of the Adam Walsh case at the time Ottis Toole had first come forward with his confession back in 1983.

After the first night of classes concluded, Matthews and Haggerty were relaxing over a drink when the Walsh case came up. While Matthews had maintained an interest in the investigation, there was really little he could do—he was a homicide cop working for another police department.

Matthews was intrigued to know what the Bureau's take on the matter had been—the Feds might not have wanted to get directly involved for various political and practical reasons, but that didn't mean they hadn't provided peripheral consultation. And indeed the agency had, the retired agent assured Matthews. In fact, when Ottis Toole surfaced as a suspect back in 1983, Haggerty told Matthews that he had eliminated Toole as a suspect almost immediately.

"Oh yeah," Matthews said, curious. "Why was that?"

The agent leaned forward, his face a sage mask. "Think about it," he said to Matthews. "A guy takes a bus ride all the way from Virginia to Jacksonville, maybe sixteen, eighteen, twenty hours. No way he's going to get in a car and drive another five or six hours all the way to Miami or Fort Lauderdale and spend the night hustling gays."

Matthews stared back at his federal counterpart, not sure if he wanted to start up with the guy. After all, they had a couple more days together. What was to be gained? But was this the kind of thinking upon which an FBI agent had based his investigation of the Adam Walsh case?

As Matthews saw it, Ottis Toole was the kind of guy who slept on park benches and on plastic bags in mulch piles. On a good night, he'd get blasted and sleep in his car. A twenty-hour ride on a plush reclining seat in an air-conditioned bus would be like a stay in the Ritz-Carlton to Toole.

Besides, what on earth had such off-the-wall suppositions to do with whether or not Ottis Toole had committed the crime he said he had? Matthews could only hope that the guy sitting across from him had not been the lead FBI investigator on the case.

Matthews was well aware that no one had ever conducted a proper investigative interview with Toole—after all, he was in Tallahassee to explain the very concept. All that Toole had ever provided were statements. For the most part Toole talked, and instead of asking questions, detectives simply listened, taking notes, following the agenda set by the suspect. It was the opposite of effective investigative interviewing in Matthews's book, but with Toole that is what had happened.

What's worse, Toole had never been polygraphed, not once. On a number of occasions he said he killed Adam Walsh, a couple other times he said he didn't. It seemed to leave a lot of people in law enforcement guessing: On which days had he been deceptive?

But you didn't have to guess, Matthews reminded himself, shaking his head at the smug agent sitting across the table. There was this scientific instrument called a polygraph that could help you learn the truth, and when he got back to South Florida, he would give it one last shot to see if he could put it to use on Ottis Toole.

Late that month, motivated by nothing more than his sense of duty and an innate desire to do the right thing, Matthews drove to the headquarters of Hollywood police, where he met with Captain Gil Frazier, who was then in charge of the Criminal Investigations Division. Matthews pointed out his concerns over the handling of Ottis Toole as a suspect and made a simple request of Frazier: let Matthews conduct a formal investigative interview of the type that had never been performed on the suspect. "What do you have to lose?" he asked.

Frazier thought about it for a moment, then nodded. Matthews was right; why not give it a shot? As Matthews looked on, the captain got Detective Hoffman on the phone. He wanted Hoffman and Matthews to travel to Starke, Frazier said, where Matthews would interview Toole about the Walsh case. Hoffman acknowledged his superior's order and suggested that Matthews give him a call in a day or two to arrange a date.

Things couldn't have gone more smoothly, Matthews thought, until he began trying to set a date with Hoffman. He left several phone messages for the lead detective, all of which were ignored. Finally, Matthews drove back to Hollywood PD headquarters and confronted Hoffman at his desk. When were they going to go interview Toole? Matthews wanted to know. "Soon," Hoffman assured him, but right now he was busy with a million things. He'd get back to Matthews as soon as he possibly could.

Matthews was frustrated, certainly, but since he wasn't signing Hoffman's paycheck, there was little he could do. Without the detective in charge of the case, Matthews had no access to Toole.

Toole, meantime, was convicted in late September of three more homicides in Florida's Jackson County, a rural enclave bordering Alabama and Georgia, and had returned to Starke with yet another life sentence tacked onto his list. Other jurisdictions seemed happy to investigate, charge, and convict Toole of murders he had confessed to, Matthews thought. What was the problem at Hollywood? Why on earth wouldn't you want to do anything you could to try and solve this case?

On October 16, 1991, Matthews was back in Tallahassee, team-teaching another course with Bill Haggerty, the retired FBI agent whose misguided notions had provoked him into making his request of Captain Frazier at Hollywood PD a couple of months before. During a break, Haggerty mentioned to Matthews that he might not be in class the following day— he'd promised to drive the two hours to Starke to help out on a case.

No problem, Matthews assured his counterpart. He could handle the class on his own. But just what was it that was calling the agent away?

Oh, just a pain in the ass, really, Haggerty replied. He'd received a call from Jack Hoffman down at Hollywood PD. Hoffman's boss wanted Hoffman to reinterview Ottis Toole for some reason, and Hoffman had asked Haggerty to accompany him. "Big waste of time, if you ask me," the agent told Matthews, "but hey, I'm always ready to lend a hand."

Matthews listened, then excused himself to make a phone call. When he reached Hollywood PD, he asked to speak with Gil Frazier. He couldn't believe what Hoffman was trying to pull, Matthews thought. But Frazier would put a stop to it. The captain had been 100 percent in support of his request, Matthews was certain of it.

Abruptly the connection went through, and Matthews took a breath, about to launch into the summary of what he had learned. "Captain Frazier is on vacation," an assistant's voice said before he got a word out. "He'll be gone for the next six weeks." Matthews replaced the phone and leaned back in his chair, releasing a pent-up breath. Unless everything he knew about cops was wrong, Matthews told himself, Hoffman had simply waited for his boss to go on vacation, then purposefully ignored his order to have Matthews interview Toole. Apparently, Hoffman was bound and determined to make sure nothing ever moved forward on this investigation.

"Told you so," Matthews's fellow instructor reported when he returned from Starke the following afternoon. He explained to Matthews that Toole had informed them that he hadn't been involved in the Walsh kidnapping back in July 1981. He'd returned to Jacksonville from Virginia and had not left. As to why he'd told some people otherwise back in 1983, Toole said it was "for his own personal gain." He got taken out of jail for a while, ate real food, got to smoke cigarettes.

He'd also been approached by another inmate, a guy named Gerald Schaffer who wanted to write a book about the killings that Toole and Henry Lee Lucas had been involved in. Schaffer was working with some author, Toole said, and this guy would funnel monthly payments to them both if Toole would sign over the rights to his story. That sounded fine and dandy to Toole, but, he claimed, he had told Schaffer at the time that he didn't kill Adam Walsh. Toole omitted any reference to the letters that Schaffer had helped him write in 1988, as well as any mention of such details as the bayonet that he and Schaffer had dangled before the Broward County investigators at the time.

Toole told Hoffman there wasn't any reason for him to be withholding information at this time, not when he was already facing multiple life sentences. Hoffman, without bothering to bring up the fact that there might be several reasons for an incarcerated felon not to confess to the abuse and murder of a six-year-old child, took Toole's word on the matter. "Based on the interview with Ottis Toole," he wrote in summary, "it is this detective's opinion that Ottis Toole was being truthful and sincere about his noninvolvement in the Adam Walsh homicide."

And Haggerty, the retired agent who had witnessed this most recent exchange between Hoffman and Toole, agreed, or so he told Matthews that afternoon when he returned from Starke. "Ottis is telling the truth."

"Oh yeah?" said Matthews, who could hold his tongue no longer. "Would that have been today he was telling the truth, or the twenty-one other times when he said he did it?"

For Matthews, it wasn't an accusation, but an honest question. The two of them were in Tallahassee to instruct other detectives in proper investigative methods. Matthews believed that it was vital to understand the difference between listening passively to a statement and a proactive investigative interview, where the questioner, not the subject, controls the agenda. Left to his own devices, a suspect might change his story concerning a crime for any number of reasons.

Jack Hoffman had not found physical evidence that tied Toole to the crime, but there was a mountain of circumstantial evidence that did, and Hoffman had certainly not found any evidence that excluded him from the crime. In the end, it seemed to Matthew, he had simply "decided" that Toole was not involved.

Matthews, on the other hand, felt certain that if Toole were properly interviewed and his responses subjected to polygraph examination, the question of his involvement could be determined once and for all. Not to have done so in all this time seemed simply unfathomable.

Which begged the question as to why Hoffman seemed so dead set against allowing Matthews access to Toole. If Matthews discovered that Toole was in fact being deceptive when he spoke of matters related to the crime, it would only support what Hoffman had apparently chosen to believe long ago. But if Matthews found good reason to believe that Toole was being truthful when he spoke of killing Adam Walsh, it would mean the virtual ruin of a detective who had been unable to make any headway on the most celebrated crime his department had ever encountered. He had staked his career on his steadfast refusal to arrest the only viable suspect who had surfaced during his ten-plus years of investigation, and he still had his job. Why on earth take any chances? Meantime, Adam Walsh's seventeenth birthday passed in November 1991 without further progress on the case.

As evidence that he was still on the job and willing to pursue any lead, Detective Hoffman at the request of John Walsh traveled to Madison, Wisconsin, in the late summer of 1992, where he interviewed Jeffrey Dahmer, who had been arrested for a series of gruesome murders the previous year. While most of the seventeen killings Dahmer was charged with took place between 1987 and 1991, he had taken his first victim in 1977. Some of his victims were as young as fourteen, and many had been spectacularly tortured, abused, and dismembered. Moreover, when he'd been discharged from the army for alcoholism in 1981, Dahmer had spent some time in Miami Beach. It seemed, at the very least, a lead worth pursuing.

Accordingly, Hoffman interviewed Dahmer in his Wisconsin prison on August 13, 1992. At that time, Dahmer assured Hoffman that he was not involved in the abduction and murder of Adam Walsh. No polygraph examination was administered to Dahmer regarding the case. Hoffman returned to South Florida, advised John Walsh as to what he had found, and recorded the information in the case file, where it would reside as the only record of note for the next two years.

Adam Walsh's eighteenth and nineteenth birthdays passed in 1992 and 1993, and nothing new had turned up to suggest who might have taken his life. Still, if the calendar pages seemed to be flipping with no apparent concern for the answer to that question, the steady beat of those tsunami-causing butterfly wings continued.

In 1994, there was something of a startling development within the Hollywood Police Department, where a new command staff was assigned to take over the Criminal Investigations Division. Major Brian Maher and Lieutenant Debbie Futch were placed in charge, and one of the first things they agreed upon was the transfer of Jack Hoffman out of their arena. Hoffman was sent summarily to the Patrol Division as a uniform cop.

As part of her own skills improvement program, Lieutenant Futch attended a homicide investigation seminar being conducted at Broward Community College by Harry O'Reilly, a retired NYPD homicide detective and a well-respected instructor in death investigation technique. Futch told O'Reilly of her own frustration with her department's failure to progress with the Adam Walsh case, and O'Reilly had a quick suggestion: "Why don't you call Joe Matthews over at Miami Beach PD?"

O'Reilly knew and respected Matthews and had heard him talk about the various miscues in the Walsh case on more than one occasion. He was sure that Matthews would welcome the opportunity to involve himself formally, and he assured Futch that there was no better investigator in South Florida to aid in the investigation.

Lieutenant Futch told her boss Maher about the conversation, and Maher thought it was an excellent way to restore credibility to the investigative division. They called Matthews and asked if he'd be willing to consult with their department if they reopened the investigation of the Adam Walsh case. It was a welcome overture to Matthews, who was grappling with grief over the recent death of his father Al, following a fall and a forty-day stay in an intensive care unit.

The opportunity to busy himself in pursuit of a case he'd always been passionate about promised a way to displace a portion of his misery, and he agreed without hesitation. Then–chief of Hollywood police Dick Witt made the request of Miami Beach Police that Matthews be formally assigned, and the deal was done.

Detective Mark Smith—who in 1981, as a rookie cop seated behind the wheel of a patrol car, had assured John Walsh that he and every one of his fellow officers were doing everything they could to find his son—had been assigned to oversee a new cold case squad at Hollywood PD, and among the first he was assigned to reopen was that of the murder of Adam Walsh.

As ordered, Smith met with Matthews to discuss a game plan for how the homicide would best be investigated. From the outset, however, Matthews had his concerns. Smith seemed much more protective of his department's image than Maher and Futch had been, and while he made many of the case files available to Matthews, he held back certain reports and memos that he assured Matthews were inconsequential.

To Matthews, nothing was inconsequential, especially files that might shed light on mistakes and oversights made early on in the investigation, but there was little he could do about it. He set aside his doubts and discussed with Smith the interviews that should be conducted and the evidence that could be reexamined, especially in light of the newly advanced DNA testing now available.

Smith assured Matthews that he would pass along a summary of their recommendations to his superiors and that as soon as he got approval, they would move forward. To Matthews, it sounded good. Just possibly, a new era was about to dawn at Hollywood PD where the Adam Walsh case was concerned. Though he doubted that he and Smith would ever become bosom buddies, he judged that at least he would be working with a competent, hardworking cop. Quite understandably, he looked forward to the day when he could report to John and Revé Walsh that at last significant progress was being made in finding the killer of their son.

On Monday, August 15, 1994, Detective Smith composed a memo to deputy chief Mike Ignasiak outlining what he thought could be done to revive the Walsh case. In his memo, however, he noted that "due to the amount of time since the incident, it would be virtually impossible to set out and try to establish new suspects or motives," an odd position for a cold case investigator to take, given that the aim of such undertakings is to consider the possibility of new suspects or motives.

Smith also suggested in his memo that one thing that they might do was to conduct a follow-up inspection of the area around mile marker 126 on Florida's Turnpike to try and determine why that might have been selected as a place for the killer to dispose of Adam's head, though he doesn't make clear exactly what significance he attributed to that question. More important, Smith recommended to his superiors that "a re-interview" be scheduled with Ottis Toole, "to either eliminate him as a suspect or reaffirm his involvement." This was necessary, Smith said, because it seemed that the "original investigators" believed that Toole was confessing for publicity reasons and had been furnished confidential case file information by "an overzealous Jacksonville detective."

Despite Hoffman's reluctance to pursue the matter, Smith said, "Toole has not been successfully eliminated as a suspect in the case," and he recommended that Miami Beach detective sergeant Joe Matthews be involved in the interview of Toole. "Mr. Matthews has agreed to accompany this agency in an interview with Toole free of charge," Smith explained, before adding something of a curious addendum. "Although he may have ulterior motives for his willingness to assist, I feel Matthews is a resource that could be beneficial to this investigation."

As it turned out, Matthews would not view this memo until ten years after it was written, and when he did see it, he found it mystifying, to say the least. For one thing, the very notion of compensation for his involvement was ludicrous—he was in the paid employ of the Miami Beach Police Department, and he had been assigned to work with Hollywood PD at the latter's own request. Furthermore, he was not "Mr." Matthews, but "Detective Sergeant Matthews"—a small point, but police protocol is unwavering when it comes to distinguishing ordinary civilians from officers in formal correspondence of any kind.

Most troubling to Matthews was the offhand mention of "ulterior motives." To Matthews, it smacked of Jack Hoffman's accusation that Buddy Terry had signed a book contract with Ottis Toole, an unfounded charge that not only besmirched a good cop's career but hobbled the Walsh investigation.

Of course, he could give credit to Hollywood PD for reopening the investigation, but he could only view Smith's comments as symptomatic of an entire department's unspoken wish that the case simply go away, once and for all.

In order to understand what makes Matthews tick, it may be worth a brief return to the detective's early days as a beat cop on the Miami Beach force. Matthews had joined the force in 1967, shortly after his twenty-first birthday, following a chance encounter with a cop during a stint as a security guard at the Miami Beach Convention Center. Why be busting your ass for a buck and a quarter an hour? the cop asked. Matthews seemed like a smart kid. There was a shortage in the department. If he passed the test, the cop told him, he could be knocking down $500 a month.

It seemed like a fortune at the time, and Matthews decided to follow the advice. He took the entrance exam, placed second among applicants, and soon was enrolled in the Dade County Police Academy.

From the first, there were indications that Matthews was not going to be your ordinary cop. His outspoken nature and will-ingness to question his superiors earned him respect in some quarters, but not everyone appreciated his candor. One morn-ing during training, he returned from class to his locker to find it yawning open, his holster dangling inside, his department-issued pistol missing. Though losing your weapon was just about the worst offense a cadet could commit, Matthews knew there was no avoiding the matter. He marched himself to the training sergeant's office and made his report.

He'd left his locker on "day-lock," he explained to Sergeant, meaning he'd closed his locker, spun the dial, then clicked in the first number of the combination and the second, leaving the dial a few spots shy of the third. It was the sort of thing many cadets did, for there was little time allotted between training sessions, and being late for roll call too often could mean wash-ing out of the program. You'd hurry back to your locker, move the dial a few notches, grab what you needed, and hurry off.

His supervisor might have been aware of the practice, but it didn't mean he condoned it. "You lost your fucking fire-arm?" the sergeant bellowed. "Do you know who cleans those locker rooms? The fucking jailhouse trusties. If you don't come up with that pistol, we're going to have to empty every cell and strip-search every inmate." With that, he snatched up the phone and asked for Major Sandstrom, chief of the Dade County Corrections Department, to explain the situation. "Yes, that's M-a-t-t-h-e-w-s," he told Sandstrom. "No, not from Dade County. From Miami Beach."

After a bit more consultation with his colleague, Grant hung up the phone and turned back. "Do you know what a colossal pain in the ass this is going to be? We'll wait a few hours. Go find your goddamn gun. If you come up with it, we'll save a hell of a lot of trouble. And if you don't—" The sergeant broke off, shaking his head. Matthews had little doubt as to what the consequences would be.

Following lunch, the forty-man cadet class was once again assembled before the training sergeant, who wanted to make an announcement before they got back to their regularly scheduled business for the afternoon. Grant proceeded then to give the cadre a detailed account of Matthews's profound screwup, and called for him to stand. Matthews rose, ramrod-straight, ready for the worst. "Have you found your firearm yet?" the sergeant demanded.

Matthews felt every eye in the room upon him. Many of his fellow cadets were squirming, well aware that there but for the grace of God they might be. "No sir," Matthews responded, "but I have identified a suspect, sir."

Grant shared a sadist's smile with the others in the room. "Oh yeah?" he said. "And who might that be?"

"It's *you*, sir," Matthews responded.

There was a momentary silence, then a murmur swept the room. The sergeant's face contorted. "Me? What the fuck are you talking about?"

"I went to Major Sandstrom's office during our lunch hour, sir. He told me he hadn't received any call from you regarding any missing pistol. He didn't have any idea what I was talking about."

"Are you calling me a liar?" Grant said, rising from his seat.

"I'd like permission to interview you, sir. You've been instructing us on interviewing suspects, and I think you took my pistol to teach me a lesson. I'd like to ask if you, or anyone at

your direction, might have gone to the locker room this morning
and removed my pistol from my locker."

By this point the sergeant's face was an apoplectic mask.
"Shut the fuck up and sit down, Matthews," he said.

If he had harbored any suspicion that all of this had been
something of a training exercise, the spittle flying from Grant's
lips convinced Matthews otherwise. Sometimes discretion was
the better part of valor, he decided.

On the way out of the room after class was dismissed, one
of his fellow cadets gave him a consoling pat on the shoulder.
"You've done it this time, Matthews," he said. "You're out of
here for sure."

Matthews shrugged. "Maybe you're right," he said. "But I do
know one thing. That bastard took my gun."

His fellow cadet could only shake his head, and the two hurried off to class. Later that afternoon, Matthews returned to
open his locker. Sure enough, his pistol had been replaced.

It is one of many stories reflecting Matthews's refusal to be
cowed by blowhards, but it is surely not the only one. Shortly
after he'd graduated from the academy and joined the ranks of
beat cops at Miami Beach PD, Matthews turned up at morning roll call to hear a pronouncement: there had been too many
complaints from high rollers in big cars and the owners of delivery companies with drivers trying to navigate the clogged streets
of the densely populated island. Every officer was to make the
ticketing of double-parked cars a priority.

Not a problem, Matthews thought, and set out upon his
rounds for the day. He had scarcely turned the corner of Lin-
coln Road onto Alton when he saw a big Buick pull up beside a
car parked in front of Alfie's, a mega-sized Miami version of a
New York City candy store *cum* newsstand. The driver got out
of the Buick, gave Matthews an uninterested glance, and then
strolled casually into the store. It might have been a brazen
enough action, parking your barge of a sedan in a busy traf-

fic lane while a cop approached—but on top of everything else, there were empty parking places both in front of and behind the car the guy had parked beside.

Matthews shook his head and made his own way into the store. There he found the guy from the sedan at the counter, engaged in earnest conversation with the owner. "Excuse me, sir," Matthews called. "You're double-parked outside. You'll have to move your car."

The guy kept on talking, ignoring him.

Matthews joined him at the counter, holding up his ticket book. "You're double-parked," he repeated. "If you don't move, I'll have to write you a ticket."

Alfie the proprietor gave Matthews a doubtful look from behind the counter, but said nothing. The guy at the counter turned, gave Matthews a snicker, then turned back and resumed his conversation with Alfie.

"Okay by me," Matthews said. "I'll be outside writing tickets," he went on. "And I'll still be writing them until you come out there and move your car."

He left the store and walked to the back of the car to check the plate number. Having never issued a citation for double parking, he had to consult his statute book to find the proper code, and that took him a few moments. He had completed that citation and was at work on a second—for obstructing traffic— when the door to Alfie's finally opened and the guy came out, a look of disbelief on his face.

"What do you think you're doing?" the guy said.

"Exactly what I told you I'd be doing," Matthews said. He finished the second citation and tore a copy out of his book. He thrust the two tickets at the guy, who rolled his eyes and brushed past him.

As the guy got into his car and slammed the door, Matthews approached, lifted the wiper on the driver's side of the windshield, and snapped the two tickets under the rubber blade. The driver's-side window rolled down, and the guy thrust his face through the opening. "You don't know who you're screwing with, do you?" he demanded.

By the point Matthews had had enough. He bent close enough to smell the guy's boozer breath. "You don't know who *you're* screwing with, do you?"

The guy's eyes widened in surprise momentarily. "Fuck you," he said finally, then floored the Buick's accelerator and sped away.

"Fuck *you*," Matthews called after him. He noted that Alfie had come out onto the sidewalk to witness the scene. The proprietor gave Matthews a baleful look, then went back inside. Matthews shrugged and went on about his day.

Before dismissal at the following morning's roll call, the patrol sergeant reiterated the need for them all to be vigilant about ticketing double-parkers, and then, as everyone was filing out, called Matthews to his desk. "Captain Webb wants to see you," the sergeant said.

When Matthews asked the sergeant if he knew what it was about, the sergeant gave him a look. "I think I'll let the captain explain. Just get your ass down there."

Accordingly, Matthews made his way to the patrol commander's office. As Matthews stood nervously at attention, Webb gave him the once-over, then tented his fingers and finally began.

"Since when did you start issuing parking tickets to police officers?" Webb inquired.

Matthews was genuinely perplexed. "I don't know what you mean, sir. I wouldn't do anything like that."

"Then why did you write Captain Henry Dworkin, who happens to be commander of the detective bureau, two parking tickets yesterday? One for double-parking and another for obstructing traffic?"

Matthews stared at the tickets Captain Webb had produced, a feeling of dread washing over him. "Uh . . . I had no idea he was a police officer, sir."

His supervisor stared at him. "Well, you made one hell of a mistake, Matthews."

"Yes sir," Matthews said.

"And you need to take care of these tickets," his supervisor added.

Matthews nodded. "I'll do that, sir."

"Good," his supervisor said, giving him a weary look. "Go to it. And try to keep your head out of your ass from now on, will you?"

By the time he made his way down the hallway from the squad room, Matthews's shock had abated, and resentment had begun to take its place. Why hadn't Dworkin just said he was a cop in the first place? Why be such a dick about it?

Anyway, he thought, his supervisor had told him to take care of the matter, and so he would. He'd go right to Captain Dworkin's office and do whatever it took.

At his knock on Dworkin's door, a voice issued, inviting him in. Matthews entered to find the guy he'd given the tickets sitting behind a desk. "What are you doing here?" Dworkin said, the instant he saw who it was.

"I just wanted to talk to you about those tickets—," Matthews began.

Dworkin stared as if a leper was about to climb into his lap. "Get the fuck out of my office and don't you ever come back," he said.

"Yes sir," Matthews said, and turned on his heel.

As he was making his way down the hallway in the aftermath, he heard a voice calling after him. "Hey, Matthews."

What now? he thought, as he turned to see Detective Walter Philbin stepping out of a doorway, beckoning toward him. Philbin was a lieutenant of detectives, a tall, muscular guy with plenty of swagger and the look of a ladies' man. He was a big drinker and a high-stakes gambler, but he had connections inside the department and on the streets as well. His was a legendary presence in the department's detective bureau.

"I just wanted to say you got some balls, kid. Telling Dworkin he doesn't know who he's fucking with. That's classic." Philbin laughed and clapped him on the shoulder.

Matthews stared back in some concern. "How'd you hear about that?" He glanced down the hall toward the office he'd just left. "Did Dworkin tell you?"

"Hell, no," Philbin said, waving his hand. "The guy's a total asshole. Nobody talks to him. Alfie told me what happened. He said he never saw anything like it."

Philbin was about to duck back into his office, then stopped. "By the way, go see Esther down in the traffic division. She'll tell you how to make those tickets go away."

It might have been the end of the matter, and just one more story about Joe Matthews and how his penchant for doing the right thing seemed always to land him in trouble, except for one thing. It was not long after that encounter that Chief Pomerance asked Walter Philbin to put together a task force that would do whatever was necessary to bring down the crime rate on Miami Beach.

Pomerance and Philbin were in agreement as to the kind of officers needed for such an assignment. There'd be some ticklish situations dealing with hardened criminals who'd prefer to take their chances on justice in a shootout as opposed to a courtroom, and you'd need to be able to trust your partners to stand up, during and after tough situations like those.

Accordingly, Philbin primarily chose men whom he'd known for years. Experienced and able cops, those savvy enough to understand when justice had to be dispensed with on the spot, and how to keep their mouths shut afterward. Given his dictum that you couldn't trust a man you couldn't drink with, Philbin would probably have added incipient alcoholism to his list of qualifications as well. But there was rigor in such work, and the need for a certain amount of young blood too.

It was in that way, then, that Joe Matthews found himself plucked from the ranks of the beat cops to become part of a task force that one day would be dispatched to a stakeout at the Shoreham Hotel and from there to any number of other incidents that would propel him upward through the ranks. From task force, to detective bureau, to sergeant. From homicide investigator, to polygraph expert, to Dade County Cop of the Year, and ultimately to involvement with the kidnapping and murder of Adam Walsh. Flap, flap, flap.

HOLLYWOOD, FLORIDA—AUGUST 16, 1994

Despite his "reservations" about the motives of Joe Matthews, Detective Smith proceeded with his work on the Adam Walsh case, albeit at a deliberate pace. He met with Harry O'Reilly, the retired NYPD homicide detective who had put the department back in touch with Matthews, and Smith and O'Reilly traveled to the spot off Florida's Turnpike where Toole originally said he'd disposed of Adam's head and body, to determine whether or not O'Reilly thought it might be worth conducting a second concerted search for remains. O'Reilly doubted that there was anything to be accomplished by such an undertaking, but he did return from the trip with a real concern: he called Joe Matthews to tell him about the foray, wondering why Smith had not asked Matthews to join them, a point at which Matthews realized that whatever might eventuate from his collaboration with Smith, the two were certainly not functioning as true partners.

Not until the following January did Smith take his next significant step, telephoning John Walsh to seek approval to get a DNA baseline sample using Adam's mandible as a source. A few days later, Smith wrote a memo to his superiors indicating that it had been suggested that he send hair samples from the victim, along with the bloody machete and bloodstained sheath and a sample of the carpet taken from the Cadillac, for DNA comparison testing.

Smith then called the FDLE, looking for the carpet samples that they had tested a dozen years before. But those had been sent back to the Jacksonville Sheriff's Office long ago, Smith was told, and accordingly, on January 17, 1995, he drove to Jacksonville to search the sheriff's evidence room for the carpet samples and try and discover the whereabouts of the vehicle itself.

What he discovered was disheartening, to say the least. Records showed that the Cadillac's floorboard carpets and the seven squares tested for blood had been received by the sheriff's property room on May 24, 1984, signed for with the initial "J." Whether the J stood for Jack Hoffman or Jacksonville, no one could say. Whatever had happened to the carpet samples once they arrived at the Jacksonville Sheriff's Office, only one thing was certain: eleven years later, they were nowhere to be found.

As for the car itself, Smith learned, it was sold to a dealer at auction, purchased by a man from St. Augustine, then—when it finally stopped running a half-dozen years or more before—towed to a junkyard and scrapped. Smith, distressed at such sloppy handling of key evidence in the case, filed a complaint with the FDLE, but it went nowhere.

As for the machete and its sheath, those items remained in the possession of the Hollywood PD, and Smith forwarded them for testing. Once again, the results were not what he or Matthews hoped for. Though testing on those items performed by FDLE serologist James Pollack in 1983 had confirmed the presence of small amounts of blood, the laboratory to which they were sent for DNA testing in 1995 could find no blood anywhere. "As a result of that, no additional comparisons were made," the technician advised.

While that scarcely qualified as good news, Matthews moved forward. Following ten months of effort, he was finally able to arrange an interview with Ottis Toole, scheduled for June 20, 1995. Though by this time Toole had adopted a newly stated policy that he would not grant any interviews to law enforcement officials investigating specific homicides, Matthews was able to convince him to make something of an exception.

Matthews had arranged for Toole's prison counselor to identify him in his role as a clinical research associate from Nova Southeastern University and a police detective from Miami Beach, not Hollywood, all of which was true. Toole was told that he was simply one of many convicted murderers to be interviewed by Matthews, who was conducting a study of the phenomenon of serial killing. After some consideration, Toole agreed to talk, and the interview was set to be conducted in the prison library without the use of handcuffs or restraints, so that it might seem more like a bit of academic inquiry than an interrogation.

Though it had taken some time, Matthews was champing at the bit. After years of frustration, he would finally have the chance to fix the lens of reason upon the only viable suspect in the murder of Adam Walsh.

On Father's Day, Sunday, June 18, two days before the interview was scheduled, Matthews called Detective Smith to make sure all was in order for the trip to Starke. There was an awkward pause when Smith realized who was on the other end of the line.

"Hasn't anyone called you?" he asked Matthews.

"About what?" Matthews asked, wary.

"Well . . . ," Smith fumbled, "actually Chief Witt wants me to take this juvenile division detective Navarro along to conduct the interview instead of you."

To Matthews, it seemed as if he were reliving a familiar nightmare. "You can't be serious," he told Smith.

"Look, Joe," said Smith. "I'm sorry. This was not my call. I hope you know that."

Matthews knew nothing, really, except that it had to be some giant mistake. Chief Witt had gone to Matthews's own superiors to negotiate an interagency agreement. Hollywood PD had come to *him*, not the other way around.

Since it was Sunday, however, there was no way to contact

Witt, and Matthews could only stew until Monday morning, when he called the chief, hoping to clear up the misunderstanding. When the two finally spoke, Witt quickly explained that there was nothing to explain. He thanked Sergeant Matthews for all his help and was grateful to Miami Beach PD for making him available, but, said Witt, for reasons having to do with any possible future court proceedings, he wanted Toole's confession obtained by his own personnel.

Matthews could not believe what he was hearing. So now Hollywood PD believed that Toole was guilty, but they wanted to make sure they got all the credit for making the case? He reminded Chief Witt that he had asked for Matthews's assistance, and that Matthews had been working alongside Detective Smith for more than a year, preparing for the opportunity to interview Toole at last.

How about this? Matthews suggested. I'll conduct the interview, and even if we get a confession out of Toole, you won't have to include me in the report. Just use the names of your guys, Smith and Navarro. Whoever you want.

Witt allowed that Matthews was being very generous, but he had made his decision. His own men would conduct the interview with Toole, and that was the long and short of it.

By this time Matthews was ready to lose it. "Just tell me the truth, Dick. What the fuck is really going on over there?" he blurted.

There was a moment of silence on the other end. And then Witt hung up.

Matthews sat back in his chair, literally sick at what had transpired. He'd been jerked around before, plenty of times, but never like this. A long time ago he'd become resigned to the fact that Jack Hoffman wanted no part of his involvement in the investigation, but he could chalk that up to one individual's insecurities, no matter how frustrating and tragic the consequences. But now the chief of the department was chasing Matthews off the case. And for what earthly reason?

Was it because they really thought Toole was guilty and wanted all the credit for themselves? Or was there a darker explanation? he wondered. Could it possibly be that the last thing Hollywood PD wanted was to find that Ottis Toole had been guilty all along?

Hey, the kid's been dead fifteen years, his old man's a celebrity now, the guy who claims he did it is locked up for life—why try to fix what isn't really broken and make yourself look bad in the process? Matthews shook his head at the very thought.

Matthews would never be able to answer his questions with certainty, but certain things that happened in the lee of his dismissal from the case for a third time have their implications. Late in the afternoon of the same day he spoke with Chief Witt, Matthews returned to the offices of the homicide unit, intending to pick up where he'd left off the day before on a troubling matter that had nothing to do with the Adam Walsh case.

A female police officer had filed a lawsuit against the police department for allowing a hostile work environment and, as a result of that lawsuit, had been transferred from uniform patrol to the detective bureau. Soon after her arrival, she'd complained that her new fellow officers were playing demeaning pranks and tampering with the personal effects on her desk while she was out of the office, spilling coffee on her favorite pink desk pads, placing her animal statuettes in coital positions, and the like. To Matthews, it seemed pretty trivial stuff on both sides, and he scarcely paid any attention to it.

But then, after being called in to investigate a homicide during the early-morning hours on Sunday, Matthews had returned to his office and was leaning back in his chair, trying to clarify what needed to be done regarding the crime scene he'd just left. It was then that he noticed something odd about one of the ceiling panels next to the air-conditioning vent directly overhead. He asked one of his junior detectives to place a chair on his desk and check it out.

The kid, who'd worked for the CIA out of college, took a look behind the A/C grate, and told Matthews he'd found a video surveillance camera there, trained on the complaining officer's desk but encompassing the entire room.

Matthews notified his immediate supervisor and called in the department's crime techs to remove and process the camera. Though he could not be certain, the fact that the camera bore the logo of a private security firm suggested that the transferred female officer had taken it upon herself to try and collect evidence against those moving her statues around and writing derisive notes on her desk blotter.

Whoever was responsible for hiding this camera, though, and whatever the reason, Matthews wanted the matter settled. They were a crimes-against-persons squad, with all sorts of sensitive information being discussed in that room. You couldn't have someone recording what went on there, willy-nilly, no matter how many times you found your turtle statuettes humping each other.

At least getting to the bottom of who had put that camera up there would take his mind off the fiasco with the aborted Ottis Toole interview, he thought. But such thoughts didn't last long.

He hadn't even sat down in his chair that Monday afternoon when he noticed a memo placed prominently on his desk. Something to do with the camera investigation already? he wondered. He picked up the sheet and began to read it, disbelief filling him as he digested the words. It was a notice from Patricia Schneider, the major in charge of the detective bureau. Effective immediately, a few months shy of his retirement date after twenty-nine years with the department, Matthews was being transferred back to uniform patrol duty.

Matthews couldn't believe his eyes. When he went into the office of his commanding officer for an explanation, she shrugged. It was within her power to transfer at will—she didn't have to explain anything to him.

But no one got transferred without cause, Matthews protested, the sick feeling in his stomach now an icy cannonball. Only if you screwed up big-time. Or couldn't get along with your superiors. It was the unwritten rule within any department. What was going on here? Everyone knew Matthews was the go-to investigator in the department, and he was the supervisor of the crimes against persons unit. And he got along fine with those above and below him. She knew that.

The major shrugged. She wasn't so sure. She had heard he couldn't get along very well with Dick Witt over at Hollywood PD.

Matthews was stunned. Less than six hours since he'd spoken with Witt, and already he was being torpedoed? He left the major's office without another word and made his way to the office of the chief. Matthews had known Richard Barretto for a long time, and while they weren't necessarily pals, they got along just fine. Matthews showed Barretto the memo from his supervisor, and Barretto handed it back to him.

"So?" he asked Matthews.

"So?" Matthews repeated. "What the hell is going on here? Is Dick Witt the chief of this department, or are you? I just talked with the major. She let the cat out of the bag. I give Dick Witt a little grief, and suddenly I'm being transferred back into uniform?"

Barretto stared evenly back at Matthews. "Dick Witt doesn't have anything to do with your transfer. You interfered with a sexual harassment investigation being conducted by our internal affairs division. That's why you're being transferred."

Matthews shook his head in puzzlement. "What the hell are you talking about?"

"That camera you had removed from the office was placed there by IA."

Matthews was dumbfounded by Barretto's revelation. "It was a departmental surveillance camera? You mean internal affairs took all that turtle statue shit seriously? That's still no reason for me to be transferred."

Barretto folded his hands and leaned across his desk. "I'm the *acting* chief," he told Matthews. "And I would like to become *the* chief. The major wants you transferred, and I can't undermine my command staff by issuing counterorders. It's as simple as that."

Matthews started to protest yet again, but what was the point? He'd simply done what any other detective who'd found a spy camera in his office would have done. All that was just a smoke screen.

He stood up and walked out of Barretto's office while the acting chief was prattling on, reminding him that he had just a few months left to retirement, and that he probably had that much leave time accrued. Matthews could in effect retire right now, no worries about uniform duty . . .

Sure, Matthews was thinking. But all he could think about was what had happened to Buddy Terry in Jacksonville. Terry was a well-respected, hardworking detective who had gotten crosswise with Hollywood PD trying to make headway on the Adam Walsh case, and look what had happened to him. Now— and Matthews was certain of it—he had made the same mistake.

When he came home that evening, Ginny met him at the door excited, waving a sheaf of photos. Joe had missed the opening of Cristina's dance recital the day before because he'd been held up at work, but that was no problem—she had these great pictures of their daughter coming out on stage. When she suddenly saw the expression on Joe's face, she stopped.

She took a closer look at what was in the box. Pictures from his office—a dozen years of the kids growing up—one of his father, who'd been so proud of his detective son, and framed commendations. When she heard Joe's account, she was stunned. That's the thanks he got for caring about a case an entire police department had botched? Finally, she took a deep breath and said, "Joe, things happen for a reason. Your family loves you. I love you. It's going to be fine."

When his brother Pete, also a Miami Beach detective sergeant and supervisor of the department's crimes against property unit, heard what had happened, he demanded a transfer back to uniform patrol as well. "You don't need to do that," Matthews protested to his brother, but Pete was having none of it. It was all bullshit, and everyone knew it.

Sure enough, when Matthews turned up at roll call on his first day back in uniform, the entire shift stood to give him a lengthy ovation. They all knew it wasn't much, but it was the very least they could do.

RAIFORD, FLORIDA—JUNE 27, 1995

On Tuesday of the following week, Detective Smith did in fact travel to Raiford, Florida, with Detective Navarro, where they sought to interview Ottis Toole at the Union Correctional Institution. "Toole had no initial response to the introduction," wrote Smith in his report, "until he was informed of the purpose of the interview." Once he realized that the two were there to question him in regard to his involvement in the abduction and murder of Adam Walsh, Toole became "disturbed," Smith said, "and stated that he had no involvement in this case or any other cases, including the ones of which he was convicted."

Adam Walsh's twenty-first birthday passed later that year, and then, less than a month later, on Tuesday, December 5, convicted serial killer Gerald Schaffer, former cellmate and erstwhile legal adviser of Ottis Toole, was found dead in his cell at Starke, stabbed several times in the eye, his throat slit. In an interview with the *Palm Beach Post*, Schaffer's mother and sister said to reporters that he had told them that he was about to cooperate with detectives on the Adam Walsh case. He had agreed to testify in an upcoming proceeding, he confided to them, and explained that he hoped to gain early parole as a result. That explained why he'd been killed, the women told reporters.

If the bits and pieces of the case against Ottis Toole already seemed to be dissolving, what happened in early 1996 appeared to be the death knell for the matter altogether. In early May 1995, the *Mobile Press-Register* had filed a request under the Freedom of Information Act, asking that the contents of the Hollywood Police Department file on Adam Walsh be made public.

As often happens in any missing child case, there had always been a certain amount of innuendo involving the parents. There was the scandal involving Revé's short-lived affair with Jimmy Campbell, and the bizarre suggestion made by Hoffman's partner Hickman that God would bring Adam back if Walsh would only repent for his misdeeds.

Also, as armchair theorists warmed to their work over the long history of the failed investigation, the notion was kicked around that John Walsh had become involved with the mob as a result of his work with an international hotel chain. He'd either screwed up some drug deal—or, more charitably, refused to partake in one—and the killing of Adam was payback.

The real reason that the case had failed to progress, such thinking went, was that Walsh had himself obstructed the investigation and pressured the Hollywood police to drag their feet. Conspiracy theorists everywhere were licking their chops at having the case files laid bare—all the dirt could finally be revealed. And what ace reporter would not dream of being the hero who finally revealed what police couldn't or wouldn't prove in this case of cases? In any event, and whatever they hoped to discover as a result, three other newspapers—the *Fort Lauderdale Sun-Sentinel*, the *Palm Beach Post*, and the *Miami Herald*—joined the *Mobile Press-Register* in its suit.

Walsh was dismayed at the prospect, for he knew what opening police files would mean to any serious ongoing investigation. Accordingly, he went directly to Chief Witt to press for assurances that the department would fight the request. Meantime, Walsh suggested, during a May 15 meeting at which Joe Matthews and Mark Smith were present, that perhaps Witt could issue a statement that suggested how ridiculous the rumors were that tied him to the Mafia. Witt seemed a bit befuddled at the request, however. As Joe Matthews and Walsh stared expectantly at Witt, the chief answered by saying that in his opinion anyone who frequented a certain well-known Fort Lauderdale restaurant for lunch—as Walsh did—"must have something to do with the Mafia."

"With friends like Dick Witt," Matthews told Walsh on the way out the door, "you don't need any enemies."

And then in December, the Walshes received more disturbing news from Hollywood police, when Mark Smith called to check on something. John Walsh listened patiently to a rambling preamble before finally asking the detective to get to the point.

"Well," Smith said, "they did show you these green shorts and that sandal they found back in 1984, didn't they?"

Walsh assured Smith that he had no idea what he was talking about, and Smith finally explained. An FDLE team had dug up the items on Ottis Toole's property in Jacksonville, Smith told him. The shorts and a child's yellow flip-flop had been sent to Hollywood PD, where they'd been in the evidence room ever since.

Walsh, as might be expected, went ballistic at the news. The "Missing" posters that were issued in the wake of Adam's disappearance had described him as wearing green shorts and yellow flip-flops. Now Smith was saying that the detective in charge of the case had discovered such items on the property of the only serious suspect who had ever been identified and had not called him in to see if they belonged to Adam? How could such behavior be explained?

Smith, obviously, could not explain it, but he did arrange a meeting at which the Walshes could view the items. It took nearly a month, but finally, on January 16, 1996, John and Revé

Walsh met with Detective Smith and Chief Witt in a conference room at Hollywood PD. Chief Witt began the meeting
with a long-winded preamble in which he proclaimed the untir-
ing efforts of his department to solve the case. No effort had
been spared, the chief said, no tip had been ignored. Finally, he
paused, holding up a large evidence envelope, and gave Revé a
glance meant to be solicitous.

"Would you and John like to take a minute?" he asked.

Revé stared back, doubfounded. *Good lord*, she thought—
they'd already been kept waiting for fifteen years.

"Just show us what you've got," John said.

Witt seemed taken aback by Walsh's tone, but he broke off to
open up the envelope with a flourish. Revé took one look at the
muddy shorts and the tiny shoe that was barely bigger than one
an infant might wear and shook her head quickly. No way had
these items come from Adam. "They're not his," she told John.

The collective disappointment in the room was palpable.
Once again, it seemed, Ottis Toole had slipped from a snare.

Despite the letdown, Detective Smith did his best to put
a positive spin on matters for the Walshes. He and Sergeant
Matthews had made very real progress on the cold case investigation, he insisted. He mentioned the fact that Sears security
guard Kathy Shaffer had finally admitted sending Adam outside the store through the door where Toole claimed he'd picked
the child up. And he also pointed to the significance of the fact
that when Toole made his first confession, no news report had
mentioned the site near mile marker 126 where Toole later took
detectives. As further corroboration that he knew details that
had never been reported in the press, Toole had spoken several times of driving no more than ten minutes farther north
on the turnpike before disposing of the head in the canal. As
Smith pointed out, the spot where fishermen had discovered the
remains was four miles north, at mile marker 130—ten minutes
was just how long it would take to turn around on that deserted

service road, make your way back to the turnpike, and drive to the spot where Adam's head had been found.

Smith then turned his attention to Witt. All these details that Toole had dropped into his multiple confessions were unknown to anyone outside the circle of law enforcement. If they were divulged publicly, however, that evidence would become readily available to any deranged soul who wanted to claim responsibility for the crime. Anyone could say, "Actually it was me who pulled off there at mile marker 130 and tossed that head in the canal." Surely, Smith said, Witt understood the importance of standing up against the request to open the files.

Witt nodded, tenting his fingers thoughtfully. "I suppose you could look it that way," he said, "but I think it is just as likely that opening up the case files would put pressure on Toole to break down and confess."

Though no one in the room had the temerity to point out that Toole had already broken down and confessed on several occasions, one thing seemed clear: even though no ruling on the matter had been issued, Witt had already decided to release the files. As the meeting was winding down, in fact, Witt made the offhanded remark that he already had aides working to transfer the materials onto microfilm, all ten thousand pages of it.

In the aftermath of this disclosure, an angry Walsh went immediately to Michael Satz, head of the Broward County State Attorney's Office, to plead that Satz intervene. If the state attorney announced imminent plans to bring a suspect to trial, then it would be a good bet no judge would allow potential evidence to be revealed in public. Walsh begged Satz to review the case file, and asked for an explanation why no one in all this time had been willing to prosecute a case against Ottis Toole.

What Satz had to say in response floored Walsh. There was a simple reason why the case had not gone forward, Satz said. Since the day in 1983 when Chief Martin of the Hollywood Police Department had announced that Ottis Toole was their prime suspect in the case, not a shred of evidence had been presented to Satz's office. In fact, the HPD hadn't shared its full case file on the investigation until just five days ago, Satz said.

Walsh shook his head in disbelief. And what did Satz think about the extortion letter in that file—the one that Toole had sent to him, offering to lead Walsh to where Adam's body had been buried for $50,000? Satz had no idea what Walsh was referring to—there was no such letter in the file that had recently been presented to him.

When Walsh showed Satz the letter that described his son as crying for his mother as Toole had sodomized him, the state attorney was stunned. He set the letter aside and stood to apologize to Walsh. Of course his office had been insistent that Hoffman and his team present evidence linking Toole to the crime back in the 1980s, but what he had just read was all a competent attorney needed, Satz said.

"I could get a jury conviction on the strength of this letter alone," he told Walsh.

Furthermore, he said, his office *would* intervene immediately to prevent the opening of the case files to the media on the grounds that a prosecution against Ottis Toole was now imminent, and that opening the evidence to the public would compromise the prosecution's ability to prove its case against Toole.

On February 16, 1996, a hearing was set on the matter, with Revé Walsh present to add a personal plea. But Judge Moe would not allow her to speak—he wanted no appeals to emotion in his court, he explained. And then, after listening to brief presentations by both sides, he issued his order. The case file would be released.

With every detail known to investigators—including all crime scene photos—now a part of the public record, the possibility of ever corroborating any future confession against matters known only to police ended.

Yet, whatever hopes the media might have had as to their

own analysis of the case files, they came to very little. There was no "hidden" evidence concerning John Walsh's ties to the Mafia, nor was there any suggestion that he had meddled with the investigation of the Hollywood police in any way, though the spectacular lack of progress might well have warranted it.

There was a brief flurry of indignation when reporters realized that key evidence—the bloody carpet samples taken from Toole's Cadillac, as well as the car itself—had been lost. As to that matter, the Jacksonville Sheriff's Office was quick to deflect responsibility onto the Hollywood PD. No evidentiary hold had been placed upon the car by the principal investigators, the sheriff's office said, so they were only following proper procedure in returning the car to its owner, Wells Brothers Used Cars. As far as the carpet samples were concerned, the sheriff admitted having destroyed them, but again, that was normal procedure for dealing with what were reclassified as "non-evidentiary materials"—since the original testing was inconclusive, no one had seen any point in keeping them. As to what had become of the sections of the floor carpets that had not been tested, no one could be sure . . . perhaps only the mysterious "J" who signed for them could say.

Whatever the validity of the various claims and counterclaims of the agencies involved, anyone who read the various accounts published in the wake of the release of the case files could be forgiven for assuming that the matter was finished. Propriety and impropriety of procedures aside, it simply looked as if police would never find out who had kidnapped and murdered Adam Walsh.

And yet, even with Hollywood PD apparently at a standstill and Joe Matthews retired from Miami Beach PD, there was still desultory work on the case. In September, investigator Philip Mundy of the Broward County State Attorney's Office took the sworn statement of Bobby Lee Jones, a former cellmate of Toole's in the Duval County Jail, who claimed to have worked with Ottis Toole at Reaves Roofing in 1982. In late July of that year, Jones said, Toole began to talk to him about various crimes he had committed, including the killing of a little boy. Jones recalled Toole telling him he'd lured the child into his car, and had intended to take him home and "be his father." But it had not worked out, Jones said. Toole told him he'd cut the boy's head off and tossed it into a creek, then cut up the body and burned it.

Jones's statement might have had greater impact were it not for the inconsistency suggested by the dates he gave Mundy. Company records indicate that the last day of Toole's employment at Reaves Roofing was June 4, 1981, several weeks before the killing. Furthermore, he drew only one day's pay from Southeast Color Coat in December.

Of course, fourteen or fifteen years had passed, and Jones might have been mistaken about exactly when he'd heard all this from Toole. The conversation could have taken place when they were incarcerated together in 1983. And there was no doubt that many details of Toole's confession had been recounted by the media when the case files had been opened earlier that year. Still, if Jones was being truthful—if he'd heard about it from Toole at work in December 1982, or simply as they chatted on the streets or in a bar—it would mean that Toole had begun talking to others about killing Adam Walsh long before he first admitted it to police in 1983.

Meanwhile, John Walsh had decided to take matters into his own hands, even if it was a stinging blow that led him to do so. In May 1996, as he was on his way to a Washington, D.C., gathering of missing children who had been reunited with their families as a result of *America's Most Wanted*, Walsh received an unexpected call on his car phone. He didn't have to bother coming to New York next week to talk about next year's episodes, a spokesman explained. After eight years, the Fox network had abruptly decided to cancel the show. He'd be kept on contract as a consultant and producer, but the decision was final: *America's Most Wanted* was finished.

Though stunned at the news, Walsh had little choice in the matter. And after it had finally sunk in, he realized that the appropriate way to close the program was with an episode on the one case they had never featured: that of Adam Walsh.

The program, which ran on September 21, 1996, was put together by John Turchin, a reporter for WSVN, Channel 7, the Fox affiliate in Miami, and was based on information and tips gathered by Joe Matthews and Mark Smith, the detective with whom Matthews had worked the cold case investigation at Hollywood PD. Turchin interviewed Sears security guard Kathy Shaffer, who spoke candidly for the first time about her role in the incident back in 1981. She'd just started the job, she told Turchin, and when she realized that big trouble had indeed unfolded on that day, she was overwhelmed. While she had said otherwise, shortly after Revé Walsh showed her the pictures of her son she realized that Adam had in fact been in the store that day. It was also true that she had made him leave, along with all the other kids who were causing a fuss at the video game display. But she hadn't wanted to admit it—after all, if she hadn't sent him outside, he might still be alive.

Turchin also brought up the fact that the cops had recovered the car that was thought to have been used to abduct Adam, but sadly, it had been scrapped. And he pointed out that the cops had seized bloodstained carpeting from that car, as well—also lost, unfortunately.

Turchin also interviewed William Mistler, who recounted testimony that he had provided to the Hollywood police five years previously: he had seen a scruffy-looking man leading a little boy to a white Cadillac parked outside a Sears store on July 27, 1981. Mistler identified the boy as Adam Walsh, and the man who'd kidnapped him as Ottis Toole. The program concluded with some footage the Walshes had stumbled across by accident a few weeks before: six-year-old Adam Walsh in his baseball uniform, full of life, mugging at the camera, swinging his bat, getting a hit, rounding the bases. The stuff of which heartbreak is made.

Shortly after the show aired, Walsh received a call from Peter Roth, president of the Fox Entertainment Group. Hundreds of thousands of letters had been pouring in. Fifty-five members of Congress had complained, as had thirty-seven governors and every attorney general in the fifty states. The FBI had written as well. The network had reconsidered, Roth told Walsh. *America's Most Wanted*—the show that had resulted in the capture of some four hundred fugitives, including eleven on the FBI's "Most Wanted" list, the show that had recovered twenty missing children and led to the apprehension of scores of child molesters—was going to remain on the air.

WASHINGTON, D.C.—SEPTEMBER 23, 1996

John Walsh was heartened by the news from Fox, and he was proud of the way the program on Adam had turned out. How could anyone who had seen it doubt what had really happened? he thought. He and Revé had not yet found closure in a court of law, perhaps, but this was damned close. And as for bringing Ottis Toole to justice, he had plans for that as well.

He'd received word from sources that Ottis Toole had been diagnosed with hepatitis and AIDS by prison doctors at Lake Butler. Toole knew he was dying, Walsh was told, and it was suggested that the convict might be willing to talk to the right person. Walsh, who knew of the calamitous outcome of Mark Smith's visit to Toole the previous year, thought he had the "right person" for the task in the person of Joe Matthews, who had retired from Miami Beach PD in the spring and had volunteered to help Walsh on the case in any way he possibly could.

And by this point, Walsh had formed a substantial network

of friends in law enforcement, including the FBI and the FDLE. He was going to stop mincing around and use some of his influence to get Joe Matthews in to talk with Ottis Toole, once and for all. If Matthews could get a deathbed confession out of Toole, then he and Revé could rest with that, Walsh thought. Certainly, the prospect was worth using every favor he might call in.

Word that *America's Most Wanted* would live on was not the only news that arrived in the wake of the September 21 program featuring Adam's case. A number of tips were phoned in that suggested that Walsh and Joe Matthews were right about the killer's identity.

While Matthews followed up most of the leads at Walsh's request, one tip bypassed *AMW* entirely and went straight to the Hollywood PD: the caller's name was Mary Hagan, she told police, and though she now resided in a retirement community in upstate Florida, she had been living in Hollywood not far from the Walshes at the time of Adam's murder. She had seen things inside the Sears store that day he disappeared, she explained, and hadn't realized until she'd seen that TV segment on Adam that police still hadn't caught the killer. Perhaps what she had to tell them would help.

Phil Mundy, the investigator for the Broward County State Attorney's Office, followed up with Hagan, seventy-six at the time. She told him that on the morning of July 27, 1981, she had noticed an ad for a lamp sale at Sears, and decided to go have a look. She entered the store through the garden department entrance and passed the video game display, where several kids were gathered, including Adam, whom she recognized from the neighborhood. Also standing there talking with the boys, said Hagan, was a "rancid-smelling" man who seemed out of place to her. He was filthy, and she could smell him—"overpowering, like beer and onions"—from several feet away.

The guy had to step out of her way so she could get past,

Hagan said, and when he did, he smiled at her, a goofy-looking expression that exposed a big gap in his front teeth. She hurried on past, she said, and checked out the lamp section, where she couldn't find anything she liked. There wasn't a clerk around—only one customer, an attractive younger woman who seemed to be waiting on something—so Hagan decided to leave. As she passed the video display on the way out, she noted that it was deserted.

She explained to Mundy that she had thought about coming forward when she later learned what had happened to Adam, but wasn't sure what good it would do. By that time, there was all that news about people who'd seen Adam being dragged into a "blue van," so what she had seen didn't seem all that important. "Leave it alone," her husband Lou told her. "Let the police do their job."

And she assumed that is just what happened, she told Mundy, until she watched the episode of *America's Most Wanted* and saw the picture of Ottis Toole displayed on-screen. Oh my God, she thought, You mean he's still alive—they never got him?

To Mundy, Hagan's story was provocative. True, she might have pieced together much of what she'd told him from various reports. But there was one thing that had never been included in any account of Toole's involvement with the crime, and that was his terrible, overpowering body odor. No one who had ever been in Toole's presence for a moment failed to mention just how bad the guy smelled—as if there was something rotting inside him, bursting to get out.

Another particularly provocative call came directly to the *AMW* hotline, from a young woman named Sarah Patterson, the individual listed as "next of kin" on prison records. Patterson was the recipient of Toole's few personal effects: his prison-issued Bible, some letters, and a few photographs.

In years past, she'd also received a lot more from Toole,

though most of it was an unwelcome legacy. As she explained to Joe Matthews, she was Ottis Toole's niece, the older sister of Frieda "Becky" Powell, who had been murdered by Henry Lee Lucas.

After her mother's death, she had been raised by her grandmother and by Ottis Toole, if "raising" was what you could call it. Uncle Ottis, as Sarah called him, favored her younger sister, treating Becky like a daughter and Sarah "more like a friend," though a curious friendship it seemed.

He taught her to drink and smoke dope and they partied hard together. "By the time I was ten, I was a whore," Sarah told Matthews, "and I still am a whore. Back then, Uncle Ottis would turn me out to his friends for $10. He'd watch me fuck them and give them head and beat off while I was doing it."

She never had sex with Ottis, however, because he was as queer as anyone could be, she explained. He shaved his legs, wore stockings, panties, and a bra. He dressed in drag, got shots "for boobs," Sarah said, and wore a wig. That was the way he liked to dress "when he hustled other fags," she said.

He could get mad, Sarah recalled, but he had a good side, too. Even if he only had enough money for one six-pack, he was always willing to share it. And when she got married at age seventeen, Ottis came to the wedding dressed as her bridesmaid.

As to the matter of Adam Walsh, Sarah had some pertinent information for Matthews. Some time around Christmas in 1995, she heard that Ottis was pretty sick and went to see him in prison. During that visit, she said, she asked him directly, "Uncle Ottis, are you the one that killed Adam Walsh?"

"Yeah," he told Sarah. "I killed the little boy. And I always felt kinda bad about it, too." As to why he hadn't confessed to authorities, he told her that he had talked enough about the murder of Adam Walsh and he just didn't want to talk about it anymore.

When Matthews asked Sarah if she believed it, Sarah gave a

bitter laugh. She had no doubt about it. "I know my uncle too well," she said.

The *AMW* segment also resulted in a call from a young South Florida man named Joel Cockerman. Cockerman explained that until he had seen the show, he did not realize it—but he was calling now to report that he had actually witnessed the kidnapping of Adam Walsh.

As he later explained to Joe Matthews, Cockerman, eight at the time, was in the Sears store and was the other boy playing Asteroids with Adam Walsh when the trouble started with the kids who wanted to take the controllers away. When the security guard heard the commotion, she kicked them all out of the store, Cockerman said. Shortly after they made their way outside, Cockerman's mother came and picked up him and his sister, Mia, nine at the time. Cockerman told his mother that he wanted to stay with his little friend until his parents came for him. In all likelihood, it is Cockerman and his mother and sister whom Bill Mistler had witnessed standing on the sidewalk when he viewed the same scene from his vehicle.

But his mother said it wasn't necessary for them to wait. "Look," she told Cockerman, "his dad is there now." She pointed to where a disheveled-looking man was leading Adam from the curb and into the parking lot. When they saw the photograph of Ottis Toole flash on the screen, during the *AMW* segment, Cockerman's sister clapped her hand to her mouth. "That's him," she told Cockerman. "He had more hair then, but that's him."

Neither Cockerman nor his sister had reported the incident before. They simply did not realize the importance of what they had witnessed until the program aired.

All of this seemed to Walsh and Matthews like fuel that might possibly reignite the investigation, until *AMW* producers fielded yet another call on the Monday following the segment. Just how stupid were they? a caller wanted to know. When asked what he was talking about, the caller passed along what no one at *AMW* had realized until that moment. "Ottis Toole is dead and already in the ground at Raiford Prison, down there in Florida."

As it happened, Barry Gemelli, the health services administrator at the Union Correctional Institution, had been in his office at the prison infirmary one day the previous week, completing the paperwork necessary for the transfer of patient Ottis Toole to the nearby hospital unit at Lake Butler, when he got a summons from an aide. Ottis Toole had taken a sudden turn for the worse. The aide thought Gemelli ought to have a look.

Gemelli hurried to find Toole raving in his bed, begging God to forgive the many bad things he had done in his life. Gemelli had witnessed such scenes before—he knew there were no atheists in foxholes, and it was his experience that even the most hardened of criminals find salvation as the end approaches. But Toole caught Gemelli's attention when he began to tell God about the worst thing he'd ever done. He had killed that little boy named Adam Walsh down in Broward County, Toole said, and he was very, very sorry that he did it.

After Toole had been stabilized and was transferred to the hospital unit, Gemelli notified the prison's investigative unit of what he heard Toole say about killing Adam Walsh, and a report of the matter was entered into prison files. Though Joe Matthews had urged Mark Smith to make his own foray to Lake Butler in the hopes of obtaining a deathbed confession, Smith never followed through. As far as deathbed confessions, what Gemelli heard that day would have to suffice.

On September 15, 1996, Ottis Ellwood Toole, a three-times convicted killer, died of cirrhosis of the liver at the age of forty-nine, in Lake Butler Prison Hospital. His body was unclaimed, and four days later—unbeknownst to John and Revé Walsh, Joe

Matthews, or anyone at *America's Most Wanted*—Toole was buried, in a cloth-covered casket, on prison grounds.

John Walsh was stunned by the news. Over the years, one piece of evidence after another that might have helped link Toole to the crime had somehow disappeared, and now even the perpetrator himself was no more. Some might have theorized that Toole's death would have marked the end of the matter once and for all. The guy who did it is dead. What's left?

Justice, John and Revé Walsh might have answered. And the right of any victim for the chance to know what had happened. An end to the feeling of helplessness. An end to the rage over the actions of a police force that had bungled this investigation from the beginning and now seemed intent on forgetting that the murder of Adam Walsh had ever happened.

Furthermore, the Walshes had spent fifteen years dedicating their lives to the cause of victimized children and their parents everywhere. To simply throw up their hands in the pursuit of justice for their own child's death would make a mockery of everything they'd been fighting for.

In this light, and though it might seem strange to say so, his own death might be the most provocative action a killer could take to elude responsibility for his crime. One can imagine Toole leering from his grave, "You'll never catch me now."

And were those who had pursued him for so many years any less driven, that imagined taunt might have proven true.

Even though the man himself had died, the evil that he had wrought had a way of living on. Not quite a week after Toole was buried, on September 25, 1996, an Associated Press reporter published an interview with Henry Lee Lucas in which Lucas told the writer that he was certain that Toole was responsible for the killing—he had seen blood all over the car after Toole used it. Lucas also said that a couple of months after Adam's death, he and Toole were back in South Florida one day when Ottis decided to drive him over to the Sears Mall and show him where he had picked "that kid" up. At that time, Lucas said, Toole took him through a step-by-step re-creation of the abduction and the killing.

From his cell in Texas, Lucas told a reporter that he had actually seen Adam's body in the shallow grave where Toole had buried it. "He kicked it uncovered and showed it to me," Lucas said. "I got sick about it. I said, 'Let's get the hell out of here.' I left. I never heard no more about it until '83."

That interview, startling as it was, prompted no action from law enforcement despite what seemed a compelling offer from Lucas. "If they want to talk to me and take me down there, I'll show them where it's at," he said. He described the burial site as being located in an isolated area off a freeway. "We got to an old foundation in there, either a barn or a house. There was nothing there, just a foundation. There was an old oak tree or pine tree and that's where the body was at."

At the time, Hollywood spokesperson Todd DeAngelis told reporters, "None of it is news to us," but there is no mention of Lucas's claims anywhere in the case file. Furthermore, it would mark the last significant public mention of the case for a very long time.

In fact, were it not for the simple axiom that the truth has a way of making itself known when someone wants to find it badly enough, the case of Adam Walsh—its files laid bare for anyone to see, the only suspect of substance to have surfaced in fifteen years now dead—might have also been laid to rest forever.

CHAPTER SIX

Thunder from Heaven

Q: So you admit that you're a cannibal?

A: I have eaten some parts of them. And the skin.

Q: Did you eat them raw?

A: Oh no. You can't eat that without cooking it. Are you crazy?

—OTTIS TOOLE, WITH TEXAS RANGERS,
MARCH 24, 1984

HOLLYWOOD, FLORIDA—OCTOBER 1, 1996

In early 1996, following an acrimonious investigation into irregularities in the department's hiring practices, Hollywood police chief Richard Witt was fired by city manager Sam Finz. "Just say I'm leaving due to health reasons," was Witt's parting shot. "The city manager is sick of me."

Finz appointed deputy chief Mike Ignasiak as interim chief while a national search was conducted for a permanent replacement for Witt. On October 1, the city hired Rick Stone, a veteran cop from Dallas who had recently retired as a chief with the Wichita, Kansas, PD.

Soon after Stone came on board, in early February 1997, former chief Sam Martin died of a heart attack, and in the story that accompanied that news was a reminder of how profound the impact of one case had been: "Although his 11-year tenure as chief was marked by rapid modernization and a raising of educational standards on the force," the *Herald* reporter noted, "it was marred by a still-unsolved crime that shocked and horrified the nation: the kidnapping and murder of Adam Walsh."

Nor was Chief Stone immune from reminders that his department had failed in the matter. In September 1997, stung by charges of "laziness, stupidity and arrogance" against his department made by John Walsh in his own recently published chronicle of the case, *Tears of Rage*, Stone told reporters, "I'd like to go back and start from scratch, but none of us can do that." While he would not acknowledge that the department had made mistakes in the investigation of the case, he did assert that with contemporary technology and the "professional team I have today, it's possible things could have turned out much differently."

Stone refused to address specific blunders Walsh pointed out in the investigation of the crime, choosing instead to focus on the fact that nothing could have saved Adam's life: "The FBI didn't kill Mr. Walsh's son," Stone said. "The media didn't kill Mr. Walsh's son. And the Hollywood Police Department didn't kill Mr. Walsh's son." While true, it might have sounded a bit callous of the new chief, who was quoted in closing, "I've spoken with the few people who are still here who worked the case, and they feel they bent over backward to help the Walshes and investigate this case."

Undeniably, "bending over backwards" and "doing one's best" are admirable traits, but when it comes to assessing the quality of the investigation of a murder case, questions of capability are more germane. In any case, Stone would not last much longer at the top in Hollywood. He may have gotten along well with his own superiors, but before another year had passed he had begun to clash with the police union, and in late 1998 he was dismissed.

At that point, Finz approached Broward sheriff Ken Jenne for interim help, and Jenne assigned Major Al Lamberti as temporary chief while commissioners launched another search. Finally, in July 1999, they were successful in luring James Scarberry, assistant chief for the city of Miami Beach, to the position. Scarberry, a twenty-seven-year veteran with a reputation as a "cop's cop," was endorsed by the police union and was capable as an administrator as well.

Nor was Scarberry confronted in any meaningful way regarding the Adam Walsh case, though reminders of its enduring power continued to surface. The March 14, 2001, death of Henry Lee Lucas, serving a life term in a Texas prison, prompted a call to Hollywood PD for a comment on Lucas's onetime role as a suspect in the case, but Detective Sergeant Mark Smith, by then in charge of the department's homicide unit, reminded reporters that Lucas had been in a Maryland jail at the time of Adam's disappearance. When questioned about the status of that investigation, Smith said simply, "It's still an open case."

In July 2001 the *Miami Herald* ran a pair of lengthy articles by staff writer Daniel de Vise concerning the case, concurrent with the twentieth anniversary of Adam's disappearance. The first focused on the impact of the case on the nation's attitudes, rewriting laws and redefining relationships between adults and children. Many tragic child murders had faded from the public consciousness, de Vise wrote, "but Adam Walsh's endures."

That was likely due to the indefatigable John Walsh, de Vise opined, who included in his piece criticism directed at Walsh by some experts. "In some ways, he's taken his personal tragedy and inflicted it upon the nation," a Mount Holyoke College sociologist was quoted as saying. "He's made all kids afraid." Noted pediatrician Benjamin Spock had also criticized the practice of placing the pictures of missing children on milk cartons, said to have begun at Chicago-area Hawthorn Mellody Farms and copied by legions of others across the country, including South Florida's McArthur Dairy. While Spock understood the impetus behind such efforts, he worried that it turned breakfast into a ritual of terror for the young and impressionable.

But others, particularly the parents of children lost and missing, praised Walsh's work in redefining a nation's indifference to a significant problem. As a spokesperson for the National Center for Missing and Exploited Children put it, "Before the Adam Walsh case, it was easier to locate a stolen car than a missing child."

That first piece ended with a reprise of milestones to date in what de Vise referred to as the "missing-children movement," including the FBI database established by the Missing Children Act of 1982, and the 1984 legislation establishing the National Center for Missing and Exploited Children. Also referenced was "Megan's Law" of 1996, named after Megan Kanka, a New Jersey seven-year-old raped and murdered by a child molester who had moved into the neighborhood unbeknownst to residents. That measure required the notification of communities when a freed sex offender moves into a neighborhood.

De Vise also cited the AMBER Alert system, named for Amber Hagerman, a nine-year-old resident of Arlington, Texas, kidnapped while riding a bicycle near her home, her body later discarded in a ditch. It began as a grassroots movement in 1996 and has since been formalized nationwide, with bulletins interrupting radio programming and emblazoned on highway alert displays and elsewhere during the first hours following an abduction. Also mentioned was the Jimmy Ryce Act, the Florida measures named after a young Homestead boy taken and killed by a handyman, allowing law enforcement to publicize the identities of sexual offenders and extend the sentences of the most violent sexual predators.

On July 27, 2001, de Vise's follow-up piece centered on the

status of the long-stalled investigation. De Vise cataloged the emergence and dismissal of various individuals considered as suspects, including the quickly cleared John and Revé Walsh and Jimmy Campbell, who, de Vise pointed out, not only passed his polygraph examinations but also had an alibi. De Vise also rehashed the brief flurry caused in November 1981, when a drifter in a Broward County lockup claimed his cellmate Edward James had confessed to the crime. As it turned out, however, James, who passed a voice stress analysis test, was proven to be at work the day of the crime.

And in 1995 there were reports in an Alabama newspaper contending that Michael Monahan, the younger son of Walsh's former boss John Monahan, might have murdered Adam Walsh as a favor to his pal Jimmy Campbell. After all, police records showed that just three days after Adam's disappearance, the younger Monahan had slashed through a door of a Broward County home with a machete during a dispute over a stolen skateboard.

But that also came to nothing. Tests on the machete revealed no evidence, and Monahan had an alibi for his whereabouts at the time of Adam's death. Once he passed a polygraph exam, police quickly cleared him as well.

Ottis Toole remained the most likely suspect, de Vise wrote, before adding the familiar saw, "But there is no hard evidence to support it." For his story, de Vise tracked down former Hollywood police chief Richard Witt, who acknowledged in an interview that the department could have done a better job. Focusing on Jimmy Campbell had probably been a mistake, and, given their relative inexperience in such matters, they might have tried harder to get the FBI involved at the outset. "Within the first few months of this case," Witt told de Vise, "it was really screwed up to the point where obtaining a conviction had been compromised."

A companion piece in the *South Florida Sun-Sentinel* (Fort

Lauderdale was replaced in the paper's title in 2000) quoted Hollywood detective Mark Smith as admitting that the case was "probably too big for us at the time," and while he stopped short of criticizing those who had preceded him, he did say, "The investigation was not handled to my satisfaction. Let's just leave it at that." While Smith stoutly proclaimed that he "really believed" that his department would close the case someday, he admitted that he had not interviewed anyone concerning the matter in more than three years. Attempts to solicit comment from former detective Jack Hoffman, still on the force but scheduled for imminent retirement, went unanswered.

In the end, and following a rehash of missed opportunities and dead-end investigations, *Herald* reporter de Vise concluded, "The prospect that it will ever be solved has never looked so dim."

So it had always been at Hollywood PD, it seemed, and so it would remain for most of Chief Scarberry's tenure as well. Despite Detective Smith's upbeat contentions, five more years would pass without further pronouncements on the case, until the *Miami Herald* published yet another milestone story, this one proclaiming the twenty-fifth anniversary of failure, though this time there was a positive coda to add: "25 Years after Crime, a New Federal Law." The piece, mirrored by many in South Florida and around the nation, recounted the grim outline of Adam Walsh's kidnapping and murder, calling it "a crime that would change the nation."

Few parents would ever again leave their children alone or unattended in public places, reporters noted, pointing to such widespread practices as the "Code Adam" alerts broadcast by big-box retailers such as Walmart and Home Depot any time a child is reported lost in their stores.

In addition, laws had changed to help police mobilize and defend on behalf of children, including the new Adam Walsh Child Protection and Safety Act, legislation that President Bush was poised to sign on the twenty-fifth anniversary of the tragic event. The act mandated ten-year prison sentences for sex crimes against persons under the age of eighteen, created a uniform sex offender registry in every state, and outlawed any depiction of sexual abuse of children and its dissemination.

As to the case itself, however, commentators held out little hope for a solution. "The Walshes—and all families of missing children—never get closure," said Bill Fleisher, a Philadelphia forensic scientist and commissioner of the Vidocq Society, a cold case investigative group. Despite the likelihood that their son's murderer would never be found, Fleisher called attention to the good that had come out of personal tragedy. "They are likely the most important advocates that the country has ever had for preventing and solving crimes against children."

Still, there was always reason to hope, some opined. Detective Mark Smith again told reporters of his hopes that someone might come forward one day with information that would allow him to close the case, a prospect echoed by noted criminologist Vernon J. Geberth. "A new witness could come forward," said Geberth, former commander of the NYPD Bronx homicide unit. "A relative of the killer who knows about the crime may want to finally unburden himself."

The Walshes had survived on such hopes for a quarter of a century, of course, and while John had assumed a role as a celebrity crime fighter in his own right, the years in the spotlight had not always been kind. In 1983, just a few weeks shy of the statute of limitations in such matters, the couple had contemplated suing Sears over what they considered shortcomings in store security, including the fact that six-year-old Adam had simply been turned out on the street without so much as a "Where are your parents, little boy?"

However, attorneys for the company countered by saying that if the Walshes sued, they would parade details of Revé's affair with Jimmy Campbell in court and paint her as an unfit mother.

It wasn't really a threat, a Sears attorney told reporters—he was just trying to save the Walshes some embarrassment. Faced with such a prospect, the Walshes dropped the suit.

And in 1999, as if following the statistical mandate that more than half of the couples who lose a child to tragedy will split up (some studies have put the figure as high as 80 percent), Revé filed for divorce from John. However, there were three children still at home at the time—Meghan, then seventeen, Callahan, fifteen, and Hayden, fourteen—and four months later, Revé rescinded her petition. Eventually the couple smoothed over their difficulties and resumed a united place at the forefront of efforts on behalf of missing and exploited children.

As for Joe Matthews, his days following his retirement from Miami Beach PD remained full as well. He joined the faculty of the Center for Psychological Studies at Nova Southeastern University in the 1980s and he continued on there, lecturing on investigative interviewing and clinical polygraph. He also traveled extensively about the United States speaking at universities, police departments, and corporations on behalf of DNA LifePrint, a company formed to offer child safety programs and distribution of an inexpensive home DNA identification kit developed as a result of the difficulty he encountered in identifying "Baby Lollipops." And while he had stepped away from his interest in polygraph services and instruction, he continued as an investigative consultant to law enforcement agencies and the private sector across the United States and in Canada.

In 1999, when John Walsh asked if he might be interested in doing some investigative work for a new "cold case" component for *America's Most Wanted*, Matthews—a detective through and through—jumped at the opportunity. The producers expected that Matthews might present evidence pertaining to various cold cases and let the audience theorize for themselves what might have actually happened, but Matthews took one look at the known elements of the first case suggested to him, one involving the year-old death of a former high school wrestling champion in eastern Pennsylvania, and decided he could do better than what was proposed. After nearly two years of digging, he unearthed evidence proving the involvement of four drug-dealing University of Lock Haven football players in the killing. Having solved the first cold case investigation in the show's history, Matthews secured his career as an on-screen investigator.

From time to time during their association, both Matthews and Walsh would reflect on the one case that had baffled authorities and galled them both, and they each vowed on more than one occasion that one day they would see justice served. In fact, from the time of the airing of the first *AMW* show on Adam in 1996, Matthews had followed up every tip concerning the case submitted to the program, calls that came on the average of two or three a month. The former homicide detective traveled around Florida and as far away as the prisons of Colorado and California in search of viable leads, but nothing panned out.

And Matthews admits that if it hadn't been for the boorish reporter who buttonholed John Walsh in January 2006, just a few months before the signing of the Adam Walsh Child Protection and Safety Act, things might have stayed that way forever.

When Joe Matthews got the call from John Walsh to let him know he was coming to South Florida for an *AMW* shoot in early February 2006 and would like to get together, the detective didn't think too much about it. Matthews was still working regularly as an investigator for the show and simply assumed that Walsh wanted to run an idea for some new investigation past him.

Even when Walsh added that Revé would be with him and that they wanted to talk to him about an important matter, it still didn't register. Most of the time John traveled by himself for the shoots, but since this one was in South Florida, it made sense that Revé would come along, and Matthews, who enjoyed her company, was happy to hear it. Walsh suggested that they meet at the Atlantic Hotel on Ocean Drive in Fort Lauderdale, where the crew would be set up, and Matthews said he'd be there with bells on.

When he walked into the hotel's second-floor conference room on the afternoon of February 20, Matthews found John and Revé waiting, along with Lance Heflin, then executive producer for *AMW*, and Heflin's wife, Jan. John invited Matthews to sit and began to explain why they'd asked him there that afternoon. It was only when Revé put her hand on John's arm and cut in that Matthews began to understand that something out of the ordinary was afoot. In all his years around the Walshes, he'd found that John usually did most of the talking, while Revé listened patiently. She would have her incisive piece to add, to be sure, but it was almost always after John had led the way. As she began to speak on this day, Matthews was still trying to remember the last time he'd seen her interrupt her husband.

"Excuse me, John," Revé said, then cast an apologetic glance at Heflin's wife. "But I'd like this to be a closed meeting. I'm sorry, Jan. It's just that it's a very sensitive matter."

By the time that Heflin's wife had left the room, every cop instinct in Matthews was on alert. Again, John Walsh started his preamble. They'd been up in Washington a few days ago, working the Hill on behalf of the Adam Walsh Child Protection and Safety Act, when he'd been confronted with the question that had plagued him most of his adult life. As always, Walsh said, he realized the futility of trying to explain the million and one screwups involved . . .

Then Revé interrupted again. "Joe," she said, "we've heard the question a hundred times, and we'll hear it again on July 27 when we're back in Washington to watch the president sign the bill—'Why can't you find out who killed your son?' And you know what? I'm sick of it. Do you think I don't *want* to find out?"

There were tears in her eyes by that point, and Matthews stole a glance at John and Heflin, two guys accustomed to riding in the front seat. But they were way, way in the back right now, he thought.

"For twenty-five years, my husband has been pretty much in charge of this matter, protecting me from things. He's shielded me from the awful details, and he's minimized all the incompetence we've had to deal with from the police. He's done it because he loves me and doesn't want me to have to hear horrible things about what happened to our baby, particularly when he worries that they can't be proven. And he hasn't wanted to make me any more angry than I am already when the cops throw up their hands over and over again. But I am here to tell you that all that has come to an end." She glanced at her husband, then turned back to Matthews.

"When I left Adam that day, I told him, 'Honey, I'll be right over there in the lamp department,' and he looked back at me and said, 'I know where you'll be, Mommy.' Those are the last words I ever heard him say. That's the moment I've lived with for twenty-five years, and that is worse than anything some sick son of a bitch could ever say to me."

Revé leaned across the table toward Matthews, who was riveted in his chair. By this point, the tears were streaming down her face. "I've known you a long time, Joe, and I think you're one of the few cops ever involved in Adam's case who knows what the hell he's doing."

Matthews might have mumbled his thanks at that, but Revé held up her hand to stop him. "But it's been twenty-five years," she said, her voice rising, "and nothing has happened. I still don't know who killed my little boy. I want *you* to investigate. I want to know every detail. I want to know who did what and who didn't do what."

She was wiping away tears with the heels of both hands now. "This has nothing to do with the show. For John and me, for our sake as parents, I want you to prove once and for all who killed our son. We *think* we know who did it, but we want you to *prove* it. And we want the cops to clear this case. Until that happens, we won't have peace. It doesn't matter that Ottis Toole is dead. He died without ever being charged, and as far as John and I are concerned that's the same thing as going free. Our baby was murdered, and someone has to be held accountable. That's not too hard to understand, is it?"

She paused, still wiping at her tears, and fixed Matthews with an even gaze. "Joe, will you do this for me?"

At this point, everyone in the room was choked up. John Walsh leaned to comfort his sobbing wife, and Matthews struggled to get his voice under control. He'd spent his whole life trying to bring criminals to justice, and he knew exactly how Revé felt. Her words spoke to the core of his reason for being.

"I'm honored that you'd even ask," he told Revé quietly. He would start immediately. He would investigate as he would were he a police officer assigned to a cold case, and he would bring to the job all that he had in him. He couldn't predict the outcome, of course—no one could—but at least this time there'd be no one there to throw him off the case.

HOLLYWOOD, FLORIDA—FEBRUARY 21, 2006

The resurrection of the Adam Walsh case had never been a matter high on Hollywood police chief James Scarberry's priority list. Still, Scarberry knew that Matthews had put in a good word on his behalf with the Hollywood police union while he was being considered for the job, and he was also well aware of the blemish the high-profile matter had left on the record of his new department. Furthermore, Scarberry knew from his time in Miami Beach that Matthews was an accomplished cop—whatever the public thought, you didn't get to be Officer of the Year by accident. Thus, when Matthews showed up in his office on

February 21, 2006, some five and a half years after he'd taken over the reins in Hollywood, Scarberry knew enough to listen.

He was there for important reasons, Matthews told Scarberry, and then got quickly to the point. Almost twenty-five years had passed since Adam Walsh went missing, and were he still alive, he would have been looking forward to celebrating his thirty-second birthday. Nearly ten years had passed since the record of the failed investigation in his abduction and murder had been made public—effectively putting an end to its investigation—and nearly ten years had passed since the only viable suspect ever identified had died while imprisoned for other killings. There'd been any number of lurid stories concerning the disappearances and deaths of children splashed across the pages of the newspapers of the nation and the region—those of Jimmy Ryce and Shannon Melendi, a young South Florida woman kidnapped and slain by a softball umpire, among them.

There might even be a few people who'd forgotten all about Adam Walsh, just one more unfortunate kid in what had become a long line of them. But Adam Walsh was really the first kid in that line, Matthews pointed out. Before Adam, there really wasn't much attention paid to the problem of missing and endangered children. And now, due in large part to the efforts of Adam's parents, John and Revé Walsh, the issue had become one of the most important priorities of law enforcement and society as a whole.

Yet for all that John and Revé had accomplished, *they* had certainly not forgotten about Adam. Furthermore, as every new day dawned, they thought about the son whom they had so tragically lost, and they were reminded that his killer had yet to be brought to justice. Matthews recounted the recent incident in Washington, where John Walsh was confronted by a reporter who wanted to know if it ever "bothered" him that he had been unable to find the killer of his own son.

If that reporter had any idea what John Walsh had gone

through, Matthews reminded Chief Scarberry, he would have been running for the doorway before he finished his question. It was true that Walsh had heard such things before, and though he had placed his trust in the Hollywood PD for many years, he felt a certain amount of guilt that he hadn't done more to move the investigation forward earlier. He'd even felt bad that the baseless innuendo regarding his lifestyle and his ties to organized crime might have somehow affected the conduct of the case. And certainly there was a point to the reporter's question, offensive as it was. John Walsh had helped to apprehend a lot of bad guys in his time, but the worst one of all had gone scot-free.

"That's why I'm here today," Matthews told Scarberry. He'd been asked by John and Revé Walsh to reopen the case and to conduct a complete, independent investigation to prove once and for all who had kidnapped and murdered their son. And Matthews—who was doing this as a favor to people he cared about, and for the sake of justice—was asking for Scarberry's help. The files had been opened to every reporter under the sun ten years ago, Matthews pointed out, though the motivations of those who wanted them opened were somewhat dubious and their abilities to evaluate what they were looking at just as questionable.

Matthews was an experienced investigator with a single aim in mind: to reexamine files and statements, reevaluate evidence, and reinterview witnesses, and, where new leads presented themselves, to follow them wherever they might go. As Scarberry well knew, Matthews had solved any number of cases thought to be unsolvable before. Surely, said Matthews—who had not come to take no for an answer—it was time to give him his final shot. John and Revé and Adam Walsh deserved that much, at least.

Scarberry heard Matthews out, then sat back in his chair, considering things. He glanced away for a moment, then turned back to Matthews and gave his okay. If Matthews thought he could manage to prove anything after all these years, who was Scarberry or his department to stand in the way?

He would have access to everything in the department's files, Scarberry told him. And he further assured Matthews that now-captain Mark Smith, the detective who had opened the cold case investigation with Matthews back in 1995, would provide whatever help he could. Godspeed and good luck.

The promise of "help" from Mark Smith was a favor that Matthews could have just as well done without, he thought, but at least this time there was no selective withholding of files.

The transfer of all case file documentation, including myriad reports, statements, memos, photos, and interviews—including those filmed and on CD—began the following day, February 22, 2006. Day after day, Matthews (convinced by their disarray that he was the first to do so) combed through the voluminous files, refreshing himself on details, cataloging crucial information and evidence, building for the first time a comprehensive chronology of events and identifying key witnesses who had never been interviewed, or who were never asked the necessary questions in the first place.

On Thursday, February 23, Matthews—backed by a film crew *AMW*'s Lance Heflin had been happy to provide for the purposes of documentation—interviewed retired Hollywood detective Larry Hoisington regarding the things Ottis Toole had told him on October 21, 1981, when Hoisington had been the driver for the team taking Toole around to the various scenes connected to the crime. Hoisington told Matthews that on that day, while Hoffman and others were busy with other things, Toole had given him a complete and independent confession to the crime, the gruesome details of which he recounted for Matthews. Hoisington also recounted Hoffman's treatment of Toole and repeated what he'd told Leroy Hessler year before: "I'm surprised Toole cooperated at all."

Hoisington reiterated his conversation with Deputy Chief Hessler at the time and recounted Hessler's response that Hoisington simply tell Hoffman about it. Matthews pointed to the files, shaking his head. Despite Hoffman's assurances that he would include what Hoisington told him in his report, no such mention of Toole's confession to Hoisington existed there.

On Saturday, February 25, Matthews interviewed Arlene Mayer, who had identified Ottis Toole as the man who accosted her and her daughter Heidi at a Hollywood Kmart store two days prior to Adam's abduction. They both recalled the incident vividly and confirmed that they had identified Toole from a lineup of photographs shown them by Hollywood police. For all the good it did, Matthews thought. Had Hoffman bothered to confirm Toole's encounter with the Mayers when he had the chance, all this could have very likely been concluded back in 1983.

The likely reason why Hollywood police had placed so little credence in what the Mayers had told them had to do with the timing, Matthews understood. Arlene had been sure that their trip to Kmart to place on a Friday or a Saturday night because those were the only nights they ever went shopping. But the fact that her husband wouldn't go into the store with them because he had just gotten off work suggested to detectives that it had very likely been a Friday night when the Mayers had their frightening encounter. That, of course, would have ruled Toole out of the scenario, since he would have been on a bus somewhere between Newport News and Jacksonville at the time.

However, Matthews had since spoken with Susan Schindehette, coauthor of John Walsh's *Tears of Rage*. She'd wondered about that seeming inconsistency, too, she told Matthews, until she asked Wayne Mayer a simple question, one that the detectives never had. Did he ever work at his construction job on Saturdays? "Oh, sure," Wayne told her. "All the time."

The simple questions, Matthews thought to himself, as he finished up his notes on the Mayers. When you forget to ask them during an investigation, that's when things go south.

On the following Tuesday, February 28, Matthews got in touch with prison hospital administrator Barry Gemelli, who confirmed that he had overheard the unsolicited confession to the crime by Ottis Toole as he was lying on his deathbed. The two made arrangements to meet the following week.

In the meantime, Matthews conducted an interview with Kathy Shaffer, the Sears security guard who had ordered Adam Walsh out of the store that day. "His mom showed me two pictures of Adam that day," Shaffer told Matthews, "and I really wasn't sure about the first one. But then she made me look at another one, and I knew right then. I was chilled. One hundred and ten percent, I knew it was him."

But she had lied to Revé that day and said she didn't recognize Adam because she was just seventeen, and she was scared. She thought Revé would get mad at her for throwing Adam out of the store, Shaffer said, and besides, at first she thought he was just some kid wandering around and he was going to turn up just fine without any help from her.

By the time detectives arrived and were beginning to question her, she realized the enormity of what had happened. This child had really, truly disappeared. She couldn't own up to what she had done by then, she said to Matthews. She had started to feel truly responsible for Adam's disappearance. Eventually she came to feel responsible for his death.

"I still do," she told Matthews, tearfully. "Not a day has gone by in twenty-five years that I haven't thought about it. If I had just said, 'Where's your mama?' he might still be here today." She had to pause to gather herself before she could get her last words out, and even then Matthews had to ask her to repeat them. "I pray every night that his mom and dad will forgive me."

Matthews tried to console Shaffer, but he felt like the little Dutch boy his mother used to tell him about, only this wasn't some storybook problem where you could just plug your finger in the leak and wait for help to arrive. Woulda, coulda, shoulda. Once upon a time, what was so terrible about letting your kid play a video game while you walked fifty feet away to buy a frigging lamp? And yet Revé Walsh had been tying herself in knots ever since, thinking *she* was somehow responsible for what had happened. Or how about her husband John, who put the whole idea of going to Sears in her head in the first place—"Hey, honey, we can save a couple of bucks if we just act now"?

Or how about Joe Matthews, for that matter? Maybe if he had simply cold-cocked Jack Hoffman the first time the know-it-all SOB had insulted him, the guy would have ended up in the hospital and somebody else would have taken over the case. Which of course wouldn't have changed anything, really, because Adam Walsh would still have been dead.

The fact is that one person, and one person only, was responsible for what had happened to Adam. One person had taken that little boy and done unspeakable things to him, and Matthews was going to prove who that person was, because, quite frankly, that is the only way he knew how to give meaning to his life.

On Tuesday, March 14, Matthews met with Barry Gemelli, the former health service administrator at the Union Correctional Institution. Gemelli, himself suffering from advanced leukemia, recounted the details of the confession he heard from Toole just before he died, and confirmed that he had followed up with the criminal investigation unit at the facility both verbally and with a follow-up written report. Gemelli told Matthews that Toole seemed well aware that he was dying. He was sad and scared, and there seemed to Gemelli no reason on earth for the man to be lying. He had done something particularly terrible, and he wanted to get it off his chest. As far as Matthews was concerned, Gemelli was only underscoring what Toole had told officers when he originally confessed in 1983: "It was the youngest person I ever killed and I feel bad about it." Even ghouls sometimes feel a pang of conscience, he thought.

And then, on the following day, Wednesday, March 15, Matthews conducted an interview that would cast new light on a matter that had seemed to color Ottis Toole's confessions so profoundly. Despite the fact that Toole had divulged details of the crime that only Hoffman and his fellow detectives could have known at the time, including the place where he had disposed of Adam's head, Hoffman had stuck to his accusations that Detective Buddy Terry had struck a book deal with Toole and was feeding him privileged information.

However, in the course of going back through Toole's movements in Jacksonville, prior to and just after the time of the crime, Matthews had occasion to speak with John Reaves Jr., son of the owner of Reaves Roofing at the time. Yes, he'd verified all those dates pertaining to Ottis Toole's work history at the company, Reaves told Matthews. And he also confirmed that his aunt Faye McNett had sold Toole the Cadillac, later repossessing it when Toole couldn't keep up the payments. For a time, though, Toole had used it as his work vehicle, and usually kept it full of rakes and shovels and other gardening-type tools. Toole didn't like heights, Reaves explained, so he was always doing cleanup and other such work around the job sites.

Maybe he didn't like to climb because of his eyes, Reaves theorized. Toole would be looking at you and suddenly one eye would go floating in another direction, Reaves said, accounting for the odd-looking expression that other witnesses had noted.

All that was interesting enough, but it wasn't until Matthews asked the obvious question that Reaves dropped his own bombshell. Did he have any knowledge of Toole's involvement in the abduction and murder of Adam Walsh? Matthews wanted to know.

Actually, he did, Reaves responded. In fact, Toole had admitted the whole thing to him in great detail, during a visit they'd had in the Duval County Jail. Ottis had told him he'd taken the kid from a store, though he didn't mention Sears. It was down around Miami, somewhere, Reaves remembered Ottis saying, and that while he was driving them back to Jacksonville, the kid wouldn't stop crying. Ottis hit him hard in the stomach, and when the kid starting gasping for air, Ottis said he put his hands around his neck and choked him until he was dead. Then Ottis said he cut his head off and threw it, or the body, into a canal. There was a lot of blood in the Cadillac as a result, Ottis told him.

And why was it that Reaves had not told detectives this back in 1983 when they questioned him? Matthews asked. Well, because they never asked, Reaves replied. He and Ottis had their conversation about the killing a few days after the detectives had called about the dates of Toole's employment, Reaves said, and he'd just never seen the point of calling the cops back on his own.

And besides, there was the matter of the book contract that he and Ottis had worked out, Reaves added.

Really? Matthews replied, blandly, trying to conceal his eagerness. Just what book contract was Reaves talking about?

It took Reaves, who was undergoing treatment for lymph node and prostate cancer, a bit of time to find the document in his files, but finally he came up with a copy for Matthews. Dated October 29, 1983, shortly after Ottis made his first confessions to detectives from four separate jurisdictions (Steve Kendrick of Brevard County, Jay Via from Louisiana, Buddy Terry of Jacksonville, and Jack Hoffman from Hollywood), the agreement gave John Reaves Jr. the exclusive rights to any film and book adaptation of the "life and deeds of Toole." Ottis and Reaves would split any profits fifty-fifty, the contract stipulated, and even if something happened to Toole, his surviving brothers and sisters would reap the rewards. In return for affixing his signature at the end of the document, Toole received an immediate advance against earnings of $10.

So indeed there had been a book contract, Matthews realized. Reaves was just a businessman who'd recognized a good possibility when he'd seen one.

Matthews would never know why Hoffman was so reluctant to pursue Ottis Toole, but if it truly was his belief that Buddy Terry had struck a book deal with the killer, what a shame it was that he'd never taken the trouble to have a follow-up conversation with John Reaves Jr. It would have dispensed with the chief ostensible reason why Hollywood PD and others in law enforcement and the media were so reluctant to believe Toole's account of the killing, and it very possibly could have changed the course of the investigation.

On the following day, March 16, 2006, Matthews interviewed Sarah Patterson, the woman who called *America's Most Wanted* following the 1996 segment on Adam, indentifying herself as Toole's niece and claiming that he had confessed the killing to her. Patterson, the last person to visit Toole in prison before his death, reiterated her account of her uncle's confession during that visit. Nothing had changed in the ten years that had passed, she said. There was no doubt in her mind that he had done exactly what he said he did.

She did not mean to be unfaithful to her uncle, who had always been good to her, but Patterson simply felt that after Ottis's mother died, he lost what tenuous grip he might have had on self-control. "When Grandma Sarah died," Patterson said, "this whole family went to hell."

There were some good moments, however. During his stay with her just prior to her wedding years ago, he had offered to bake a cake for the occasion, but then he'd dropped it right before the reception. Uncle Ottis had spent his last $20 to buy her another, she recalled. But right was right, and the parents of that poor boy down in Hollywood deserved to know the truth.

At the end of her interview with Matthews, Patterson said she wanted him to have something her uncle had given her the last day they'd talked. She handed over a sheet of paper and Matthews found himself studying a multicolored drawing signed by Toole.

It was a clown's face, Patterson said, and a clown's face should make you happy. But this clown's face haunted her. Looking at its dark-circled, bulging eyes and its protruding tongue reminded her of what evil her uncle did by taking the life of Adam Walsh. As much as she had once loved her Uncle Ottis, she now wanted only to forget him.

JACKSONVILLE, FLORIDA—MARCH 17, 2006

The day after his interview with Sarah Patterson, Matthews interviewed retired Jacksonville sheriff's detective Jesse "Buddy" Terry. Terry had known Ottis Toole for nearly twenty years prior to his arrest for the murder of George Sonnenberg, Terry told Matthews. A lot of cops knew Ottis Toole—he had been a fringe dweller in Jacksonville from the time he was a kid. As an adult, Toole—openly gay, and prone to dressing in drag—had been picked up several times for prostitution and various petty offenses, and was a suspected arsonist as well. No one, however, made him for a serial killer until James Redwine, the delinquent son of Toole's landlady, fingered Toole in the arson-murder of George Sonnenberg, and Toole began to talk.

Terry recounted to Matthews the details of the various interviews he had witnessed where Toole confessed to the abduction and murder of Adam Walsh, and went back over the visit he'd made to South Florida, accompanying Toole on his tour of the crime scenes. From the outset, Terry said, he was not sure why Detective Hoffman was so reluctant to view Toole's confession as truthful, for it seemed clear to every other detective who'd been involved that Toole knew things that only Adam's killer could possibly have known.

As to Hoffman's accusations that he had cut a book deal

with Toole, Terry was comforted to hear what Matthews had discovered about the real partners in that undertaking, but he was still indignant. He felt that he'd been used as a scapegoat in the matter, Terry said—there was so much public outcry at the lack of progress in the case that his own department was happy to let Hoffman's claims go unopposed. Though an internal affairs investigation eventually cleared Terry of Hoffman's allegations, and the detective was offered his old job back, the department never issued a formal statement on the matter. To Terry, it seemed that the Jacksonville Sheriff's Office was perfectly willing to have it seem as if he had manufactured Ottis Toole's various confessions out of whole cloth.

Yes, practically speaking, the investigation was in the hands of Jack Hoffman and Hollywood PD, but if his own superiors had been more forceful in refuting Hoffman's trumped-up charges, more attention might have been given to Toole's statements that clearly proved his involvement in the crime.

To that day, there remained no doubt in Terry's mind that Toole was responsible. "He even drew us a little stick-figure diagram of the area where the killing took place and how he stood over Adam with his machete to cut his head off," Terry told Matthews. Hoffman took the diagram away with him, Terry said, but as Matthews discovered, no such drawing had found its way into the case file. Somehow, he was not surprised.

When he had concluded his interview with Detective Terry, Matthews once again pulled out copies of the various interviews that Jack Hoffman had conducted with Toole at the Duval County Jail: the first had taken place just before midnight on Wednesday, October 20, 1983, and during that conversation Toole had described the Cadillac he was driving, the Sears store from which he took Adam, and the force he employed in rendering Adam unconscious. He had used a "bayonet" to decapitate Adam, Toole told Hoffman, and during that interview, he also claimed that Henry Lee Lucas was present during the abduction and killing, and that Lucas had sex with the decapitated head.

In the course of his statement, Toole told Hoffman that he had been "window shopping" in the mall before he made his way to the Sears store and remembered looking at some of the wigs displayed in a nearby shop. Broward County state attorney's investigator Phil Mundy had later ascertained that there was indeed a wig store operating in the Sears Mall at the time of Adam's abduction. It might have seemed an inconsequential detail, but Matthews knew there had been no mention of "wig shops" in any of the press coverage of the case. How could Toole—cross-dresser and wig fancier that he was—have known there was a wig shop in that mall unless he'd been there and seen it with his own eyes?

When Hoffman and his partner Hickman left the room following that first interview, Detective Terry had confronted Toole about his contention that Henry Lee Lucas had taken part in the crime. Toole admitted lying about that and asked to speak with Hoffman and Hickman again to clarify the matter. Shortly after midnight, the Hollywood detectives took their second statement from Toole, during which he once again described using "four or five" blows to sever Adam's head from his body, though in this interview Detective Hoffman began to refer to the weapon as a machete instead of a bayonet. For a second time, then, Matthews noted, Toole had confirmed detailed autopsy findings that had not been made public. And later, when Toole was trying to broker his way out of Raiford, his jailhouse lawyer Gerald Schaefer would tell Broward County investigators that Toole had used *both* a bayonet and a machete in the murder.

Following those statements, on Friday, October 21, Hoffman flew with Toole to South Florida, where Toole guided detectives to the Hollywood Sears store where Adam was taken, and then to the spot near mile marker 126 on Florida's Turnpike where he said he had decapitated and dismembered Adam. Finally, he identified the canal at mile marker 130 as the spot where he disposed of Adam's head. At the time, Matthews noted, the only person in the party who knew Toole had ID'd the very place where fishermen had found the severed head was Jack Hoffman.

It could have been the end of the matter then and there, Matthews thought, but it was not to be. On the following Wednesday, October 26, Hoffman returned to Jacksonville to take a fourth statement from Toole, ostensibly to clarify the suspect's movements from the time he left the hospital in Newport News, Virginia, and his arrival at the Sears store in South Florida shortly thereafter. It was during that fourth statement that Toole broke down and told Hoffman, "I'm not really sure that I really did kill Adam Walsh."

It occurred to Matthews that Hoffman might well have responded by asking Toole how he could have known, for instance, where Adam's head was discarded or how many blows it took to sever his head from his body, but he did not. Instead, Hoffman concluded his interview and walked out, leaving Buddy Terry to calm Toole down.

Not fifteen minutes later, Toole asked Hoffman to return so that he could tell the truth. Indeed, he had committed the crime, he assured Hoffman. He'd simply been upset there a few minutes ago: "I couldn't get my head together," he said. In this fifth statement, Toole went once more through a detailed account of the crime, including a graphic description of his disposal of Adam's head. After he'd driven north for five or ten minutes following the dismemberment, Toole said, he pulled off the turnpike again:

"I seen a little . . . a little bridge down there and I walked down there and I throwed it in, throwed it in the water."

And what happened next? Hoffman wanted to know. He probably meant to ask what Toole did after he threw the head in the water.

But Toole took Hoffman quite literally. The head sank, he said, simply.

There was a pause. "You're positive about that?" Hoffman asked.

"Positive." Toole replied. And shortly thereafter, the interview was concluded.

Matthews tossed the transcript down on his desk, shaking his head. That exchange might as well have been typed in red, with double underlining. If a cop needed any further assurance that Toole had done just what he said he'd done, there it was on the page before him.

"*It sank*," Matthews repeated. Yes, that's exactly what would have happened. Adam's head would have hit the water and sunk like a stone. If Toole had been making his story up, he'd have probably said something like, "It went floating off," or "It went under for a second and then it bobbed right back up."

Matthews had investigated a murder case once and had known something was wrong from the moment he heard the tape of the 911 call. "Help. I think my husband's dead. He's just floating there facedown in the pool." *Yeah? Not unless he was lying on the bottom for a couple of days first, lady. Dead bodies—and body parts—hit the water and go down like lead. After a couple of days and enough decomposition, gases form in cavities and then gruesome things float to the surface.*

Nor were such oversights the only oddities Matthews found during his examination of Hoffman's records. Along with the failure to include Toole's drawing in the case file and the failure to request that the Walshes come in to identify the items of clothing found during the search of Toole's mother's yard, Matthews discovered another startling inconsistency.

As Matthews worked his way through the case documentation, he eventually came to a mention of the polygraph examination that he had administered to Jimmy Campbell during the early hours of August 8, 1981. Following that examination Matthews had his first conversation with Detective Hoffman regarding his polygraph examination of Campbell. Prior to that conversation, Hoffman had not even known Campbell's name, but within moments, the Hollywood detective was declaring his virtual certainty that Campbell was the perpetrator. And following the heated exchange with Detective Matthews, Hoffman tracked down and interviewed Campbell as to his alibi for the time of the kidnapping.

All that was clear in Matthews's memory. However, as he studied Hoffman's files more carefully, Matthews discovered something dumbfounding: Hoffman had filed a report claiming that he had interviewed Jimmy Campbell on Friday, August 7— *the day before* Matthews had alerted Hoffman to Campbell's very existence. Nor was there mention of the fact that Matthews had already conducted a polygraph examination that cleared Campbell of any guilty knowledge concerning the crime. The report suggested that Hoffman had tracked down Jimmy Campbell on his own, and *then* ordered Matthews to call Campbell in for a polygraph exam the following week.

Furthermore, while Hoffman had assiduously recorded all other interviews he conducted in the course of his investigation, the one with Campbell was not recorded. That was for one simple reason, Matthews theorized: the date recorded on the tape would have determined when the interview actually took place. Most disturbing to Matthews, however, was a supplemental report that Hoffman filed on August 8, where he falsely stated that the results of Matthews's polygraph examination of Campbell were "inconclusive."

To Matthews, all this was evidence that from the beginning Hoffman had seen Jimmy Campbell as the perfect suspect and had set about constructing a scenario where he would seem a supersleuth for having deduced things about the case that no one else had. By switching the dates of his interview with Campbell,

Hoffman made it seem that he had smoked Campbell out, then ordered Matthews to administer a test that incriminated him.

Later that evening, as Matthews made a visit to the unmarked grave site of Toole's mother, a call came from Vinetta Syphurs, Toole's sister and the owner of the Japanese bayonet that Broward County detectives had questioned her about a decade before. Matthews had left a message for her earlier that day that he was hoping to talk with her about the matter.

She was suffering from cancer, Vinetta told Matthews—in fact she was dying. Her husband Rodney had recently died as well, and somehow the timing of Matthews's phone call, after all this time, suggested to her that it was a message from the grave, her Rodney suggesting that she tell police the truth about the things she knew.

She told Matthews that she and Ottis were the closest of all the nine children, especially after their mother died, and that he often confided to her about some of the things he'd done. She had visited Ottis in prison—a fact noted by Toole in one of his letters to John Reaves Jr.—and during that visit he told her, without expressing remorse, that he had murdered Adam Walsh. This confession had so disgusted her that she disowned her brother and refused to visit or correspond afterward. She had lied to Broward detectives when she'd told them she had that bayonet mounted above her mantel, she told Matthews. She wasn't even sure where it had come from or when she got it. It had just been stuck on a shelf somewhere.

If Ottis had taken the bayonet and replaced it some time later on, she would have never known. She'd been trying to protect her brother at the time she spoke to detectives, but when she asked him point-blank and he admitted the killing, she'd been sickened. She wanted Matthews to pass on what she'd told him to the Walshes. She was sorry she had not come forward sooner, but now she felt at peace.

. . .

It was a score for Matthews, one more suggestion that the original investigators had been more intent on proving Ottis Toole's innocence than his guilt, but he would have to keep going until he'd picked through the case file from top to bottom and—if possible—found that elusive piece of evidence that had so consumed his predecessors.

On Saturday, March 18, Matthews met with retired Brevard County sheriff deputy Steve Kendrick, the first police officer to whom Toole had confessed. Kendrick took Matthews back through his initial interview with Toole and the chance confusion with Broward County that had set twenty-five years of history into motion.

Thank God the dumb bastard couldn't spell, Kendrick said, or else the whole thing might never have come out. When Matthews reminded him that actually the thing had not yet "come out," Kendrick nodded in commiseration. Still there was not a doubt in his mind. Toole wasn't the kind of guy who would have seen any value in confessing to such an awful thing unbidden. He'd confessed the crime to him twice, offering details that Kendrick realized—once the Hollywood police finally shared their information with him—only the killer could have known at the time.

In the weeks that followed, Matthews continued to pore through the voluminous file, and in late May he began to work back through an analysis of the physical evidence. In 1986, while still with the Miami Beach Police, Matthews had supervised the investigation of a case that stymied detectives until he ordered a tool marking analysis comparing a knife found in possession of a suspect and the wound in the deceased's chest. As a result, the killer was convicted, among the first to be solved by such means.

Accordingly, on Thursday, May 25, he coordinated a reexamination of Adam's skull for tool markings by the Miami Dade crime lab and the Broward County medical examiner's office.

Once again, however, though the markings showed "some similarities," the results were inconclusive.

That same day, Matthews asked that Hollywood Police turn over certain evidence that it appeared they had not yet shared with him: Matthews wanted to examine copies of the photos taken by the FDLE, specifically those of the search and analysis of Ottis Toole's Cadillac. Sergeant Lyle Bean, the Hollywood officer in charge of the file, checked, but then told Matthews that there were no such photos to be found.

Well, Matthews told Bean, FDLE reports indicated that five rolls of film had been shot documenting the search. If in fact the photos were not in Hollywood's files, perhaps Bean would be willing to call the FDLE and find out what had happened to them.

Bean told Matthews he would place the call, and Matthews waited a week to follow up. On June 1, he called back. "They haven't found them yet, but they're still looking," Bean said.

On June 19, Matthews placed yet another call to Bean, asking for an update on the status of those misplaced photographs. The FDLE had told him that no such photos existed in their files, Bean said.

Matthews hung up and sat pondering the situation for a moment. Twenty-three years had passed. Witnesses had died, the likely killer of Adam Walsh had died, and a great deal of evidence had disappeared as well. If the bloody carpet samples had vanished, along with the 4,200-pound automobile from which they'd come, why couldn't five rolls worth of photographs have vaporized as well? Still, Matthews was not the sort to leave stones unturned. If you were a good cop, you turned them all over. And sometimes, if you were lucky, you found exactly what you were looking for.

He reached for the phone then and called the FDLE crime lab himself. He'd have to speak to someone in the photo lab, a voice told him, and Matthews waited patiently while he was transferred. When an attendant answered, he explained that he was simply following up on the request of Sergeant Bean from Hollywood PD. Were they absolutely certain that no copies of the photographs taken of Ottis Toole's Cadillac back in 1983 existed in their files?

There was a pause on the other end. No one in the office seemed to know what Matthews was talking about. There'd been no request for any photos from anyone at Hollywood PD.

Matthews nodded and hung up. He'd played this game before. Except the last time around, the joker on the other side of the table had been a guy named Jack Hoffman.

In the end, Matthews spoke to an FDLE public information officer, Sharon Gogerty, who checked the files in reference to Hollywood PD case #81-56073. Yes, she told Matthews, they had ninety-eight photo negatives pertaining to the processing of suspect Ottis Toole's vehicle.

Well then, Matthews asked, would it be possible for him to obtain copies of the prints? Gogerty paused, then said a surprising thing. There were no prints, she told Matthews. The film had been processed into negatives for the purposes of storage— standard operating procedure at FDLE—but never in twenty-three years had any prints been developed.

Matthews paused. In other words, he asked, no detective has ever requested or looked at the photos taken of Ottis Toole's Cadillac?

"That would seem to be the case," Gogerty replied brightly. "But you can be the first."

On Tuesday, June 27, 2006, an FDLE regional legal adviser, John Kenner, sent ninety-eight photographs copied from lab case file 831043357 to Matthews at *America's Most Wanted*, where staffers in turn forwarded them to his offices in Davie, a few miles northwest of Hollywood. Matthews, who had come in early that Wednesday to work on his report, glanced up as his longtime secretary Mary Alvarez came through his door with a hefty UPS envelope in hand. "Were you expecting something in the overnight?" she asked.

Indeed he was, Matthews assured her. He set his coffee aside and quickly spread out the thick sheaf of three-by-five-inch prints on his desk, trying all the while to keep his expectations under control. He was excited to have unearthed the photographs, but he had suffered his share of setbacks on this case before—in all honesty, it wouldn't have surprised him to find he'd been sent a series of shots of an FDLE employee's birthday party.

This time, though, he'd hit pay dirt. He was looking at the outset for any shots of the rear bumper of the Cadillac. When he quickly found three that depicted the sizable dent described by both William Mistler and Bobby Lee Jones, Toole's coworker from Jacksonville, Matthews nodded with satisfaction. It was confirmation that indeed it was Toole's car that Mistler had seen in the Sears parking lot the day that Adam had been taken.

"Good, good, good" is Matthews' characteristic way of expressing enthusiasm, and that is what he murmured as he turned to see what other treasures might have come his way. There were other shots of the Cadillac's exterior, dashboard, and seats, but he expected nothing of real import there. Of far more interest were a series of dark shots that resembled negatives, dotted here and there by objects that glowed a psychedelic blue.

In fact, these were a set of specially processed shots taken by FDLE crime scene investigators using luminol technology to identify or enhance the presence of blood traces on items of evidence. In this process, ordinary photographs are taken of objects, then chemicals that become luminescent when in contact with blood are applied to those objects, and the photographs taken again. The second series of photos are shot in darkness, with a wide aperture setting and the lens open for a minute or more. The only images that appear are special luminescent markers that orient the viewer and any part of the item where blood residue—invisible to the naked eye—might exist. Anything that retains the presence of blood will show up in a ghostly metallic blue.

Matthews first went about arranging a comparison of a set of photos taken of the front driver's-side floorboards. Given all the disappointments of the past quarter-century, he expected little. But now he sat staring in disbelief at what was laid out before him.

The pictures of the front floorboard carpeting shot in ordinary light showed nothing beyond the ordinary dirt and dings he might expect, except for the presence of the orienting marker the technician had placed along the edge of the carpet. But as Matthews placed the corresponding luminol-enhanced shot alongside the first, he could hear Ottis Toole's reply to Jack Hoffman during his confession of October 20, 1983, ringing in his mind:

> *Hoffman:* Did you get blood all over you from the child?
> *Toole:* I got it on my shoes. I threw my shoes away
>   too, and I put another pair of shoes on.

So you did, Matthews murmured to himself, so you damned well did. There in the photograph before him glowed a blood-engendered image of a pair of shoeprints firmly planted on the driver's floorboards.

Matthews set those images aside, well aware of the significance of the discovery. At long last, here was physical evidence tying Ottis Toole to the crime.

He set aside the images of the bloody footprints, and turned to another set of prints of the machete that Detective Terry had confiscated from Toole's car-dealer associate in Jacksonville. In one of his confessions, Toole had mentioned wrapping tape around the handle of his machete to keep from getting blisters, and the luminol shot of the machete with its taped-up handle showed nothing.

But in a second image, taken after the tape had been removed from its handle, the wooden grips of the blade glowed from blood as if radioactive. Matthews studied the image, compared the location of the marker in the luminol image with that in the original again, then exhaled deeply and leaned back in his chair. There before him was a photograph of Ottis Toole's machete, taken from his car, its handle soaked in blood.

Matthews turned back to what was left of the photographs, then, riffling through a set taken from the rear floorboards. At first he saw nothing of interest, just some streaky, vague imagery, nothing to compare with that bold set of footprints or that pulsing machete handle; then he stopped himself and looked closer at the photograph in his hand.

He studied the image for a moment, glanced away, then turned to look closely again, not sure whether to trust his eyes. He double-checked the markers to be certain—but indeed he was looking at a shot of the carpet directly behind the driver's seat. The image taken in ordinary light revealed nothing. But as to the luminol-enhanced image . . .

In all his years as a cop, Matthews had never seen anything like it—though having been raised as a Catholic, he was more than familiar with similar images preserved by church fathers over the centuries. What he was looking at chilled him—but there was more to the feeling than that. From this image there emanated reassurance, and a strange kind of peace, and the blessed feeling that twenty-six years of effort had not gone in vain.

Unless he was just finding images in clouds, that is.

He tucked the photographs into a folder and hurried out of his office with a distracted wave for Mary. Once in his car, he paused to dial his old friend Pat Franklin, also a former Miami Beach detective and now a private investigator with his own firm. The two of them often met at a cigar bar far north on Biscayne Boulevard for a smoke and a coffee on the way home from their respective offices, but Joe was an hour or more ahead of the usual curve.

"Something wrong?" Franklin asked when he picked up. He'd recognized who it was from the caller ID. Neither one of them bothered with unnecessary pleasantries anymore.

"You gotta meet me right now," he told Franklin.

"It's a little early," Franklin said.

"I'm not kidding," Matthews said. "I need you to see something."

There was a pause, and some rustling of papers. "Give me fifteen minutes," Franklin said.

When he caught sight of his still-trim friend entering the bar, Matthews felt the urgency rising in him again. He hadn't dared to look at the photograph since he'd left his office.

"Take a look at this," he said, thrusting the folder at Franklin.

Franklin smiled at him quizzically. "Good to see you, too," he said, opening the folder. He glanced at the photo, then looked back at Matthews. "The light's for shit in here." He stepped closer to the window in the front of the place and Matthews tagged along after him.

Franklin studied the photo for a moment and Matthews watched his face. Franklin was well aware of what he was working on, and knew the last detail of every roadblock and frustration he'd encountered over all the years. Finally Franklin closed the folder and handed it back. They'd both learned how to play poker as cops. If Franklin didn't want you to know what he was thinking, you could beat your brains out wondering.

"You weren't going to ask me what I see there, were you?"

Matthews gave him something like a shrug. "I wasn't sure, that's all."

Franklin nodded. He might have smiled, except for the horror of what they'd been looking at.

"The hell of it is, I have to show the Walshes," Matthews said. "But right now, let's have us a cigar."

Throughout the course of his two-year reinvestigation of the case, Joe Matthews met regularly with John and Revé Walsh to update them on his progress, but despite Revé's insistence that he share *everything* with her, he hesitated about showing her and John the images from the machete and the floorboards of Toole's Cadillac. Still, he could scarcely keep such a discovery from them. Furthermore, he needed their corroboration of the results.

Accordingly, he arranged for a meeting in the law offices of Kelly Hancock, John and Revé's attorney and longtime friend. Hancock, a former Broward County prosecutor, had already spoken to Matthews and knew what to expect, but he, too, understood how tough it would be for any parents to view what Matthews had uncovered. While Matthews explained the luminol process and tried to prepare John and Revé for what he was about to show them, Revé cut in. "Let me see the photographs, Joe," she said, her face set.

Matthews hesitated, but finally handed over the packet. Revé studied the photos for a moment—first those of Toole's machete, then his glowing footprints, and then the stunning image taken from the rear floorboards. With her eyes welling, she turned and handed them to John.

John took his own hard look at the photos, lingering over the last, then glanced up at Matthews and nodded briefly. Finally, he turned and wordlessly embraced his anguished wife.

Twenty-seven years of not knowing, Matthews thought, looking on. And now they finally did.

FORT LAUDERDALE, FLORIDA—JULY 14, 2006

As Matthews left Kelly Hancock's law offices that day, he knew well that he had settled the first of the items on the investigation's agenda. If there had ever been a doubt in the minds of

John and Revé Walsh as to what had happened to their son, not a shred now remained.

But still before him was the matter of presenting an investigative file that would convince the Hollywood police to name Ottis Toole as the person responsible. Until the killer was charged—and never mind that he was dead, and no matter how many other slayings he had been convicted of—John and Revé Walsh could never rest.

Especially not after what they'd seen that day. As a law officer and a father of four himself, Matthews understood well the importance of the task that remained. One last bit of business, and then, just maybe, he could rest.

There were several items Matthews wanted to bolster in his report, but one of the first things he did was to place a call to Reaves Roofing in Jacksonville, seeking information on the employment records of Bobby Lee Jones, the man who said he had put the dent in Ottis Toole's bumper and who had told Broward County State Attorney's Office investigator Philip Mundy in 1996 that Toole had confessed the crime to him as early as 1982. When Matthews finally reached family member Alan Reaves at the company offices, Reaves explained that John Reaves Jr. had recently died of cancer. Alan Reaves said that he'd be happy to help, but that no records prior to 1986 were any longer in existence. They had been eaten by termites while in storage, Reaves explained.

Matthews briefly contemplated the fact that even insects seemed to have conspired against him in his pursuit of the investigation, but it was not in his nature to dwell upon disappointment. He simply shook his head and moved on, intent upon building a body of evidence that would compel any law enforcement agency to conclude that a certain individual had committed this crime and that a successful prosecution could be carried out.

Still, events around him were a constant reminder that time

had its own way of imposing a statute of limitations on a case. In July 2007, former Hollywood police chief Dick Witt, who had ordered Matthews off the cold case investigation back in 1996, died in Ormand Beach, where he had retired. And in early November, current Hollywood chief James Scarberry, the man who had authorized opening his department's files to Matthews, retired, hounded by accusations that he had tipped off his command staff that several corrupt Hollywood detectives had been targeted by an FBI sting operation.

Scarberry's departure was no great disappointment to Matthews, for while the chief had posed no impediment to his investigation, he was clearly not greatly interested in the matter either. In fact, as Matthews reviewed the files that had been turned over to him, it became clear that even though every tip that had come to *America's Most Wanted* over the years since the airing of the Adam episode in 1996 had been passed along— leads that Matthews had pursued all the way from Florida to Colorado and points in between—*not one* had ever been pursued by Hollywood PD.

Still, he reminded himself, that was all water under the bridge. The more pressing issue now was the inclination of Scarberry's successor, Chad Wagner, who'd risen through the ranks at Hollywood PD, beginning as a patrolman in 1983 to become assistant chief under Scarberry.

Would Wagner prove to be another in a long line of administrators who would rather the matter were simply buried once and for all, or would he throw the roadblocks up once again? The answer was not long in coming.

In December, Mark Smith of the Hollywood PD, now a captain of detectives at Hollywood PD, called Matthews. By this time Matthews had come across the "ulterior motives" memo Smith had written years before, but Matthews said nothing. Smith was either going to be a help or a hindrance, and bringing up the matter would accomplish nothing.

Smith explained that he was calling on behalf of the newly appointed Chief Wagner, who wondered whether or not Matthews might be able to provide him with an address for John Walsh. Wagner wanted to introduce himself, Smith said, and he also wanted to extend his personal condolences to the Walsh family. Matthews held the phone away from his ear to stare at it for a moment, not sure he had heard correctly.

He gave Smith the address, then went back to work, wondering if he might have imagined the incident. A few days later, however, he got a call from John Walsh, who began by saying, "You're not going to believe this letter I just received . . ." Matthews said nothing, just listened quietly as John Walsh described the contents of the first unsolicited communication that had ever passed from the Hollywood PD to him and his family in more than twenty-six years. Matthews could hear it in Walsh's voice—how much that gesture meant to a still-grieving family.

Then, in late January of the following year, at a reception following a Broward County Police Academy graduation, Dick Brickman, the president of the Broward County Police Benevolent Association, took Matthews by the arm and introduced him to Chief Wagner. Matthews let Wagner know how much his letter meant to the Walsh family, surprising the chief when he mentioned the fact that it was the first such gesture they had ever received from his agency.

Matthews also told Wagner that he was well along on a cold case investigation of the murder of Adam Walsh that had been authorized by Chief Scarberry. Matthews explained that his progress had been delayed by the fact that his ninety-four-year-old mother was now confined to the hospital, where he sometimes took parts of the Walsh case file to work on at her bedside. Still, he looked forward to presenting his report to Chief Wagner soon.

For his part, Wagner seemed glad to hear the news. "I'll read every page," he assured Matthews. They were heartening words, and Wagner seemed sincere enough, Matthews thought, but he had heard a lot of promises in his day.

Still, he continued with work on his report, obsessed with checking every fact, tying up every loose end, reducing his findings to their essence. He prepared a meticulous timeline of the case drawn from the myriad agency reports and supplemental memos, for the first time placing the events and discoveries in order from first to last, and providing a context from which patterns of cause and effect might be discerned.

As an investigator, Matthews was most concerned with the assemblage of evidence. But he also understood that unless he was able to convey those facts in a compelling way, all his hard work was likely to go for naught. He had a natural gift for storytelling and was entirely at ease in front of an audience or a camera, but laying a story out on paper, he soon discovered, was another matter altogether.

On the most basic level, he'd never been the greatest at grammar, and when his mother, Margaret, who'd had a long career as a librarian and was still keen and vibrant despite her years, offered to proofread for him as he went, Matthews was glad to have her help. She had always been interested in the stories he brought home from work, and this was the story of them all.

From time to time, she'd glance up from the pages to offer advice that went beyond matters of the comma splice: "Are you sure you're not being too tough on this fellow here, Joey?" she might ask. And usually, she was right.

One day in March, Matthews arrived at the hospital to find one of his mother's doctors waiting to speak with him outside her room. His mother had a lot of life left, the doctor agreed, but her heartbeat was acting up. She needed a pacemaker implanted, a relatively minor procedure, if any operation could be called minor when the patient was ninety-four.

"You can blame it on my son," Matthews's mother told the

doctor when the pair came into the room to discuss the matter with her. "If you were reading what I've been reading, your heart would be racing, too."

That might be, the doctor allowed, but there was no question in his mind that the operation would make her much more comfortable. They talked it over with Matthews's brother Peter and younger sister Mariann once they arrived, and in the end, the procedure was agreed to.

At first, word from surgery was positive. The operation proceeded without a hitch. Then, suddenly, there were complications. And just as suddenly, on March 18, 2006, his mother was dead, stunning everyone. Michelina Militana "Margaret" Matthews, the daughter of Sicilian immigrants, had led a long and loving life, but if anything, all those years had only suggested to Matthews that somehow she always would be with him.

A few days after the funeral, Matthews forced himself back to his office, where his still-unfinished report lay on his desk. How many people had died in the quarter-century-plus he'd worked on this case? Matthews asked himself. Now even his mother had gone to her grave, with her sticky notes still attached to the pages in front of him.

Another victim of the case, you might call her, he found himself thinking. And when you came right down to it, how much time did he have left? If he croaked, what the hell would happen to all this work then?

With such thoughts in mind, he pinched the bridge of his nose between his forefinger and his thumb, closed his eyes briefly, then took a deep breath and went back to his report.

HOLLYWOOD, FLORIDA—APRIL 30, 2008

On a bright spring afternoon late in April 2008, Joe Matthews appeared at the office of Hollywood police chief Chad Wagner with a thick bound sheaf tucked under his arm. He wished with all his heart that his mother could have looked over his shoulder just once more before he handed the document over, but he had assembled the evidence to the best of his ability, given the writing all he had, and it was time to put up or shut up.

When he handed over the report to Wagner, he stressed the importance of the FDLE crime scene photos he'd had developed for the first time. Wagner was curious as to why such evidence had not been examined before, but Matthews couldn't explain that one. He had had the devil's own time even getting hold of the photos, he told Wagner, explaining that when he'd found them missing from the Hollywood file, he'd had to go to the FDLE himself to find the film and get the prints developed.

Why didn't Sergeant Lyle Bean get these prints added to the department file? Wagner wanted to know. But again, Matthews couldn't answer. Bean had claimed he'd requested the photos several times from the FDLE and was told that the photos did not exist, that's all Matthews knew for sure. He tapped his report. "In the end, we got what we needed."

"That may be so," Wagner said. "But I'll find out why it took so long to get those photos, rest assured of that."

Whatever the upshot of any conversations with Bean regarding the matter, Wagner did not share it with Matthews, though the irony that it took an outsider to accomplish what no detective had in twenty-five years was clearly not lost on the chief. Matthews took the opportunity to point out that while he had gone back through the tool marking test procedures regarding the machete to no avail, DNA testing on that clearly blood-soaked handle had never been performed. Matthews could not authorize such testing, but the weapon was still in possession of the Hollywood PD, and the chief surely could.

And he would, Wagner assured Matthews. The day following, Matthews got a phone call from Sergeant Lyle Bean. The chief wanted that machete tested for DNA, Bean explained, and he was calling to talk about the matter with Matthews before he sent it out.

So far, Wagner had been as good as his word, Matthews thought. Matthews then explained to Bean that he'd spoken to a forensic geneticist after he'd seen the luminol indications on the wooden handle of the machete. That specialist suggested that the handle be drilled for samples, and not scraped as was normally done, based on the assumption that the blood had soaked into the wood over time. Matthews would never learn whether or not Bean passed his expert's suggestions along, and furthermore, the results seemed to take forever in coming back. It was not until October 14 that Chief Wagner called Matthews to let him know the disappointing findings. The results were, in a word, "inconclusive." Not negative. Not positive. Just, maddeningly, "inconclusive."

All the while, Matthews continued to pore over the files, wondering if he might have missed something that, however small, or seemingly unimportant, might lead him to an unexpected find. He was reviewing the phone and e-mail tips that had come in to *America's Most Wanted* following the airing of the episode on Adam in 1996, when one phone intake sheet caught his eye. On September 21, at 11:10 p.m., a call had come from someone named Wendy Sapp, identifying herself to an operator as a niece of Toole's. The operator had noted, "In 1982 Ottis told caller and relatives that he killed Adam." Matthews racked his brain, trying to remember. He'd talked to Sarah Patterson and to Joel Cockerman at some length, but as to a Wendy Sapp, he was drawing nothing but blanks.

There was certainly nothing in the file to suggest that anyone at Hollywood PD had followed up on this or any of the other tips *AMW* had supplied, but he could certainly talk to her now. He picked up the phone and launched into a series of calls, until finally he found himself talking to one Wendy Sapp Fralick. And, yes, her mother had been previously married to a man named Dickie McHenry, who, she believed, was a cousin of Ottis Toole.

"Uncle Ottis" had often babysat for her and her sisters, Fralick said, and she remembered quite clearly that one night he had told her that he killed Adam Walsh. She was a bit hazy on any details that he might have given, for that was a long time ago. Besides, she told Matthews, she was only eight at the time and didn't truly comprehend the magnitude of his statements.

However, Fralick said, about four years ago she had spent some time with her cousin Erica Toole, the daughter of Howard and Georgia Toole, from whom Ottis had stolen the truck back in June 1981. During that 2004 visit, Fralick brought up the subject of Adam Walsh, and Erica replied that her father Howard, Ottis's brother, had told her that Ottis did in fact murder Adam.

With Fralick's help, Matthews then tracked down her mother Linda, who was by then remarried to a man name Gerald Orand. It was Orand who answered the phone, explaining that his wife was recuperating from a stroke. She had difficulty being understood at times, but she very much wanted to communicate with Matthews, presuming he was who he claimed to be, that is.

After Orand called *America's Most Wanted* to verify Matthews's identity, he got back to the detective, along with his wife Linda. Linda explained a bit of the family tree at the outset of the conversation. She had first been married to a man named Willie Sapp, the father of Wendy. After divorcing Sapp, she married Dickie McHenry, the brother of Georgia Toole, who was married to Ottis's brother Howard.

As to the things that Wendy had told Matthews about Ottis and Adam Walsh, Linda did have a few things she would like to add. On an early winter afternoon in 1981 or 1982, she said, she and Dickie took her kids over to Howard and Georgia's for a visit. Ottis happened to be there that day, and was sitting out in the backyard, drinking beer. While Georgia stayed inside to feed the kids and Howard took a bath, Linda and Dickie went out to the yard to sit with Ottis. He offered them both a beer, she told Matthews, but neither one of them felt like drinking that day, and they declined.

Ottis started talking about how he missed his niece Becky Powell, Linda said. He told them that both he and Henry Lee Lucas liked to fuck her, but Henry Lee had run off with her. After contemplating that dismal fact for a bit, Linda recalls that Ottis then announced to them that it was he who "took" Adam Walsh.

"Who is Adam Walsh?" Linda asked Ottis. She had never heard a thing about the matter at that time.

"The one who's been missing," he responded.

Linda told Matthews that Toole went on to recount how he kidnapped this little boy down in Broward County, fucked him in the butt, cut his head off, cut his body up in pieces, then put the pieces in plastic bags and dumped them. The descriptions were so vivid that Linda stood up and vomited into some nearby bushes.

Ottis watched her wiping her mouth and laughed. "You pregnant or something?" he asked.

"No," she answered. "You make me sick, that's all."

A bit later, Linda said, Ottis offered to take Wendy and her two sisters out for ice cream. "Here's Ottis," she said to Matthews, her outrage palpable still, "who just got through talking about raping Becky Powell and some little boy and then chopping him up in pieces, and he wants to take my kids out for ice cream?"

After that, she made sure her children were never left alone with Ottis Toole. And that is also why Howard and his wife moved up to Georgia soon after, to get away from Ottis. Everyone in the family knew Ottis had killed Adam Walsh, she said. It was simply common knowledge.

Then why on earth had she never told anyone about these

things? Matthews asked. Linda didn't miss a beat. "Because no one ever asked," she said. "You're the first that ever did."

Matthews sat back in his chair and stared at the ceiling for a long time after his conversation with Linda McHenry Orand. Common knowledge among the members of a family that one of their own had kidnapped and killed Adam Walsh. And because no one had ever asked, not one of them stepped forward to tell.

Matthews wrote up a summary of his interviews with Wendy Sapp Fralick and her mother Linda and added them to the list that had been with Chief Wagner for several months now. He also pointed out that the 1996 tip from Sapp had been passed along to the Hollywood PD at the time, just as every tip involving the case had been.

All the while, Matthews couldn't help thinking about Ottis Toole's reply to Linda's question, "Who is Adam Walsh?"

"The one who's been missing," she claimed Toole told her. Not, "The one they found."

Finally, it struck him. If Linda Orand had all her facts straight, if those were indeed Toole's words, then this conversation had taken place *before* Adam's remains had been found, less than two weeks after the killing. Of course Linda wouldn't have heard about "Adam Walsh" all the way up in Jacksonville. At that point, before the fisherman had made their startling discovery, the Walshes were having a difficult time getting anyone outside Dade and Broward Counties to realize their son had been abducted. And there was Ottis Toole sitting in a lawn chair, swigging beer and calmly recounting to his own sister the details of the crime.

Two years before, in a newspaper article commemorating the twenty-fifth anniversary of the crime, criminologist Vernon Geberth had a rhetorical-sounding response for reporters who wanted to know if he believed the Adam Walsh case could ever be solved: "A relative of the killer who knows about the crime may want to finally unburden himself." Or *themselves*, Matthews thought.

The statement might have been only Vernon Geberth's wishful thinking at the time, but Wendy Sapp Fralick and her mother Linda Orand had just become an investigator's wish come true.

Linda McHenry Orand's statement—along with the extortion letter Toole had sent John Walsh and the damning images developed from the FDLE negatives—might have seemed yet another finding upon which a successful prosecution could have been based all by itself, but as Matthews well knew, there is a vast difference between real life and film and television drama, where justice is served up in a moment—one witness breaks down in racking sobs or a single, searing image is produced.

Nowhere had that distinction been made more clear than in the long history of this matter. If it was as simple as dropping one bombshell, then this case would have been closed long ago. Of course, charges are filed readily when an officer catches a perpetrator in the act, or when a suspect is apprehended and confesses. In this instance, however—where a suspect already in custody had confessed to the crime—the state attorney's office asked accordingly that evidence corroborating that confession be presented by police in a form that would suggest any charge as well founded. And no one in law enforcement had ever gone to the trouble of such a submission.

For that reason, Matthews did not for a moment contemplate fashioning a report that did not take into account every shred of evidence that had accumulated concerning the matter. The bombshells would have to take their places in the long chain of evidence, items both great and small. This wasn't a movie, this was life . . . and death.

Accordingly, for two years and nine months Matthews labored on his review of the 10,000-page case file. He reexamined all the taped interviews conducted with Toole and others and conducted his own independent searches, interviews, and analyses of materials pertinent. He found new evidence, and with all the disparate pieces assembled in narrative order for the first time—the many materials upon which this account is based—everything pointed to an inescapable conclusion: Ottis Toole was the man who'd committed the crime.

Certainly, Joe Matthews had long suspected Toole, and it was to his everlasting dismay that he had not been given the opportunity to conduct his own interview with the man and extract and nail down Toole's confession himself. One of the most powerful pieces of evidence that he'd come across in the course of his investigation came from a former Texas Ranger who sent Matthews a videotaped interview conducted with Toole by a former colleague who—shortly after Henry Lee Lucas was arrested—had flown Toole out to that state to try and clear a murder case in their jurisdiction. The interview took place on March 26, 1984, several weeks after Jack Hoffman had accepted Toole's recanting of his various confessions.

During the interview an avuncular Ranger draws Toole out about his typical modus operandi for murder, and Toole rattles on readily—almost cheerfully—about the thrill of shooting old ladies hanging out laundry and garroting unsuspecting drag queens. But when the questioning turns to the case of Adam Walsh, Matthews points out, everything in Toole's demeanor suddenly changes.

"You can see it in his body language," Matthews says, and indeed the signs are apparent to anyone. As Toole (who had offered few specifics in many of the other cases brought up that day) leads the Ranger through the details—the kidnapping and the beating and the effort involved in the decapitation, the wrapping of Adam's head in his shirt and its disposal and the disposal of the body—his shoulders tense and round inward, the cadences of his speech slow, his tone becomes serious, even plaintive, his gaze is suddenly evasive. What Matthews wouldn't have given to be able to climb into the frame and attach Toole to his polygraph instrument!

At one point, when the Ranger interrupts Toole to ask if he

had done anything to Adam's body before he began to burn it, Toole's response is electric. "Oh no," he says, as his eyes roll and his head snaps in emphatic negative.

In place of needles dancing across a polygraph scroll, Matthews had to be content with the reaction of the Ranger. Following the conclusion of Toole's account of eating a few of Adam's ribs before scattering the charred remains, the burly veteran turned away, his disgust scarcely concealed: "Well, that's pretty stout."

As far as his report, Matthews felt that he had done everything he could under the circumstances, and in his opinion, it was far more than enough. His opinion was not the one that mattered any longer, though. He could only wait and see what the response of Chad Wagner might be. If his report was deemed sufficiently convincing, then Wagner might carry it to the Broward state attorney and recommend that Ottis Toole be charged with the crime. But Wagner might not do that, no matter what he thought of the quality of the report.

The new chief seemed a decent man, but he was also the preeminent representative of an entire police force, and—by extension and association—of the governing structure of an entire community. If he swept aside Matthews's report, he would only be doing what many before him had seemingly chosen to do. In weighing the good to be done by naming a killer against the harm it would do to the very institution one was hired to champion, they had all apparently decided in kind: such a blow to the established order could not be justified by the closure it might provide to a family or the vague sense of justice it might provide to the world at large.

In any case, Matthews thought, it was not his call. He could only sit and wait. If Wagner didn't want to proceed on the basis of what he'd presented, maybe there was a way he could get it straight to the state attorney's office himself.

On Friday, November 14, 2008, Adam Walsh's thirty-fourth birthday passed, and, then, six days later, on November 20, Matthews realized that he would not have to worry about moving things forward himself: Chief Wagner had called a meeting at the Broward County State Attorney's Office.

Present on that day with Wagner were second-in-command state attorney Chuck Morton, assistant chief of Hollywood PD Louis Granteed, Captain Mark Smith, and Hollywood Police legal adviser Joel Cantor. Also present were John and Revé Walsh, their attorney, former Broward prosecutor Kelly Hancock, and Detective Sergeant Joe Matthews.

Wagner had called the meeting to discuss the report compiled by Sergeant Matthews, he explained. Would anyone in the room, Wagner wanted to know, object to the conclusions in the report that Matthews had placed before them? Bits and pieces were familiar to many in the room, and were branded indelibly in the minds of others, but here laid out in Matthews report was the full story:

- Toole's knowledge of crime scene details only the killer could have known
- Dismissal of the theory that a "book contract" tainted Toole's confessions
- Multiple eyewitness identifications of Toole taking Adam from Sears
- Arlene and Heidi Maier's ID of Toole at Kmart the night before Adam was taken
- The damning extortion letter Toole wrote John Walsh offering to lead him to his son's body
- Twenty-five independent confessions to the crime made by Ottis Toole, including that to family member Linda Fralick before Adam's remains were found
- The never-before-seen luminol images of the bloody machete handle and footprints on the carpet of Toole's Cadillac
- And the most damning image of them all . . . which had both haunted and sustained Matthews since the

moment it had wavered into focus on his office desk months before, as powerful to him as the Shroud of Turin:

Traced in the blue glow of luminol was the outline of a familiar young boy's face, a negative pressed into floorboard carpeting, eye sockets blackened blank cavities, mouth twisted in an oval of pain.

Ottis Toole had told detectives time and again. He'd hacked off Adam's head and decided to keep it for a while. Perhaps he'd had sex with it, perhaps he hadn't. He'd tossed it into the back of his car and driven up the turnpike, before it dawned on him that this might be a bad idea.

Why hadn't the men in charge of the investigation taken Toole at his word? Matthews wondered as he stood among those gathered in the state's attorney's office and stared at the image once again. Why?

Still, as the ancients understood, truth has its implacable force. One of the most haunting of the tales told by the Brothers Grimm is that of the "Singing Flute," in which a craven man kills his younger brother to steal his bounty and buries his body beneath a bridge. Years later, a shepherd discovers a snow-white little bone on the sand beneath the bridge and carves a flute out of it. But when the shepherd begins to play, what issues is not music. Instead it is the voice of the long-dead boy, thanking the shepherd and telling the truth at last. "Ah, friend, thou blowest upon my bone! Long have I lain beside the water; my brother slew me for the boar."

What Joe Matthews had produced—the terrible image which he'd had to show to John and Revé and which everyone in the room around him now viewed as well—was no less powerful in its effect. The glowing blue image pressed into the carpet—the outline of Adam's face, etched in his own blood—was as stark as any fragment of bone; and the cry that issued from his battered lips was as damning an indictment as anyone might ever hear. Poor Adam, friend Joe, the truth singing to the world at last.

Following the summary of Matthews's findings, everyone in the room had the opportunity to respond. As to the image of Adam's face branded into the floorboards of Toole's Cadillac, it was an emotional haymaker, of course, but as he described in his report, Matthews had gone to some lengths to bolster its significance. Shortly after he'd made the discovery, Matthews met with Miami Dade crime lab analyst Detective Thomas Charles to discuss techniques of blood transfer that he might use to duplicate that final image he'd found in the FDLE photographs. As a result of that discussion, Matthews conducted a series of experiments using paint of various consistencies, plastic facial masks, and auto carpeting of the type that was in Toole's Cadillac.

As he detailed, Matthews employed eight different means of transferring paint from saturated plastic face masks onto carpet. And each resulted in the transfer of images to the carpet that were remarkably similar to the one that Matthews had found on the rear floorboards of Toole's car. So far as his research could determine, no crime scene investigator had confirmed such blood evidence previously.

After everyone in the room had delivered their estimations of all that Matthews had presented, Wagner had his mandate, and it was unanimous. All agreed that the investigation of the homicide of Adam Walsh would—pending the final approval of Broward County state attorney Michael Satz—be "exceptionally cleared." Translated, the phrase meant that were Ottis Toole still alive, he would be charged, arrested, prosecuted, and, in all likelihood, convicted of the abduction and murder of Adam Walsh.

Matthews watched on, scarcely able to believe what he was witnessing. For many years, he'd hoped to find a partner, one individual at Hollywood PD who seemed as determined to solve this case as he. In Chad Wagner, it seemed he finally had.

On Wednesday, December 10, Chad Wagner called Joe Matthews with the news. He had just received a letter from the state attorney's office. Michael Satz—the man who had been Broward state attorney in 1981 when Adam disappeared, and who had held the post ever since—had made his call.

Would Matthews like to be the one to let John and Revé Walsh know? And did he mind asking if the Walshes could be present at Hollywood police headquarters on the afternoon of December 16, 2008? Wagner wanted to hold a press conference to announce the decision to the world.

HOLLYWOOD, FLORIDA—DECEMBER 16, 2008

As promised, the press conference Wagner arranged took place at department headquarters the following Tuesday afternoon, with reporters from every major news organization in the United States jostling for space in the crowded training room. More than twenty-seven years had passed since Adam Walsh went missing and was found brutally murdered, and in spite of all the time that had gone by—or perhaps because of it—the case still had the power to mesmerize a nation. This was, after all, an event that had changed how every parent in America viewed the world.

Among the myriad, unkillable pieces of spam that circulate through the Ethernet is one that invites readers of a certain age to "remember when." Popular songs once had melodies, we are reminded, and stores were once closed on Sundays, and "underwear" meant exactly that.

But there are more poignant notes on the list, including an invocation of those innocent summer days when kids blew past a banging screen door with a shouted promise to be "home by dark," and who ever worried about that? Today, of course, such carelessness upon the part of parents is unthinkable, if not vaguely criminal in itself. Perhaps, once upon a time, parents only worried about their kids when they took them to the beach or to the pool, or hiking along some steep path. Now vigilance begins at birth, if not before, and for most the worry never ends.

In his book *Tears of Rage*, John Walsh gave his own account of how the apparently unsolvable case had impacted his life and that of Revé. He said then that though it was terribly painful to revisit such loss, he wanted to do so in hopes that it might help others who had lost children to senseless tragedy. Mostly, he said, he wanted to talk about "how to come to terms with life when you think you're dying of a broken heart."

At that same time, Revé spoke of the helplessness they felt in the aftermath of Adam's disappearance and the subsequent string of failures by law enforcement. "I remember thinking, 'Our son's been murdered, and now *we've* got to be the ones to do something about it?' " she said.

"It was a sad thing for this country that the fight had to be led by two broken-down parents of a murdered child," she added. "But we had to, because no one else was going to do it."

Imagine then, the anticipation of John and Revé Walsh as the chief entered the room and called for order. He was there to announce that the 1981 murder of six-year-old Adam Walsh had been solved, "a day that's long overdue," Wagner said, before adding, "This case could have been closed years ago."

Furthermore, he was not there to brandish news of some "smoking gun" unearthed miraculously after years of fruitless gumshoe work, he said. Rather, his announcement was the result of the assembly and examination of evidence that had been there all along. "What was there was everything that was in front of our face for years."

His department had been too defensive about its mistakes in the past and could well have arrested the chief suspect for the crime before he died, Wagner said, apologizing to the Walshes for those lapses. But make no mistake about it, were Ottis Toole alive today, he would be arrested and charged with the crime.

And—Wagner was certain—he would have paid for it with his life.

As might be expected, the announcement prompted a barrage of questions from the assembled media. A choked-up John Walsh told reporters that the announcement was a reaffirmation of the fact that Adam didn't die in vain. "For all the other victims who haven't gotten justice," he added, "I say one thing: 'Don't give up hope.'"

When reporters turned to Revé Walsh, she spoke simply and poignantly. "This is a wonderful day, in spite of why we're here. Nothing will bring back our beautiful little boy," she said, "but at least the knowing will close this chapter of our lives."

In that same vein, John Walsh added that while the family would never recover from Adam's death, they could finally move on. Still, he noted, "It's not about closure; it's about justice."

Maybe it was a little of both—closure *and* justice—Joe Matthews thought, as he watched from the wings. As a friend of John and Revé, he understood how important this announcement was—we now know who killed your son, and we should have found out sooner. And as a cop, Matthews also reveled in the fact that a killer had finally gotten his due.

As to the fact that his own name had not been mentioned prominently on this day, that was at his own request. The moment was for the Walshes. His wife Ginny had been in the room as Wagner made his announcement, and as she observed of the family, "It looks as if they're taking their first deep breaths in years."

To Matthews the words rang particularly true. Wagner's pronouncement wasn't going to change the Walshes' lives in an instant—he was reminded of something Revé had once told him when he'd asked her about her grieving:

"It's like you've been in a terrible accident and had your arm amputated," she told him. "After a while, the pain goes away, and eventually you even learn to get along without your arm.

Some days you're sad that you're missing your arm, and some days you're angry about it, and some days you're okay. But, no matter what, no matter how long it's been, you never stop missing your arm."

The simple observation had jolted Matthews at the time. But still, he thought, this day *was* a milestone, a place from which a new journey could begin.

Matthews had overheard Ginny bidding Revé farewell. "I wish you and your family a truly wonderful and Merry Christmas," she said simply.

Revé paused and took her husband's hand. "Thank you," she told Ginny. Her eyes were brimming, but she managed a smile. "This *will* be our first Merry Christmas in twenty-seven years." Even Matthews found himself choked up at that one.

And if anyone present chose to assume that it was Chad Wagner and his men who'd finally put two and two together, that was okay, too. Wagner was, in Matthews's eyes, deserving of plenty of credit. There were surely many of the chief's own men who would have preferred that he simply do as all his predecessors had done. But Chad Wagner was a stand-up cop.

Furthermore, John and Revé Walsh knew how this day had come to be, as did Matthews's own family and all his friends in law enforcement, and that was fine by him. Most important, Matthews felt the presence of his mother in the room, gazing at him with pride, nodding her approval. He'd done his job, banging away at the case for twenty-seven years, and justice had prevailed.

So now, he'd go down to the beach, treat himself to a good cigar, and watch the waves roll in and out. He'd earned it.

As John Walsh made the rounds of the talk shows in the following days, he was quick to point out that were it not for Joe Matthews, he would not be having those conversations, and he reiterated his praise for the retired homicide detective at the close of the year-end episode of *America's Most Wanted*. But even there, it was hardly possible to explain what was really a twenty-seven-year process. Chief Wagner gave hints at the news conference, alluding to the fact that much of the evidence that prompted the closing of the case had been available all along; but he did not go on to add the obvious—"available had anyone competent been in charge of the search and the effort to put a case together."

Furthermore, when Wagner said to reporters, "If you're looking for that magic wand or that hidden document that just appeared, it's not there," his intent was likely to defuse the sort of "Perry Mason" effect engendered by years of exposure to manufactured drama. Still, while neither Wagner nor anyone else wanted any part of a trial by media on that day, one might speculate as to what the effect would have been had he filled a screen with the images of Ottis Toole's bloody footprints glowing on the floorboards of his Cadillac or the rendering of a silent scream from a young boy's severed head.

Along with reminders of how important the Walshes' good works had been—"If people hold their kids a little bit closer in crowded stores these days, thank the Walshes," one writer said—there were also, predictably, a few doubters who surfaced in the wake of Chief Wagner's announcement. A *Miami Herald* story published on December 28, 2008, quoted a Washington criminal profiler as being "appalled" by the decision to close the case without more proof. The story rehashed the reluctance of Hollywood police to charge Toole at the time of his first series of confessions, and also quoted Ron Hickman's 2001 statement to reporter de Vise, "I spent 100 hours with that individual. I'll tell you right now: He didn't do it."

There was "no new evidence" presented, the *Herald* story said, suggesting that either the reporter had not bothered to read the same evidence file that Joe Matthews and Chief Wagner had, or he was simply longing for that "magic wand" that Wagner referred to. The story referenced the various inconsistencies in Toole's own confessions—including his erstwhile claims that Henry Lee Lucas had taken part, and his varying reports of where he'd disposed of Adam's body. And it also quoted a Broward assistant state attorney as saying that while his office had indeed supported the closing of the case, all the mistakes made by police would have made a successful prosecution difficult were Toole still alive.

Joe Matthews might have agreed, though he might have also pointed back to the successful prosecution of Dieter Reichmann, where prosecutors had even less physical evidence and two dozen fewer confessions on the part of the perpetrator. While any prosecutor might like to have a videotape of a killer in the act to carry into court, the truth is that many celebrated cases have resulted in convictions based almost entirely on circumstantial evidence—from which jurors must *infer* a perpetrator's guilt.

Despite any public perception to the contrary, the U.S. Supreme Court long ago established the precept that "circumstantial evidence is intrinsically no different from testimonial [direct] evidence" (*Holland v. United States*, 1954). As any competent prosecutor knows, the distinction between direct testimony and circumstantial evidence has little practical effect in the presentation or admissibility of evidence in trials. And while the so-called *CSI* effect might suggest that anything less than a mountain of forensic evidence tying a killer to the crime is insufficient, a number of recent studies have shown that jurors have not changed—even if prosecutors may feel the need to introduce high-tech data, juries remain as likely to be persuaded by logical argument as anything else.

In another piece published soon after the announcement, a veteran South Florida columnist expressed his own doubts about Hollywood PD's willingness to put an end to the matter. He'd been one of the reporters who had trooped to the multijurisdictional press conference called in Monroe, Louisiana, back in 1983, where authorities were quick to attribute a raft of unsolved killings to Henry Lee Lucas and Ottis Toole. The columnist said that he and his colleagues had been too eager to believe cops back then, when they blamed Lucas and Toole for various crimes that were later attributed to others or which were never successfully prosecuted. Thus, why after all this time believe that police had finally found the killer of Adam Walsh? "It was like a miracle, conjured up with hardly anything in the way of new evidence," the column concluded, ignoring the fact that "old" evidence, even twenty-seven-year-old evidence, becomes "new" when it is finally given a logical context.

Of course, successful prosecutions are always difficult, even when the physical evidence seems ironclad—just ask those who went after O. J. And while one Broward County state attorney may have forecast a difficult time proving the case, another prominent former prosecutor interviewed by a *Sun-Sentinel* reporter weighed in that he had gone to court on several instances with much less.

In fact, FBI findings disclosed just weeks before the press conference, in the case of Caylee Anthony, the two-year-old Orlando girl thought to have been murdered by her mother, Casey, would support Matthews's analysis of the images he had found on the carpets of Toole's car. A September 30, 2008, e-mail from FBI intelligence analyst Karen B. Cowan to a fellow agency employee identified a bodily fluids outline lifted from the trunk liner of Casey Anthony's car using essentially the same methodology. "If you look closely at this photo, there appears to be the outline or silhouette of a child in the fetal position," Cowan wrote. Shortly thereafter, Casey Anthony was arrested and charged with the crime.

And as for "believing," why believe anything, Plato might respond, when the very nature of reality is—like shadows flickering on a cave wall, twice removed from the source—such a subjective matter? Had there been a dozen witnesses present when Ottis Toole carried Adam Walsh from his car, laid him on the ground, and severed his head, there would have been a dozen different accounts as to just what had occurred.

Subjectivity, along with contrariness, is a part of human nature. And when it comes to newspaper adjudications of controversial cases, as the cigar-chomping editor is quick to remind the cub reporter, "Keep the trouble coming. Good news just doesn't sell."

In keeping with that notion, as recently as March 2010, more than fifteen months after the case was cleared by authorities, the *Miami Herald* published a front-page story suggesting that indeed it was Jeffrey Dahmer who had been responsible for the killing, asserting that two new witnesses had come forward claiming to have spotted a disheveled, disturbing-looking man in the vicinity of the Sears store the day that Adam Walsh disappeared. They'd only realized it was Jeffrey Dahmer, they said, after learning of Dahmer's heinous activities a decade later in 1991.

A comparison of the mug shots of preppy-looking Dahmer—who by most accounts long eluded suspicion precisely because he appeared harmless—with those of Ottis Toole suggests the true identity of the frightening individual these new witnesses had actually seen that day in Sears. And most law enforcement officials interviewed for the story scoffed at the notion that Dahmer could have been charged, much less prosecuted, on the basis of such claims.

"The delayed Dahmer identifications certainly add intrigue and mystery to Adam Walsh's tragic death," Chief Assistant State Attorney Chuck Morton wrote in response to the questions of *Herald* reporters at the time. In his eyes, Morton said, such claims might even form the basis for the writing of a murder mystery novel, "but they do not come close to supporting the filing of criminal charges."

As Morton went on to explain, eyewitness identifications

made years after the commission of a crime are among the least reliable forms of argument in criminal prosecutions. "Such identifications would have to be corroborated by overwhelmingly credible evidence in order to have 'probable cause' to prosecute the suspect for that crime—e.g., credible admissions by the suspect or credible and indisputable physical evidence that directly links the suspect to the criminal act." Joe Matthews had finally pieced together such a web of corroborating evidence against Ottis Toole, one that had been validated by Assistant Police Chief Mark Smith and others at HPD, Morton pointed out to reporters. He reiterated his opinion that even though a successful prosecution of Toole might have been difficult, the thought of so much as filing charges against Dahmer was out of the question.

Very little of Morton's response was printed, however, and soon the *Herald* story had prompted breathless headlines of the "Bigfoot" variety in various supermarket tabloids, one of which theorized that Adam Walsh was still alive somewhere, even providing a computer-generated rendition of what he would look like as an adult so that readers could keep an eye out. Such stories might seem outlandish, but they are also proof of how deeply the psyche of the entire nation has been affected by the Adam Walsh matter and by the time it took for a credible case to be built. Indeed, unless "old news" is of the caliber of the Kennedy assassination, the paranoia-fostering tabloid press simply doesn't get involved.

When a rehash of the *Herald* story ran on a local Vero Beach station at the time, John Walsh turned to Revé and blurted, "For God's sakes, aren't the ghouls ever going to give up?"

Revé glanced at him. "Maybe not," she said. "But at least you and I know the truth now."

One of the complaints made by those who have expressed doubt as to Toole's guilt has to do with his penchant for changing the details of his story over time. But Joe Matthews sees that as a positive. Were no detail to vary in a killer's various confessions, Matthews points out, *then* you might worry that you were hearing a tale memorized and scripted for some hidden purpose.

"It happens time and again," Matthews explains to students in his classes on interrogation technique: "Stage one, you'll ask the person about the crime and you get total denial. So you talk about other things for a while, and then you come back to the crime again. The second time around, the party might allow as how he knows who did the deed and implicate somebody else. When you circle back for a third time, the guy says, 'Well, actually, I was there, but I was: (a) outside the bedroom where it all happened, (b) just driving the car, (c) didn't realize what was going to take place.' By stage four, you'll get some admission, like 'Well, actually I helped hold her down,' or 'Yeah, maybe I dug the grave.' And by the time you get to stage five, there is no other person involved, and the perpetrator is sitting there telling you he is responsible for every last thing you've been talking about all this time."

From the point at which a confession has been made, all you are likely to get from a perpetrator is damage control, Matthews says. Once a perpetrator realizes that the confession just delivered is a virtual death sentence, why wouldn't he try and reverse the process? Recanting is simply common practice.

As for the incidental details that varied in the various confessions, Toole was not the brightest bulb in the array, and given the additional burden of a lifetime of drug and alcohol abuse, his memory was often in and out of focus. And as for issues such as having implicated Henry Lee Lucas in the crime initially, Toole had a perfectly plausible reason for that. As he himself admitted, he might have been a "retard," but that did not mean he lacked cunning. Were he not street-smart, he could never have survived in the circles where he traveled for nearly as long as he did.

One of the documents that had not come to light before Matthews made his thorough search of the files, in fact, was a report filed by Deputy J. E. Winterbaum of the Duval County Sheriff's Office back in October of 1983, shortly after Toole had initially confessed. As Winterbaum was making a routine check of the cell block, Toole called him close to share a few plans he had in mind once he got out of jail.

"I am going to sue the little boy's father, the one I cut his head off," he advised Winterbaum. "And then I am going to kill him. He [meaning Walsh] is trying to pay me off, and I should have never signed the check."

Given the other documents uncovered by Matthews, it might be theorized that an addled Toole had somehow confused John Walsh with John Reaves Jr., the man who'd paid him big bucks for the rights to his life story. But to Matthews, the explanation is much simpler than that. Just as Toole had explained away a previous inconsistency in his story to an investigator: "I just like fucking with the cops."

In any event, it is hard to fathom that a police agency that had invested twenty-seven years in the hopes that the Adam Walsh case would somehow go away saw much to gain by admitting to the world the embarrassing truth as to "what had been in front of their faces" all those years, other than to see justice served, that is.

For Joe Matthews and John and Revé Walsh, justice has in fact been served in this case, and life goes on. Matthews continues as senior investigator at *America's Most Wanted,* as a contributor at Fox News, as a motivational speaker, and as an investigative consultant to television programmers, media outlets, and the private sector. He regularly tours the United States as chairman of DNA LifePrint, promoting corporate sponsorships of events that provide biometric fingerprinting, digital photographic records, and DNA identification of children to communities.

He often conducts seminars and lectures on homicide investigation, investigative interviewing, and polygraph procedures throughout the United States and Canada.

John Walsh, of course, carries on as executive producer and host of *America's Most Wanted*, the longest-running show in Fox Network history—"The good guys do their thing Sunday through Friday," he likes to say, "but on Saturday night, *I* kick ass." He and Revé also continue their work on behalf of the National Center for Missing and Exploited Children as well as on behalf of any number of national and state initiatives related to the protection of children, a never-ending process. In a recent appearance on *Oprah*, Walsh pointed out that even though Congress passed the Adam Walsh Child Protection Act in 2006, the legislation will as a practical matter cease to have any effect beyond 2010 unless government funding is reauthorized and provided.

And even if legislators are persuaded to authorize the dollars, the mere fact that juvenile sex offenders might register their addresses regularly is no guarantee of anything, as a recent *New York Times* story makes clear. For eighteen years following a rape conviction in California, Phillip Garrido reported his whereabouts to authorities in precise accordance with the schedule demanded of him. But that did not stop him from kidnapping and raping another young woman, fathering two children by her, and holding them all prisoner in the backyard of the home he dutifully kept registered all the while.

It is a chilling reminder that the threat of evil is ever-present and that all the noble deeds and intentions on earth cannot stamp out catastrophe and loss. Broward County medical examiner Dr. Ronald Wright spoke to John Walsh of such matters in the aftermath of the initial investigation, trying to give a grief-stricken parent something to cling to. In his profession, Wright had seen horror stacked on horror, plenty of evidence that there was no shortage of hell right here on earth. As to what had kept him sane in the face of all that he had witnessed, it was a simple sense of purpose. "It *is* that simple, John," Wright said. "There is evil. And there is good."

Once Adam Walsh stepped inside Ottis Toole's Cadillac on that day, almost nothing, it seems, could have saved him. And when that car's heavy door slammed shut, it seemed to mark the end of America's innocence. Can there truly have been a time when audiences believed in *The Brady Bunch*? Was there really a time when a parent could bring a forgotten lunch or book bag to school without passing through security gates and showing photo ID?

Still, the refusal of John and Revé Walsh to submit to such evil and the actions of Joe Matthews in tracing it to its source also remind us that—even in such weary times as these—goodness can prevail.

CAST OF CHARACTERS

LYLE BEAN Hollywood PD detective of little help in obtaining FDLE photos

JIMMY CAMPBELL Walsh family friend, and Hoffman's chief suspect in 1981

JOEL COCKERMAN Boy who was escorted out of the Sears store with Adam

BARRY GEMELLI Union Correctional Institution administrator who heard Toole's deathbed confession

MARY HAGAN Identified Toole in Sears near video game display

KELLY HANCOCK Walsh family attorney and former Broward County prosecutor

ROBERT HARLEY Ottis Toole's stepfather

LEROY HESSLER Hollywood PD deputy chief of police in 1981

RON HICKMAN Hollywood PD detective, Hoffman's partner

JACK HOFFMAN Hollywood PD detective in charge of the Adam Walsh case

LARRY HOISINGTON Hollywood PD detective to whom Toole confessed in 1983

DICK HYNDS Supervisor of detectives for the Hollywood PD in 1981

BOBBY LEE JONES Cellmate and former coworker who dented Toole's Cadillac

STEVE KENDRICK Brevard County homicide detective who took Toole's first confession

HENRY LEE LUCAS Toole's lover, convicted serial killer

SAM MARTIN Hollywood PD chief in 1981; retired 1986

GINNY MATTHEWS Joe Matthews's exceedingly understanding and patient wife

JOE MATTHEWS Twenty-nine years a cop and detective, Miami Beach PD

MAMA MARGARET MATTHEWS Joe's mother

ARLENE MAYER Heidi Mayer's mother, who also identified Toole at Kmart

HEIDI MAYER Twelve-year-old girl Toole attempted to abduct from Kmart

FAYE MCNETT John Reaves Jr.'s aunt, who sold her Cadillac to Toole

WILLIAM MISTLER Pest control company owner who witnessed Adam's abduction

JOHN MONAHAN SR. Hotelier and Walsh family friend

CHUCK MORTON Broward County chief assistant state attorney

PHIL MUNDY Broward County State Attorney's Office investigator

LINDA MCHENRY ORAND Toole's sister-in-law, to whom he confessed in 1981

SARAH PATTERSON Ottis Toole's niece, to whom he confessed while in prison in 1996

FRANK POWELL Ottis Toole's adolescent nephew, brother of Frieda

FRIEDA "BECKY" POWELL Ottis Toole's adolescent niece, lover of Henry Lee Lucas

JOHN REAVES JR. Owner of Southeast Color Coat, Jacksonville

JOHN REAVES SR. Owner of Reaves Roofing, Jacksonville; Toole's employer

JAMES REDWINE Troubled son of Toole's landlord Betty Goodyear

WENDY SAPP Ottis Toole's niece to whom he confessed the murder of Adam

MICHAEL SATZ Elected state attorney for Broward County, 1976–present

JAMES SCARBERRY Hollywood PD chief, 1999–2007

GERALD SCHAFFER Toole's cellmate at Starke, convicted serial killer

ELTON SCHWARTZ Miami attorney who volunteered to defend Toole

KATHY SHAFFER Sears security guard, seventeen years old in 1981

MARK SMITH Detective who conducted Hollywood PD cold case investigation in 1995, and again in 2006

VINETTA SYPHURS Ottis Toole's sister, to whom he confessed while in prison

BUDDY TERRY Homicide detective, Jacksonville Sheriff's Office

HOWARD TOOLE Ottis Toole's brother, from whom he stole a pickup truck

NORVELLA "RITA" TOOLE Ottis Toole's wife

OTTIS ELLWOOD TOOLE Drifter, pedophile, convicted killer

SARAH TOOLE Ottis Toole's mother, who died in May 1981

JAY VIA Ouachita Parish, Louisiana, detective who took Toole's second confession in 1983

CHAD WAGNER Hollywood PD chief, 2007–present

ADAM WALSH (1974–1981) Son of John and Revé Walsh

JOHN WALSH *America's Most Wanted* host and child victims' rights advocate

REVÉ (REE-VAY) WALSH Child victims' rights advocate

RICHARD WITT Martin's successor as chief at Hollywood PD, 1986–96

DR. RONALD WRIGHT Broward County medical examiner